Soul Friends

Soul Friends

A Journey with Thomas Merton

Brother Ramon SSF

Marshall Pickering

Marshall Morgan and Scott
Marshall Pickering
34–42 Cleveland Street, London, W1P 5FB. U.K.

Copyright © 1989 Brother Ramon SSF
First published in 1989 by Marshall Morgan and Scott Publications Ltd
Part of the Marshall Pickering Holdings Group

British Library CIP Data

Ramon, *Brother, SSF*
  Soul Friends: A journey with Thomas Merton.
  1. Christian life. Contemplation. Theories of Merton, Thomas
  I. Title
  248.3′4

  ISBN: 0 551 01789 9

Text set in Baskerville by Avocet Robinson, Buckingham
Printed in Great Britain by Cox and Wyman, Reading

Dedicated to the memory of
Mother Mary Clare SLG,
mother in God and soul-friend,

and to

The Sisters of the Love of God,
Fairacres, Oxford,
in gratitude for their continued
love and prayer.

AUTHOR'S NOTE: The masculine pronoun used in this book is intended to be taken in its generic, inclusive sense. I do not wish to be exclusivist.

Most honorable reader, it is not as an author that I would speak to you, not as a storyteller, not as a philosopher, not as a friend only. I seek to speak to you, in some way, as your own self. Who can tell what this may mean? I myself do not know. But if you listen, things will be said that are perhaps not written in this book. And this will be due not to me but to the One who lives and speaks in us both.

Thomas Merton, from the Preface of the Japanese edition of *The Seven Storey Mountain*.

*   *   *

The only way I could live with the man was to love him whole, as he was, with all his contradictions, and I think this is the only way to understand him. That surely is the way he loved me. For he was as merry a man as I have known, yet he had depths of sadness it were best not to mention. He loved the monastic life, and yet he lived it in a style all his own. He had a real love for the solitary life and yet no one around here has his kind of love for people, for the world God made.

Fr Matthew Kelty in a *Letter from Gethsemani*, written the day after Thomas Merton's funeral.

*   *   *

Contents

Abbreviations

AJ	The Asian Journal of Thomas Merton
BPMS	Basic Principles of Monastic Spirituality
CP	Contemplative Prayer
CGB	Conjectures of a Guilty Bystander
CWA	Contemplation in a World of Action
ESF	Emblems of a Season of Fury
FV	Faith and Violence
HGL	The Hidden Ground of Love
HW	A Hidden Wholeness
MZM	Mystics and Zen Masters
NM	The New Man
NMI	No Man is an Island
OB	Opening the Bible
PML	The Power and Meaning of Love
RT	Redeeming the Time
RU	Raids on the Unspeakable
SC	Seeds of Contemplation
SoD	Seeds of Destruction
SSM	The Seven Storey Mountain
SJ	The Sign of Jonas
TMR	A Thomas Merton Reader
TS	Thoughts in Solitude
VC	A Vow of Conversation
WChTz	The Way of Chuang Tzu
WD	The Way of the Desert
ZBA	Zen and the Birds of Appetite
ZR	The Zen Revival

Introduction:
The Dynamic Nature of Vocation

In the year that Thomas Merton died, I heard his name. And from that moment he became a kind of soul-friend – someone who could discern and interpret the profound meaning of my own life, not only as a Christian, but as a human being. There were times when his life and words spoke to me not simply as a friend or guide, but as my very self.

The exciting thing about Merton's evolving vocation was that it was never static. The dynamic nature of his vocation was a clue to the essence of vocation in its widest sense. In his early days he was obsessed with things monastic, especially after he had left the tainted world and entered into the pure and ideal monastic enclosure. How embarrassed he later became about that kind of immature evaluation in his auto-biographical *The Seven Storey Mountain*! As time went on he became a mature man, and therefore a better monk. His simple and common humanity became precious to him, both in his relationships and in his solitude.

This evolution possessed a dynamic which excited and scared me. I cannot pretend to understand all the varied aspects of Merton's creative personality, for he was a man of many parts. But my own human and monastic vocation paralleled his, and they touched and overlapped at so many points that I began to listen, to read between the lines, to feel the power of his words and actions, and become aware of his mistakes in ways that were quite scary. Merton would not have thanked me for making him an idol, for he well knew that he had feet of clay. In any case, my independent and objective judgement knew that some of his writings were forced

and flat, especially when he had to write to order. I realised
also that he didn't worry overmuch about consistency, and
sometimes overstated his position because of an exciting
discovery, or in a mood of wry humour. But his very weaknesses were a help to me, for I was aware that his bubbling
and effervescent personality, and the ability to truly give
himself to others in counselling, teaching and personal
relationships often hid an interior loneliness and desperate
need for intimate loving. But the depths of that need drove
him to understand the deep mystery of the love of God, and
kept him on the trail of the divine Lover, who would not leave
Merton alone.

I have come to the conclusion that Merton is one of the
small band of loving soul-friends who regularly pray for me
within the communion of saints. And the time has come for
me to share something of my appreciation of him, so that the
overflow of living relationship may touch other lives. The way
I have chosen to do this is first of all to include a potted
biography, outlining the early Merton – and this will lead the
reader to the necessary reading of his autobiography if Merton
is to be really understood. Then I trace his evolving development as a monk, a Christian and a human being – all the time
relating his pilgrimage to my own vocation.

From there, I take up various themes in Merton's writings
which relate the contemplative journey to the Gospel, to the
world of humankind and to the created order. These are
exciting themes in which the fire of contemplation ignites the
fuel of theology, and for me this imparts illumination and heat.
And the fire spreads!

Merton also challenges my mind. So under the section
'Wider Horizons' I include some of the stimulating themes
of his pilgrimage which are intellectually satisfying as well as
spiritually challenging. They have delivered me from a kind
of domestic Christianity in which a parochial Jesus assures
the church family of a ghetto-like security which has the smell
of death about it. Merton's understanding of the Gospel is
both evangelical and catholic, and the incarnate Christ is the
One who, as cosmic mediator, carries the believer, the Church

and the world into the experience of the universal mystery of Love.

Finally, in my personal evaluation of Merton's influence upon my life, theology and vocation, I endeavour to indicate the implications of his life and teaching for myself and for the reader. In my own case, I am about to begin a new chapter in the contemplative journey into solitude that burned within Merton's heart, and which he had hardly begun to travel. I have already tasted something of the terror and glory of the solitude that cried out in the depths of Merton's being, and concerning which he knew so much. But his life was suddenly cut off, his contemplative pilgrimage on earth came to what seemed an untimely end by his sudden death in Bangkok in 1968.

As this book comes to publication, I shall be the age at which Merton reached his death. I have learned some of the lessons which he indicates are absolutely necessary for the spiritual journey – and I hope to continue on earth that pilgrimage into contemplative prayer, and therefore into God, which Merton now continues in heaven, with all those who are caught up into the mystery of God's love.

This book, therefore, is not a biography, an academic exercise, an anthology or a eulogy of Thomas Merton. It is an appreciation, both theological and contemplative, by a monastic brother of another communion, who appreciates not only the awe and mystery of a vocation to prayer and love in God, but who appreciates, with Merton, the simple, funny, precarious and loving humanity of which we are both a part.

Brother Ramon SSF,
The Society of Saint Francis.

Part I: The Early Merton

1: A Child of the World

Born on 31st January, 1915, Thomas Merton describes the world into which he came, and of which he became a part, in the pessimistic way that he associated with his pre-conversion experience of life:

> . . . I came into the world. Free by nature, in the image of God, I was nevertheless the prisoner of my own violence and my own selfishness, in the image of the world into which I was born. That world was the picture of Hell, full of men like myself, loving God and yet hating Him; born to love Him, living instead in fear and hopeless self-contradictory hungers. [1]

This kind of retrospective evaluation contains already the seeds of a theology which proclaims the restoration of the lost image of God, deliverance from the basic worldly selfishness, and a new life and identity in Christ. The dark colours of pre-conversion pessimism only serve to highlight the brighter contrasting colours of conversion. This technique of contrast is one of the marks of Merton's autobiographical writing.

His description of childhood experiences are often intensely emotional, and frequently interpretative. His brother, John Paul, is a figure loved and mourned in the few glimpses we have of him throughout *The Seven Storey Mountain*. The introduction of this brother, four or five years younger than himself, is the occasion of a brief homily on the rejection of love. John Paul, the 'little perplexed five-year-old kid' stands at a distance from Thomas and his friends, afraid to approach any nearer because he will be stoned and insulted. Merton writes

movingly of the sadness, the indignation, the sorrow that filled
his brother's mind and heart:

> And there he stands, not sobbing, not crying, but
> angry and unhappy and offended and tremendously
> sad. And yet he is fascinated by what we are doing,
> nailing shingles all over our new hut. And his
> tremendous desire to do what we are doing will not
> permit him to go away. The law written in his nature
> says that he must be with his elder brother, and do
> what he is doing; and he cannot understand why this
> law of love is being so wildly and unjustly violated in
> his case. [2]

Merton sermonises on this incident as he remembers with
joy and sorrow his brother's visit to him at the Gethsemani
monastery many years later and the tragedy surrounding John
Paul's lonely death at sea. The incident becomes universal,
and Merton sees in it the terrible situation which is both a
consequence and parable of man's alienation from God's love:

> Many times it was like that. And in a sense, this
> terrible situation is the pattern and prototype of all sin;
> the deliberate and formal will to reject disinterested
> love for us, for the purely arbitrary reason that we
> simply do not want it. Perhaps the inner motive is that
> the fact of being loved disinterestedly reminds us that
> we all need love from others, we all depend upon the
> charity of others to carry on our own lives, and we
> refuse love, and reject society, in so far as it seems, in
> our own perverse imagination, to imply some obscure
> kind of humiliation. [3]

In a later passage Merton describes himself as the lonely
victim of such treatment as he handed out to his brother. At
eleven years of age, after the death of his mother, his father
took him to live in France, and he describes the first day at
the Lycee:

Although by this time I knew French quite well, the
first day in the big, gravelled yard, when I was
surrounded by those fierce catlike little faces, dark and
morose, and looked into those score of pairs of
glittering and hostile eyes, I forgot every word, and
could hardly answer the furious questions that were
put to me. And my stupidity only irritated them all the
more. They began to kick me, and pull and twist my
ears, and push me around, and shout various kinds of
insults. I learned a great deal of obscenity and
blasphemy in the first few days, simply by being the
direct or indirect object of so much of it.

. . . when I lay awake at night in the huge, dark
dormitory and listened to the snoring of the little
animals all around me, and heard through the
darkness and the emptiness of the night the far
screaming of the trains, or the mad iron cry of a bugle
in a distant *caserne* of Senegalese troops, I knew for the
first time in my life the pangs of desolation and
emptiness and abandonment. [4]

'Emptiness and abandonment' – these are words which are
used in quite another sense in his later spiritual teaching,
concepts which persist throughout his writings. But here, in
his childhood, he learned the rejection of fellow human beings,
the experiences of loneliness and a certain distrust of the world.
These are the kind of experiences which caused him to write
in retrospect:

As a child, and since then too, I have always tended to
resist any kind of a possessive affection on the part of
any other human being – there has always been this
profound instinct to keep clear, to keep free. And only
with truly supernatural people have I ever really felt at
my ease, really at peace. [5]

In 1929, at fourteen years of age, Merton was sent to a
private school at Oakham, Kent. It was here that he heard

of his father's illness and worsening condition, and then the implicit intimation of his imminent death. These are the kind of experiences that cause the early Merton to write again of the alienation from God and from grace in the context of human sorrow, where there is no one to comfort, and no one to turn to:

> I sat there in the dark, unhappy room, unable to think, unable to move, with all the innumerable elements of my isolation crowding in upon me from every side: without a home, without a family, without a country, without a father, apparently without any friends, without any interior peace or confidence or light or understanding of my own – without God too, without God, without heaven, without grace, without anything.[6]

The experience of living through his father's dying months marked itself indelibly upon his young mind. It was in the summer of 1930 when Merton was fifteen years old that the end came. Added to the subjective desolation that he had felt some months before is the helplessness of the universal human condition:

> What could I make of so much suffering? There was no way for me or for anyone else in the family to get anything out of it. It was a raw wound for which there was no adequate relief. You had to take it, like an animal. We were in the condition of most of the world, the condition of men without faith in the presence of war, disease, pain, starvation, suffering, plague, bombardment, death. You just had to take it, like a dumb animal. Try to avoid it, if you could. But you must eventually reach the point where you can't avoid it any more. Take it. Try to stupefy yourself, if you like, so that it won't hurt so much. But you will always have to take some of it. And it will devour you in the end.

Indeed the truth that many people never understand until it is too late, is that the more you try to avoid suffering, the more you suffer, because smaller and more insignificant things begin to torture you, in proportion to your fear of being hurt. This is another of the great perversions by which the devil uses our philosophies to turn our whole nature inside out, and eviscerates all our capacities for good, turning them against ourselves.[7]

Merton is again reading back and philosophising here, but he is reading back into an actual situation, into the existential situation of a fifteen-year-old boy of his sensitivities. The religious ethos of his new English school at Oakham could not minister to such a need as this. He criticises the English intellectual Platonism of the place, with its purposeful vagueness, commenting on the headmaster: 'It was no easier, concretely, to find out what he believed than it was to find out what anybody else believed in that place.' The chaplain, who had been a rowing 'blue' at Cambridge, had a favourite sermon on the first epistle of St Paul to the Corinthians, chapter thirteen, in which his definition of the word 'charity' stood for 'all that we mean when we call a chap a gentleman':

If I talk with the tongues of men and of angels and not be a gentleman, I am become as sounding brass, or a tinkling cymbal . . . A gentleman is patient, is kind; a gentleman envieth not, dealeth not perversely; is not puffed up . . . A gentleman never falleth away.[8]

But the experience of sadness and depression which lasted for some months after his father's death gave way eventually to what he felt was a new kind of freedom and self-will. He says that any religion which may have been in his soul previously was squeezed out of it after he got over that experience, for, as he puts it:

There was no room for any God in that empty temple full of dust and rubbish which I was now so jealously

to guard against all intruders, in order to devote it to
the worship of my own will.

And so I became the complete twentieth-century
man. I now belonged to the world in which I lived. I
became the true citizen of my own disgusting century.
A man living on the doorsill of the Apocalypse, a man
with veins full of poison, living in death.[9]

And yet, as he picks up the threads of his adolescent
experience during this time, he discerns a meaning, a pattern
to which the seemingly haphazard events conformed – the
discovery of the poetry of William Blake, for instance.
Merton's father had liked Blake and had tried to communicate
something of the power of the poet to Merton when he was
ten years old. But now, at sixteen, he began to feel the depth
and appeal of the poet, without being able to systematise or
evaluate quite what he was saying. Something akin to the
qualities of faith and love were awakened in Merton by Blake's
influence, and perhaps this was possible because Blake
deprecated both materialistic deism with its abstract natural
religion of the eighteenth century and the agnosticism of the
nineteenth, and yet rebelled against and opposed all forms
of orthodoxy.

The next event which Merton indicates as a milestone in
his pre-conversion life was a visit to Rome. He heard of his
acceptance at Clare College, Cambridge, and the day after
his eighteenth birthday, he set out on a celebratory journey
to Italy. The escapades and experience of this journey prior
to arriving at Rome are summed up:

So there I was, with all the liberty that I had been
promising myself for so long. The world was mine.
How did I like it? I was doing just what I pleased, and
instead of being filled with happiness and well-being, I
was miserable.[10]

He wandered aimlessly and miserably around Rome, but
after a week he found himself looking into churches rather

than ruined temples, and slowly be began to discover what he calls 'another and far different Rome'. He describes the effect of a great mosaic in the apse of Ss Cosmas and Damian, of Christ coming in judgement in a dark blue sky, with a suggestion of fire in the small clouds beneath his feet. He enters into a new dimension of thinking:

> The effect of this discovery was tremendous. After all the vapid, boring, semi-pornographic statuary of the Empire, what a thing it was to come upon the genius of an art full of spiritual vitality and earnestness and power – an art that was tremendously serious and alive and eloquent and urgent in all that it had to say. Its solemnity was made all the more astounding by its simplicity – and by the obscurity of the places where it lay hid, and by its subservience to higher ends, architectural, liturgical and spiritual ends which I could not even begin to understand, but which I could not avoid guessing.[11]

Therefore, without realising it, Merton became something of a pilgrim, visiting shrine after shrine. He also bought a Vulgate text and began to read the New Testament. The gospels shed their own light upon the churches and the mosaics, and he began to feel a kind of interior peace about these holy places. He views this Roman experience as the first dawnings of a true knowledge of Christ:

> And now for the first time in my life I began to find out something of Christ. It was obscure, but it was a true knowledge of Him, truer than I knew. It was there I first saw Him, whom I now serve as my God and my King, and who owns and rules my life.
> It is the Christ of the Apocalypse, the Christ of the Martyrs, the Christ of the Fathers. It is the Christ of St John and of St Paul and St Augustine and St Jerome and all the Fathers – and of the Desert Fathers. It is Christ God, Christ King.

These mosaics told me more than I had ever known of the doctrine of a God of infinite power, wisdom and love who had yet become Man and revealed in His Manhood the infinity of power, wisdom and love that was His Godhead. The mind of the artist reached my own mind, and spoke to it his conception and his thought.[12]

Much had to take place before Merton could lay claim to faith. There had been no real movement of the will, no moral or spiritual change which could be thought of as a conversion, and yet, before he left Rome, he was to have another experience which enabled him to glimpse into his own soul. This was not so much a numinous experience of the majesty of transcendence of God, but a humbling glimpse of the darkness of his own soul, and there were tears:

I was in my room. It was night. The light was on. Suddenly it seemed to me that Father, who had been dead more than a year, was there with me. The sense of his presence was as vivid and as real and as startling as if he had touched my arm or spoken to me. The whole thing passed in a flash, but in that flash, instantly, I was overwhelmed with a sudden insight into the misery of my own soul, and I was pierced deeply with a light that made me realize somthing of the condition I was in, and I was filled with horror at what I saw, and my whole being rose up in revolt against what was within me, and my soul desired liberation from all this with an intensity and an urgency unlike anything I had ever known. And now I think for the first time in my whole life I really began to pray – praying not with my lips and my intellect, and my imagination, but praying out of the very roots of my being, and praying to the God I had never known, to reach down towards me out of His darkness and to help me to get free of the thousand terrible things that held my will in their slavery.[13]

The following morning, he climbed the Aventine, took holy water at the door, went straight up to the altar rail and kneeling down, slowly said the *Our Father*. There was joy, some inner peace, and thoughts of a change in lifestyle, but the fervour, though real, was temporary, so that in September, 1931, Merton found himself in Clare College, Cambridge, and the fervour had evaporated! Apart from the slightest acquaintance with Dante, whose poetic myths and symbols entranced Merton in spite of the scholastic philosophy and theology in which they were cast, Merton felt the rest of his Cambridge experience was negative. And yet in the very negativeness of the situation his retrospective gaze confirms the grace of the negative in the misery and futility of independence:

> God in his mercy was permitting me to fly as far as I could from His love but at the same time preparing to confront me in the bottom of the abyss, when I thought I had gone farthest away from Him. *Si ascendero in coelum, tu illic es, Si descendero in infernum, ades.* For in my greatest misery He would shed into my soul enough light to see how miserable I was, and to admit that it was my own fault and my own work. And always I was to be punished for my sins by my sins themselves, and to realize, at least obscurely, that I was being so punished, and burn in the flames of my own hell, and rot in the hell of my own corrupt will until I was forced at last, by my own intense misery, to give up my own will.[14]

This writing, and more of the same kind, indicated the lapses in his moral life which one had to guess at in the immediate reading of the *Mountain*. It was not that Merton was being dishonest, but that the Cistercian censors, at the publication of the book in 1949, were not willing for him to record, in so many words, details of his immoral life during his Cambridge days. It was commonly believed that Merton had fathered a child, and that mother and child were later killed in the London blitz. Such moral laxity, together with

his spendthrift habits, caused his Guardian Tom to send
Merton to America, where he enrolled at Columbia
University. One of his friends, Ed Rice, wrote a book about
Merton called *Man in the Sycamore Tree*, which spilled the beans,
and was very critical both of the censors and Merton's
superiors at the Abbey of Gethsemani, and the whole matter
became common knowledge.[15]

During the years 1931 to 1935 Merton became disillusioned
by the capitalistic ideas which dominated the western world,
and got mixed up with communist groups in Columbia
University. This didn't last very long, for he soon saw that
the young communists who signed the 'Oxford Pledge' in 1935
'against all wars' were soon fighting for the Red Army against
France in Spain. Merton admits that his inspiration to do
something for the good of mankind had been feeble and
abstract from the beginning – he was really only interested
in doing good for himself.

At the age of twenty-one, in 1936, with the constant
reiteration of the emptiness and intolerable boredom of both
study and leisure, and the stale satiety of the social roundabout,
but with periods of activism and enjoyment, lapsing back again
into hangovers and nervous exhaustion, Merton pinpoints his
feelings after one of the hectic nights, standing tired out waiting
for a bus in the grey, silent hour before dawn, smoking the
fortieth or fiftieth cigarette of the day:

> The thing that depressed me most of all was the shame
> and despair that invaded my whole nature when the
> sun came up, and all the labourers were going to
> work: men healthy and awake and quiet, with some
> rational purpose before them. This humiliation and
> sense of my own misery and of the fruitlessness of
> what I had done was the nearest I could get to
> contrition. It was the reaction of nature. It proved
> nothing except that I had still some faint capacity for
> moral life in me.[16]

This was the negative side of the experience which

ultimately led Merton to faith and into the religious life. The first section of *The Seven Storey Mountain* concludes with a comment of his twenty-one years of life:

I had at last become a true child of the modern world. Here I was, scarcely four years after I had left Oakham and walked out into the world that I thought I was going to ransack and rob of all its pleasures and satisfactions. I had done what I intended, and now I found that it was I who was gutted. What a strange thing! In filling myself, I had emptied myself.[17]

To crown it all, he found himself involved emotionally with a girl who merely found him amusing, who caused him to behave in a most abject manner and meekness for some sign of affection, and the girl turned her back on him when she ceased to be amused. Merton says of the experience:

Such was the death of the hero, the great man I had wanted to be. No one threw any eggs at me, nobody said a word. The wounds within me were, I suppose, enough.[18]

References

1 Merton, *SSM*, p. 3.
2 *ibid.*, p. 23.
3 *ibid.*, pp. 23f.
4 *ibid.*, p. 49.
5 *ibid.*, p. 57.
6 *ibid.*, pp. 71f.
7 *ibid.*, pp. 82f.
8 *ibid.*, p. 73.
9 *ibid.*, p. 85.
10 *ibid.*, p. 81.
11 *ibid.*, p. 82.
12 *ibid.*, p. 83.

13 *ibid.*, p. 111.
14 *ibid.*, p. 123.
15 Monica Furlong relates the story of Merton's fathering
     of a child who, with its mother died in the London blitz,
     Merton: A Biography, pp. 59f. But Michael Mott, in the
     official biography of Merton, is much more cautious
     about the matter, quoting the sources, see *The Seven
     Mountains of Thomas Merton*, p. 84 and footnotes.
16 Merton, *SSM*, p. 58.
17 *ibid.*, pp. 163f.
18 *ibid.*, p. 163.

2: Conversion to Christ

'And He called out to me from His own immense depths.'
With these words Merton closes the chapter which narrates
his conversion experience. They are words which condition
his life from that time forward, and whatever changes took
place in his evolving pilgrimage, in his orientation and lifestyle
and in his manner and matter of communication, these words
hold good to the end. In *Contemplative Prayer*, published in 1969,
the year after his death, we find words which both confirm
an evangelical experience and yet reveal his continuing
pilgrimage:

> The way of monastic prayer is not a subtle escape
> from the Christian economy of incarnation or
> redemption. It is a special way of following Christ, of
> sharing in his passion and resurrection and in his
> redemption of the world. For that very reason the
> dimensions of prayer in solitude are those of man's
> ordinary anguish, his self-searching, his moments of
> nausea at his own vanity, falsity and capacity for
> betrayal. Far from establishing one in unassailable
> narcissistic security, the way of prayer brings us face to
> face with the sham and indignity of the false self that
> seeks to live for itself alone and to enjoy the
> 'consolation of prayer' for its own sake. This 'self' is
> pure illusion, and ultimately he who lives for and by
> such an illusion must end either in disgust or madness. [1]

I remember the small earthquake which erupted in me when
I first read and recognised the truth of those words, and the
gratitude to God I felt in the realisation that in Merton I had

found a man who not only wrote like this, but lived out the implications of a sinner called to a deepening vocation to contemplative prayer and mystical love.

The years from 1948 to his death are contained in the above lines. He explores in fact and in his writing, the inner wastes of his own being and faces the illusion which is himself. He learns the meaning of the emptiness and alienation of the world and of life apart from God, but he also learns that the world is meaningful and reconciled in Christ, and this sets the scene for the truly spiritual man:

The monk searches not only his own heart; he plunges deep into the heart of that world of which he remains a part although he seems to have 'left' it. In reality the monk abandons the world only in order to listen more intently to the deepest and most neglected voices that proceed from its inner depth . . .[2]

Merton's journey into Christ was at the same time an interior journey into the depths of his own being. One of the most important pieces of writing that he produced was an essay called 'The Cell' which indicates the spiritual and psychological journey into the interior wastes, involving not only the Spirit's interior work of regeneration and sanctification, but also an experience of feeling the pain and sorrow, the suffering and yearning of a humanity estranged from but loved by God. Merton's initiation into Christ was also an increasing awareness of his solidarity with all men, and a pilgrimage into a profound appreciation of his simple humanity, and the restoration of the image of God for himself and for others. 'The Cell' bears witness to the interior solitude which is the hallmark of a man of prayer and intercession, often calling for a geographical solitude and withdrawal so that the mind and heart may be stayed upon God alone, without external distractions.[3] Merton writes of his vocation in terms of a healing work:

This is the creative and healing work of the monk, accomplished in silence, in nakedness of spirit, in

emptiness, in humility. It is a participation in the
saving death and resurrection of Christ. Therefore any
Christian may, if he so desires, enter into communion
with this silence of the praying and meditating Church,
which is the Church of the Desert.[4]

The early Merton had to make a negative rejection of the
world to find it again. Perhaps it was necessary for him, but
in an early article on Merton, one of his later biographers
says: 'Finally he left himself no option but to bang the
monastery door crossly on the whole boiling of us, with our
sins and stupidities. . . . Inside Gethsemani, by contrast all
was pure and lovely. The place smelled frighteningly clean;
polished and swept and repainted over and over, year after
year. And the Cistercians, to begin with, are just as special
as he hopes.'[5]

But even in his early days, there was a profound love for
all things human in his heart. On his first trip out of
Gethsemani in seven years, he writes a beautiful description
of the experience:

We drove into town with Senator Dawson, a
neighbour of the monastery, and all the while I
wondered how I would react at meeting once again,
face to face, the wicked world. I met the world and I
found it no longer so wicked after all. Perhaps the
things I had resented about the world when I left it
were defects of my own that I had projected upon it.
Now, on the contrary, I found that everything stirred
me with a deep and mute sense of compassion.
Perhaps some of the people we saw going about the
streets were hard and tough – with the naive,
animalistic toughness of the Middle West – but I did
not stop to observe it because I seemed to have lost an
eye for merely exterior detail and to have discovered
instead, a deep sense of respect and love and pity for
the souls that such details never fully reveal. I went
through the city, realizing for the first time in my life

how good are all the people in the world and how
much value they have in the sight of God.[6]

Before we can truly understand the later Merton, we must
follow the development, the progress, noting each necessary
step, and the concrete situations which gave rise to new ways
of thinking, of living, of understanding and of being.

The events immediately leading up to his conversion
experience began in 1937, when Merton was twenty-two years
old. In Scribner's bookstore on Fifth Avenue he purchased
a book by Etienne Gilson, *The Spirit of Medieval Philosophy*, only
to be disgusted by the fact that on the way home he saw on
the first page in small print: *'Nihil Obstat . . . Imprimatur'*. He
had been cheated!

Nevertheless, this book led him into the world of
Catholicism, and the result was that he almost immediately
acquired an immense respect for Catholic philosophy and the
Catholic faith. But this was only the beginning. The effect
of the book was to create a desire to go to church, a desire
more sincere and mature than ever before. Unfortunately,
the experience at the Episcopal Church did not mean much
more than his previous visit to the Quaker meeting. Of the
Quakers, he commented:

I went out of the meeting house saying to myself: 'In
other churches it is the minister who hands out the
commonplaces, and here it is liable to be just
anybody'.[7]

and of the Zion Episcopalian Church where his father had
once played the organ, he said:

The minister was called Mr Riley. It was modern
literature and politics that he talked about, not religion
and God. You felt that the man did not know what he
was supposed to be. He had taken upon himself some
function in society which was not his, and which was,
indeed, not a necessary function at all. When he did

get around to preaching about some truth of the
Christian religion, he practically admitted in the
pulpit, as he did in private to anyone who cared to
talk about it, that he did not believe most of these
doctrines, even in the extremely diluted form in which
they were handed out by Protestants. The Trinity?
What did he want with the Trinity? And as for the
strange medieval notions about the Incarnation, well,
that was simply too much to ask of a reasonable man.[8]

The later Merton was embarrassed by such judgmental
attitudes, especially as he had many devout friends among
Quakers and Episcopalians, but the point he was making was
valid – a church and its ministry that seemed to be more
interested in politics and literature than the saving gospel and
God, a church which did not believe most of the fundamental
doctrines of the Christian Faith, did not attract him. He had
further to go.

The year 1937 was filled with friends and lectures and classes
on Shakespeare which dealt with 'things that were really
fundamental' to human life. 'I could not realize then,' says
Merton, 'but it has become very clear to me, that God brought
me and half a dozen others together at Columbia, in such a
way that our friendship would work powerfully to rescue us
from confusion and misery.' Among those friends were Ed
Rice, author of *The Man in the Sycamore Tree: The Good Times
and Hard Life of Thomas Merton*, and Robert Lax who later went
to live a secluded life first on the islands of Patmos and
Mytilini, and later on the island of Kalymnos, in Greece.

Another matter that caught Merton's attention was that
Aldous Huxley, in his *Ends and Means*, had experienced a
change of mind that almost amounted to conversion, and had
come out with the astonishing truth that not only was there
such a thing as a supernatural order, but that it was
experientially accessible through prayer, meditation and
asceticism.

The whole concept of asceticism offended Merton and his
gang, though he makes a wry comment:

It is a strange thing that we should have thought
nothing of it, when if anyone had suggested sleeping
on the floor as a penance for the love of God, we
would have felt that he was trying to insult our
intelligence and dignity as men! And yet we somehow
seemed to think it quite logical to sleep that way as
part of an evening dedicated to pleasure.[9]

So he lifted out of Huxley the two big concepts of a
supernatural order and the possiblity of real, experiential
contact with God, and left aside the asceticism! About this
time he graduated and entered his name in the Graduate
School of English, settling on the poems and aspects of William
Blake's religious ideas as a subject for his thesis. This fired
Merton:

. . . oh, what a thing it was to live in contact with the
genius and the holiness of William Blake that year,
that summer, writing the thesis! . . . As Blake worked
himself into my system, I became conscious that the
only way to live was in a world that was charged with
the presence and reality of God.[10]

This was merely an intellectual realisation at first. The
springs of will and motive had not really been touched – but
that was to come. What with the *Confessions* of St Augustine,
and Thomas à Kempis's *Imitation of Christ*, both recommended
by a Hindu monk, complementing Gilson's *The Spirit of
Medieval Philosophy* – about the beginning of September 1938,
Merton says that the groundwork of his conversion was more
or less complete. This was a little more than a year and a half
from the first reading of Gilson's book, 'to bring me up from
an ''atheist'' – as I considered myself – to one who accepted
all the full range and possibility of religious experience right
up to the highest degree of glory.'[11]

The strange mixture of motives and desires in Merton's
life at this time presented such contradictions, for he was still
completely fettered by his 'sins and attachments'. As he

maintains, his intellect was only theoretically independent of
desire and appetite in actual practice. He goes on to say that
passion blinds and perverts intellect, and self-interest is implicit
in the very claim to objectivity. Speaking of his intellectual
acceptance of religious truth, he states:

> I not only accepted all this intellectually, but now I
> began to desire it. And not only did I begin to desire
> it, but I began to do so efficaciously: I began to want
> to take the necessary means to achieve this union, this
> peace. I began to desire to dedicate my life to God.
> The notion was still vague and obscure, and it was
> ludicrously impractical in the sense that I was already
> dreaming of mystical union when I did not even keep
> the simplest rudiments of the moral law. But
> nevertheless I was convinced of the reality of the goal,
> and confident that it could be achieved: and whatever
> element of presumption was in this confidence, I am
> sure God excused in His mercy, because of my
> stupidity and helplessness and because I was really
> beginning to be ready to do whatever I thought He
> wanted me to do to bring me to Him.
> But oh, how blind and weak and sick I was, although
> I thought I saw where I was going, and half
> understood the way! How deluded we sometimes are
> by the clear notions we beg out of books. They make
> us think that we really understand things of which we
> have no practical knowledge at all. I remember how
> learnedly and enthusiastically I could talk for hours
> about mysticism and the experimental knowledge of
> God, and all the while I was stoking the fires of the
> argument with Scotch and soda.[12]

At this time, Merton had been spending his Sundays with
his current girlfriend at Long Island, but one Sunday in
August, having called her up and cancelled the weekend
with her, he decided to go to mass for the first time in his
life. This was also his first sober Sunday in New York, and

he went to the little brick church of Corpus Christi.

The church was not large, but it was full, with a good cross-section of people, young predominating. The whole atmosphere gripped Merton – the worshipful attitude of the people, the quiet dignity of the worship, and most of all the authority of the young priest and the content of his sermon:

What was he saying? That Christ was the Son of God. That in Him, the Second Person of the Holy Trinity, God has assumed a Human Nature, a Human body and Soul, and had taken Flesh and dwelt among us, full of grace and truth; and that this Man, whom men call the Christ, was God. He was both Man and God: two Natures hypostatically united in one Person or *suppositum*, one individual who was a Divine Person, having assumed to Himself a Human Nature.

And His works were the works of God: His acts were the acts of God: He loved us: God, and walked among us: God, and died for us on the Cross, God of God, Light of Light, True God of True God . . .

If you believed it you would receive light to grasp it, to understand it in some measure. If you did not believe it, you would never understand it: it would never be anything but scandal and folly.

And no one can believe these things merely by wanting to, of his own volition. Unless he receive grace, and actual light and impulsion of the mind and will from God, he cannot even make an act of living faith. It is God who gives faith, and no one cometh to Christ unless the Father draw him.[13]

As soon as the attention was focused on the altar again, Merton became frightened and left the church, and in his soul was reflected wonder and sorrow and repentance and longing. This was the turning-point, and the whole world seemed to be changed as he walked out of the church:

I walked leisurely down Broadway in the sun, and my

eyes looked about me at a new world. I could not
understand what it was that had happened to make me
so happy, why I was so much at peace, so content with
life.

All I know is that I walked in a new world. Even
the ugly buildings of Columbia were transfigured in it,
and everywhere was peace in these streets designed for
violence and noise. Sitting outside the little Childs
restaurant at 111th Street, behind the dirty, boxed
bushes, and eating breakfast, was like sitting in the
Elysian fields.[14]

Merton's reading became more catholic, the metaphysical
poets, Gerard Manley Hopkins, Crashaw, the Jesuits, and
then Hopkins again, and his letters to Newman about
becoming a Catholic, the hesitation, the decision. Soon
Merton was at the presbytery and saying to Father Moore,
'Father, I want to become a Catholic'.

There followed two months of intense instruction and
involvement on the part of Merton, with the increasing longing
for baptism, until the 16th November when the baptism took
place. Those were fearful and ecstatic moments for Merton,
and the description of his first communion which followed his
baptism is a theological exposition of the eucharistic life of
the believer and the Church, later reflected in *The Living Bread*,
published in 1955. He recalls the priest's words, with his
exposition:

'Behold the Lamb of God: behold Him who taketh
away the sins of the world.'

And my First Communion began to come towards
me, down the steps. I was the only one at the altar
rail. Heaven was entirely mine – that Heaven in which
sharing makes no division or diminution. But this
solitariness was a kind of reminder of the singleness
with which this Christ, hidden in the small Host, was
giving Himself for me, and to me, and, with Himself,
the entire Godhead and Trinity – a great new increase

of the power and grasp of their indwelling that had begun only a few minutes before at the font . . .

In the Temple of God that I had just become, the One Eternal and Pure Sacrifice was offered up to the God dwelling in me; the sacrifice of God to God, and me sacrificed together with God, incorporated in His Incarnation. Christ was born in me, a new Bethlehem, and sacrificed in me His new Calvary, and risen in me: offering me to the Father, in Himself, asking the Father, my Father and His, to receive me into His infinite and special love – not the love He has for all things that exist – for mere existence is a token of God's love, but the love of those creatures who are drawn to Him in and with the power of His own love for Himself.

For now I had entered into the everlasting movement of that gravitation which is the very life and spirit of God: God's own gravitation towards the depths of his own infinite nature, His goodness without end. And God, that centre who is everywhere and whose circumference is nowhere, finding me, through incorporation with Christ, incorporated into this intense and tremendous gravitational movement which is love, which is the Holy Spirit, loved me.

And He called out to me from His own immense depths.[15]

Merton felt that he had travelled, like the Jews, through the Red Sea of baptism and was being called by God to himself, to the promised land which is participation in his own life – 'that lovely and fertile country which is the life of grace and glory, the interior life, the mystical life'. He had the awareness that union with God was the goal to which he was called, for which he had been created, for which Christ had died upon the cross. For this he had been baptised, and had within him the living Christ, 'melting me into Himself in the fires of His love'.

But the awareness needed to be rooted into living and

habitual experience. He needed spiritual direction, frequent
communion, an understanding of sacrifice and dedication,
and the sense that his training had only just begun. Merton's
intellect was profoundly converted, he believed in God, in the
teachings of the Church and was prepared to sit all night
arguing with all and sundry, imagining therefore that he was
a zealous Christian.

The problem was the will – the *domina voluntas*. Merton
wanted to be a writer, a poet, a critic, a professor – but with
personal ambition looming large in the region of the will. He
got his master's degree, and began study for a doctorate in
philosophy. The months passed, and his predicament was
made clear to him in a simple conversation he had with Robert
Lax as they walked down Sixth Avenue one spring evening
in 1939:

Lax suddenly turned around and asked me the
question: 'What do you want to be anyway?'

I could not say, 'I want to be Thomas Merton, the
well-known writer of all those book reviews in the back
pages of the *Times Book Review*,' or 'Thomas Merton,
the assistant instructor of Freshman English at the
New Life Social Institute for Progress and Culture,' so
I put the thing on the spiritual plane where I knew it
belonged, and said, 'I don't know: I guess what I
want is to be a good Catholic.'

'What do you mean, you want to be a good
Catholic?'

The explanation I gave was lame enough, and
expressed my confusion, and betrayed how little I had
really thought about it all. Lax did not accept it.

'What you should say,' he told me, 'what you
should say is that you want to be a saint.'

I said: 'How do you expect me to become a saint?'

'By wanting to,' said Lax simply.

'I can't be a saint,' I said, 'I can't be a saint.' And
my mind darkened.

Lax said: 'No. All that is necessary to be a saint is

to want to be one. Don't you believe that God will
make you what He created you to be, if you will
consent to let Him do it? All you have to do is desire
it.'

A long time ago, St Thomas Aquinas had said the
same thing – and it is something that is obvious to
everybody who ever understood the gospels. After Lax
was gone, I thought about it, and it became obvious to
me. [16]

Merton did not immediately translate belief into action, but
quietly, inwardly, these 'principles' were being filed away.
Speculation, argument, debate, encountering Augustine, John
of the Cross, Thomas Aquinas and saints of like calibre became
part of Merton's life, especially as he spent the summer of
1939 in a cottage on a wooded mountain from which one could
see miles over New York and Pennsylvania. With him were
Bob Lax and Ed Rice, and they entertained romantic notions
of being hermits. But that is as far as it went, for they would
descend into the 'valleys' to the cinemas, the carnivals, the
slot machines and to drink beer.

The fact of these two dimensions in Merton's life at the
time was perplexing to him, and he makes a perceptive,
retrospective comment about his condition which contains
within itself the explanation of his lack of being what he should
have been:

I had accepted Lax's principle about sanctity being
possible to those who willed it, and filed it away in my
head with all my other principles – and still I did
nothing about using it. What was this curse that was
on me, that I could not translate belief into action? I
was content to speculate and argue: and I think the
reason is that my knowledge was too much a mere
matter of natural and intellectual consideration.
Aristotle placed the highest natural felicity in the
knowledge of God which was accessible to him, a
pagan. The heights that can be reached by

metaphysical speculation introduce a man into a realm of pure and subtle pleasure that offers the most nearly permanent delight you can find in the natural order. When you go one step higher, and base your speculations on premises that are revealed, the pleasure gets deeper and more perfect still. Yet even though the subject matter may be the mysteries of the Christian faith, the manner of contemplating them, speculative and impersonal, may still not transcend the natural plane, at least as far as practical consequences go.[17]

Yet there was another principle in his soul – the principle of spiritual life, the indwelling Christ. It was during such a time as described above, in the autumn of the year, just after the beginning of the Second World War, that Merton found himself tired and dishevelled after a few hours' sleep on the floor of a friend's flat. Suddenly, while sitting on the floor with his friends, eating breakfast and playing records, the idea came to him, 'I am going to be a priest'. Recalling it, he says:

I cannot say what caused it: it was not a reaction of especially strong disgust at being so tired and so uninterested in this life I was still leading. This conviction was not emotional. It was something in the order of conscience, a new and profound and clear sense that this was what I really ought to do.[18]

He eventually got away from the others and found himself at seven o'clock that evening down at the basement of the Jesuit Church of St Francis Xavier in Sixteenth Street, New York. He found, surprisingly, that a service of Benediction was taking place, and was drawing to a close. He fell to his knees, joining in the singing of the *Tantum Ergo* of St Thomas Aquinas, and he relates:

It suddenly became clear that my whole life was at a crisis. Far more than I could imagine or understand or conceive was now hanging upon a word – a decision of mine.

I had not shaped my life to this situation: I had not been building up to this. Nothing had been further from my mind. There was, therefore, an added solemnity in the fact that I had been called in here abruptly to answer a question that had been preparing, not in my mind, but in the infinite depths of an eternal Providence . . .

It was a moment of searching, but it was a moment of joy. It took me about a minute to adjust the weak eyes of my spirit to its unaccustomed light, and during that moment my whole life remained suspended on the edge of an abyss: but this time, the abyss was an abyss of love and peace, the abyss was God . . . So now the question faced me: 'Do you really want to be a priest? If you do, say so . . .'

. . . I said: 'Yes, I want to be a priest, with all my heart I want it. If it is your will, make me a priest – make me a priest.'

When I had said them, I realized in some measure what I had done with those last four words, what power I had put into motion on my behalf, and what a union had been sealed between me and that power by my decision.[19]

This is the manner in which Merton closes the second section of his first volume of autobiography. Soon he would be able to write that the life of grace had become something permanent, that God had become the centre of his existence, and that in spite of weakness he was walking the way of liberty and life. Soon he would be able to take stock and evaluate:

I had found my spiritual freedom. My eyes were beginning to open to the powerful and constant light of heaven and my will was at last learning to give in to the subtle and gentle and loving guidance of that love which is Life without end. For once, for the first time in my life, I had been, not days, not weeks, but months, a stranger to sin.[20]

References

1 Merton, *CP*, pp. 23f.
2 *ibid.*, p. 23.
3 The essay 'The Cell', (CWA, pp. 252–259), is for me, the most important piece of theological/spiritual writing that Merton ever wrote.
4 Merton, *CP*, pp. 25f.
5 Monica Furlong, 'Trappist Untrapped', *New Fire*, Winter 1970, p. 20.
6 Merton, *SJ*, pp. 97f.
7 Merton, *SSM*, p. 116.
8 *ibid.*, p. 176.
9 *ibid.*, p. 252.
10 *ibid.*, pp. 189f.
11 *ibid.*, p. 204.
12 *ibid.*, pp. 204f.
13 *ibid.*, pp. 209f.
14 *ibid.*, pp. 210f.
15 *ibid.*, pp. 225f.
16 *ibid.*, pp. 237f.
17 *ibid.*, p. 242.
18 *ibid.*, p. 253.
19 *ibid.*, p. 255.
20 *ibid.*, p. 277.

3: The Problem of Vocation

Merton was in the last months of his twenty-fourth year, and with the new awareness of priesthood and even monastic life uppermost in his mind, he turned to the man who was to point his future direction. This was Dan Walsh, a layman who lectured on St Thomas Aquinas and Duns Scotus in Columbia, a man who had revealed through his humility a real piety and spirit of discernment. He had already encouraged Merton in his studies and shown a deep personal interest in him. So it was that Merton arranged to meet Dan one evening at the close of September, 1939.

As soon as they met and walked out into the cool night, Dan turned to Merton and said: 'You know, the first time I met you I thought you had a vocation to the priesthood.'

Merton was astonished and ashamed, but from that point of contact, they talked over the whole matter. The rule of St Benedict, the Dominicans, the Jesuits, the Benedictines, the Franciscans, and the Order that filled Dan with enthusiasm – the Cistercians – were all included. But the austerity that Merton connected with the Cistercians did not appeal to him at all, and theoretically he settled for the Franciscans. Dan gave him a note for Father Edmund of the monastery of St Francis of Assisi.

Father Edmund was a big, amiable, cheerful Franciscan, and arrangements were made for Thomas to enter the noviciate in August 1940. All went well for a time – daily communion, lectures, study, disciplined prayer, and the *Spiritual Exercises* of St Ignatius as best he knew how, all in preparation for the noviciate. Then there was the giving up of teaching English at Columbia, followed by a month over an appendectomy and convalescence, and then the bracing 'Catholic' atmosphere of a holiday in Cuba.

Cuba was a place and a time of spiritual renewal for Merton, and it was in the Church of St Francis at Havana that a new realisation of the glory and the mystery of the mass was given to him. The occasion of the experience was the moment after the consecration when the priest had replaced the host and chalice on the altar, and suddenly, led by a Franciscan friar, the voices of a crowd of children burst out 'Creo en Dios' – a loud, sudden, glad and triumphant shout from the Cuban children, a robust affirmation of faith. This was a 'moment of knowing' for Merton, and he is conscious of the poverty of language as he attempts to describe the experience:

> Then, as sudden as the shout and as definite, and a thousand times more bright, there formed in my mind an awareness, an understanding, a realization of what had just taken place on the altar, at the consecration: a realization of God made present by the words of consecration in a way that made Him belong to me.
>
> But what a thing it was, this awareness: it was so intangible, and yet it struck me like a thunderclap. It was a light that was so bright that it had no relation to any visible light and so profound and so intimate that it seemed like a neutralization of every lesser experience.
>
> And yet the thing that struck me most of all was that this light was in a certain sense 'ordinary' – it was a light (and this most of all was what took my breath away) that was offered to everybody, and there was nothing strange about it. It was the light of faith deepened and reduced to an extreme and sudden obviousness. [1]

This, for Merton, was not simply an imaginative or sensual experience, but something in the realm of an 'immediate' contact, not speculative and abstract, but concrete and experimental, belonging in some sense to the order of

knowledge, but more to the order of love. The duration of
the actual experience lasted only a moment, but the consequent
joy that accompanied it remained for hours. It was 'given'
in the sense that there was no way to recapture or reconstruct
it – it had come from somewhere else beyond and above
himself.

This was an experience never to be forgotten by Merton;
not one that affirmed that he was well on the way to a deep
and settled life of prayer, but a sheer gift of grace that helped
him along this part of the road of his pilgrimage, which would
stand him in good stead when things began to go wrong – as
very soon they did.

The difficulty arose over the problem of vocation itself. It
was already the month of June when Merton returned from
Cuba. There were just two months to go before entry into
the noviciate. All his papers were in order and his application
had been successful. Not only so, but he obtained permission
to stay for a few weeks at St Bonaventure's, a college run by
the Franciscans. Here he went to mass daily, studied St
Thomas's *Summa* in the Philosophy Seminar room, and walked
in the woods alongside the Alleghany river. His only problem
during these days was the name he would take in religion.
In retrospect Merton confesses that although he had a genuine
vocation to the religious life, yet his dispositions at the time,
preparing to enter the Franciscan noviciate, were much more
defective than he was able to realise. His motives in choosing
the Franciscans were that the rule could be kept without
difficulty, and that it attracted him by the surroundings in
which he could live. He admits that God very often accepts
such dispositions as these and makes them into a true vocation
in his own time, but he goes on to say:

But with me it was not to be so. I had to follow a path
that was beyond my own choosing. God did not want
anything of my natural tastes and fancies and
selections until they had been more completely
divorced from their old track, their old habits, and
directed to Himself, by His own working. Already my

selfishness was asserting itself, and claiming this whole vocation for itself, by investing the future with all kinds of natural pleasures and satisfactions which would fortify and defend my ego against the troubles and worries of life in the world.[2]

He called to mind the words of Christ: 'If any man will come after me, let him deny himself and take up his cross daily and follow me. For whosoever will save his life shall lose it; and he that shall lose his life for my sake shall save it.' He saw that there would be no sacrifice at all entailed in his becoming a Franciscan. There was no cross, no real sacrifice, no true renunciation. Back for a while at the cottage behind Olean, one evening he began reading the ninth chapter of the book of Job. Suddenly, he began to feel 'threatened'. The peace he had known for the past months began to recede as he felt both challenged and smitten in this attentive reading of scripture. He was being asked about his vocation, was within weeks of entry into the noviciate, and all the arrangements had been carried through. But Merton writes:

I woke to find out that the peace I had known for six months or more had suddenly gone. The Eden I had been living in had vanished. I was outside the wall. I did not know what flaming swords barred my way to the gate whose rediscovery had become impossible. I was once more out in the cold and naked and alone. Then everything began to fall apart, especially my vocation to the monastery.

Not that it occurred to me to doubt my desire to be a Franciscan, to enter the cloister, to become a priest. That desire was stronger than ever now that I was cast out into the darkness of this cold solitude. It was practically the only thing I had left, the only thing to cover me and keep me warm; and yet it was small comfort, because the very presence of the desire tortured me by contrast with the sudden helplessness that had come storming up out of the hidden depths of my heart.[3]

Merton's past life rose up before him, and he realised that neither Dan Walsh nor Father Edmund really knew him. He realised that he had to go and make it clear who he was and see if they could accept him on that basis. So he packed his bag and went to New York.

It was soon over. After a day's lapse, Father Edmund told him very kindly that he should write to the Provincial and tell him that he had reconsidered his application. It is not altogether clear why the Franciscan decision was so abruptly negative. It is indicated that Merton's past moral life, together with such a short period as a converted Catholic, and the fact that the noviciate was rather full, weighed against him becoming a Franciscan novice, but the matter of Merton's possible liaison at Cambridge and the resulting child may well have been part of the consequent Franciscan refusal.[4]

He was dazed after the interview and went into the Church of the Capuchins on Seventh Avenue, taking his place in the confessional. Being so confused and miserable, he could not explain himself, and the priest thought he was some unstable and emotional character who had been thrown out of the noviciate of some religious order for good reason. The result was that he was told, in no uncertain terms, that he certainly did not belong to the monastery, still less to the priesthood, and that he was wasting the priest's time and insulting the sacrament of penance by indulging in self-pity in the confessional. The grief shows through:

> When I came out of the ordeal I was completely
> broken. I could not keep back the tears which ran
> down between the fingers of the hands in which I
> concealed my face. So I prayed before the Tabernacle
> and the big stone crucified Christ above the altar. The
> only thing I knew, beside my own tremendous misery,
> was that I must no longer consider that I had a
> vocation to the cloister.[5]

This was the beginning of the breaking-down process that would not end for Merton all the days of his life. This particular crisis taught him his own helplessness and need for God. In his utter need he turned to a consolation and a discipline which was to be the most effective he could have chosen. He purchased a set of breviaries and began to say the divine office. He then obtained a post teaching English at St Bonaventure's, and Father Irenaeus helped him find his way through the breviary.

In November 1940, he gave in his name to be drafted with the others, and thought little about it. In February 1941, he felt that he ought to make a retreat at some monastery, and so he wrote to the Trappist Abbey in Kentucky which Dan Walsh had mentioned. At this time too, he began to write more and better poetry, and at the beginning of March received a reply from the Trappists saying that they would be glad to have him for Holy Week. Almost immediately another letter arrived, this time from the Draft Board, telling him that his number was up for the army. He returned the papers seeking to be registered as a non-combatant objector, but when his medical examination took place, he was failed.

About three weeks before Easter, Merton went to the library, and taking down the *Catholic Encyclopaedia* turned to 'The Trappists' which led him on the the 'Carthusians' and the 'Camaldolese' with their hermitages. 'What I saw in those pages pierced me to the heart,' says Merton. The articles, the pictures, the whole monastic world of these monks, of this solitude, opened wide the wound that had never really healed.

The whole matter of vocation filled his heart and mind again, giving him no peace, and so the days passed, and soon he was on his way to the Abbey of Gethsemani in Kentucky.

When at last he reached the monastery and the next morning attended his first mass, the effect was electrifying for him:

How did I live through that next hour? The silence, the solemnity, the dignity of these Masses and of the church, and the overpowering atmosphere of prayers so fervent that they were almost tangible, choked me with

love and reverence that robbed me of the power to
breathe. I could only get the air in gasps.[6]

His description of the life, the liturgy, the whole ethos of
Gethsemani Abbey is full of a sense of the *numinous*, full of
yearning and constant spiritual challenge, and it mirrors the
paradox of a man who feels both the pull and the denial of
a vocation. As he thought about the Cistercians and the
Carthusians, it was no longer a matter of which Order
attracted him more, but which one tortured him the more with
a solitude, a silence and a contemplation that could never be
his.

He reflects that this kind of a retreat should have been the
place and time for him to have sorted out the problem of
vocation, but the traumatic experience of the Capuchin's
rebuke, and the inner helplessness held him back from facing
the matter squarely.

Before leaving Gethsemani, he made the Stations of the
Cross, remembering that he had been told that no petition
asked at the fourteenth station is ever refused:

And so about the last thing I did before leaving
Gethsemani was to make the Stations of the Cross, and
to ask, with my heart in my throat, at the fourteenth
station, for the grace of a vocation to the Trappists, if
it were pleasing to God.[7]

Back in 'the world' be began to feel its emptiness and
futility, which at the same time was insipid and slightly insane
to him. He wandered in the woods at the back of St
Bonaventure's, singing the Cistercian *Salve Regina*, or what
he could remember of it, and kept himself busy with the classes
and examinations.

The next significant incident which took place was his
coming into contact with the Baroness de Hueck. She worked
among the negroes in Harlem, and came to St Bonaventure's
to talk about her work, or rather to challenge with her inner
power by which she communicated. She had been born a

Russian, a young girl at the time of the October Revolution, her family and friends, together with the priests had been killed, and she had escaped to New York with nothing but her faith. Her experience had only served to deepen and intensify her faith, and Merton felt the work of the Holy Spirit in her fortitude, her peace and her absolute confidence in God.

She had realised her personal vocation while sitting on a kerbstone eating her lunch one day, when working at a laundry near Fourteenth Street, New York. She was to exercise the apostolate of a laywoman in the world, poor among the poor, living and working in the slums, the misery and the insecurity of Harlem. This is what she spoke about in the hall at St Bonaventure's, and Merton sums up the work of the Baroness and her helpers:

> They would live and work in the slums, lose
> themselves in the huge anonymous mass of the
> forgotten and the derelict, for the only purpose of
> living the complete, integral Christian life in that
> environment – loving those around them, sacrificing
> themselves for those around them, spreading the
> Gospel and the truth of Christ most of all by being
> saints, by living in union with Him, by being full of
> His Holy Ghost, His charity.[8]

And that was how Merton began to help in the work at Harlem. He depicts the Harlem scene in all its devastating sadness and glory, and the overwhelming influence of the Baroness on his life. His time at Harlem began with part-time help while he was still at St Bonaventure's, but as time passed, and he began an important correspondence with the Baroness, who had gone to Canada for a while, he began to feel a stirring of the depths of his soul again, a dissatisfaction with his present spiritual life, and the feeling that St Bonaventure's had outlived its usefulness. But what was he to do, and where was he to go?

Harlem seemed right for him, and he prepared to change his academic world of St Bonaventure's for life in Harlem.

But three questions blocked his way – and they were all the same question. They brought him to his crossroads.

The first was asked by the Baroness herself as they travelled by car to Harlem after he had met her from the train. She said; 'Tom are you thinking of becoming a priest? People who ask all the questions you asked me in those letters usually want to become priests . . .' Her words turned a knife in his old wound, but he answered; 'Oh no, I have no vocation to the priesthood.'

The second question came from Father Thomas, the President of St Bonaventure's when Merton told him that he wanted to leave to go to Harlem. There was a long silence, and then, 'Haven't you ever thought about being a priest?' And Merton comments:

> Father Thomas was a very wise man, and since he was the head of a seminary and had taught theology to generations of priests, one of the things he might be presumed to know something about was who might or might not have a vocation to the priesthood.
>
> But I thought, 'He doesn't know my case'. And there was no desire in me to talk about it, to bring up a discussion and get all mixed up now that I had made up my mind to do something definite. So I said: 'Oh, yes, I have thought about it Father. But I don't believe I have that vocation.'[9]

The third question came just before he had left St Bonaventure's. Before joining the group at Harlem, Merton went to see his friend Mark Van Doren, who knew a publisher for a manuscript that Merton had put together, *The Journal of My Escape From the Nazis*. They had been talking about the Trappists when suddenly Mark said; 'What about your idea of being a priest? Did you ever take that up again?' Merton answered with a sort of indefinite shrug. Then came the moment:

> 'You know,' he said, 'I talked about that to someone who knows what it is all about, and he said that the

fact that you had let it all drop, when you were told
you had no vocation, might really be a sign that you
had none.' . . .

. . . the reasoning that went with this statement
forced my thoughts to take an entirely new line. If that
were true, then it prescribed a new kind of an attitude
to the whole question of my vocation.

I had been content to tell everybody that I had no
such vocation: but all the while, of course, I had been
making a whole series of adjustments and reservations
with which to surround that statement in my own
mind. Now somebody was suddenly telling me: 'If you
keep on making all these reservations, maybe you will
lose this gift which you know you have . . .'

Which I knew I had? How did I know such a thing?
The spontaneous rebellion against the mere thought
that I might definitely *not* be called to the monastic
life: that it might certainly be out of the question, once
and for all – the rebellion against such an idea was so
strong in me that it told me all I needed to know.[10]

The chapter in which Merton records that conversation is
entitled 'The Sleeping Volcano', and now the volcano erupted.
On the Thursday of the following week, he suddenly found
himself filled with a vivid conviction: 'The time has come for
me to go and be a Trappist.' He picked up the little book,
The Cistercian Life, which he had bought at Gethsemani. The
pages seemed to be written in words of flame. But there was
the old business – and he hesitated. His state of mind now
caused inner determination and then hesitation, and after
getting within six feet of Father Philotheus's room in St
Bonaventure's, he turned and ran out into the darkness. He
prayed in desperation, and then:

Suddenly, as soon as I had made that prayer, I
became aware of the wood, the trees, the dark hills,
the wet night wind, and then, clearer than any of these

obvious realities, in my imagination, I started to hear
the great bell of Gethsemani ringing in the night – the
bell in the tower, ringing and ringing, as if it were just
behind the first hill. The impression made me
breathless, and I had to think twice to realize that it
was only in my imagination that I was hearing the bell
of the Trappist Abbey ringing in the dark. Yet, as I
afterwards calculated, it was just about that time that
the bell is rung every night for the Salve Regina,
towards the end of Compline.

The bell seemed to be telling me where I belonged –
as if it were calling me home.[11]

He made his way back, found Father Philotheus, asked if
he could speak with him, and says, 'That was the end of my
anxiety'.

Father Philotheus saw no reason why Merton shouldn't
enter a monastery and become a priest, and after questioning
him, he saw that only the Trappist Order would do. So a letter
went off to the Abbot of Gethsemani, asking if he might make
a retreat. At the same time two letters arrived for Merton,
as they had done a year previously. One was from Gethsemani
saying 'yes' and the other from the Draft Board for another
medical examination. He wrote to the Draft Board immediately, saying that he was entering a monastery and asking
for time to find out when and under what conditions he would
be admitted. Then he sat down to wait. It was the first week
of December, 1941.

On Sunday, 7th December, he climbed the hillside and
wandered through the woods – for the last time. As he walked
back he met two of the lay professors who were talking
animatedly. They called, 'Did you hear what happened? Did
you hear the radio?' America was in the war.

So Merton acted. He got immediate permission to leave,
packed up everything, gave it all away except the contents
of one small suitcase, and went off to Gethsemani there and
then. All his former hesitation and fear were swallowed up
in this dramatic and sudden turn of events. After a description

of his departure and the journey, he sums up his attitude of mind:

> It was a strange thing. Mile after mile my desire to be in the monastery increased beyond belief. I was altogether absorbed in that one idea. And yet, paradoxically, mile after mile my indifference increased, and my interior peace. What if they did not receive me? Then I would go to the Army. But surely that would be a disaster? Not at all. If, after all this, I was rejected by the monastery and had to be drafted, it would be clear that it was God's will. I had done everything that was in my power; the rest was in His hands. And for all the tremendous and increasing intensity of my desire to be in the cloister, the thought that I might find myself instead, in an Army camp no longer troubled me in the least.[12]

At last he reached Gethsemani. He rang the bell at the gate. Presently the window opened, and Brother Matthew looked out between the bars:

> 'Hullo, Brother,' I said.
> He recognized me, glanced at the suitcase and said: 'This time have you come to stay?'
> 'Yes, Brother, if you'll pray for me,' I said.
> Brother nodded, and raised his hand to close the window. 'That's what I've been doing,' he said, 'praying for you.'[13]

References

1 Merton, *SSM*, p. 284.
2 *ibid.*, p. 291.
3 *ibid.*, pp. 295f.
4 This matter is not certain. See Chapter 2, footnote 15.
5 Merton, *SSM*, p. 289.

7 *ibid*., p. 332.
8 *ibid*., p. 343.
9 *ibid*., p. 359.
10 *ibid*., p. 362.
11 *ibid*., pp. 364f.
12 *ibid*., p. 370.
13 *ibid*., p. 371.

4: Pilgrimage and Paradox

Brother Matthew closed the gate behind Merton, and a new pilgrimage of enclosure and freedom began, reflecting all the paradoxes and tensions of a man on a spiritual journey. When Edward Rice, his former companion, came to write of Merton in 1970, he subtitled his book, *The Good Times and Hard Life of Thomas Merton*.

For Merton, this spiritual pilgrimage was to lead him into solitude, into silence, and deeper into God. And yet it was also to lead him back to the world, into print, and to become, as someone has called him, 'the most popular monk in the world'.

St Benedict calls the monastery the 'school' of prayer and spirituality. The learning, according to Merton, is the healing of our true nature, made in the likeness of God, and the healing power is love, and the love overflows to other men. 'The beginning of love is truth,' he says,

> and before He will give us His love, God must cleanse
> our souls of the lies that are in them. And the most
> effective way of detaching us from ourselves is to make
> us detest ourselves as we have made ourselves by sin,
> in order that we may love Him reflected in our souls
> as He has re-made them by His love. That is the
> meaning of the contemplative life. [1]

and this is what Merton sees as the end and goal of life in a contemplative monastery.

The apprehension about whether he would be accepted into the noviciate soon evaporated as Merton was received by Father Joachim who grinned and said, 'Oh, it's you', and by the Master of Novices who eventually led him, with another postulant, to Dom Frederic, the Abbot.

As a postulant, Merton began to feel his way around, looking at things from the noviciate wing instead of the guest house. He was now almost part of the community that he had seen functioning as a unity, but which now he saw broken up into its constituent parts. As he comments:

> It can be said as a general rule that the greatest saints are seldom the ones whose piety is most evident in their expression when they are kneeling at prayer, and the holiest men in a monastery are almost never the ones who get that exalted look, on feast days, in the choir. The people who gaze up at Our Lady's statue with glistening eyes are very often the ones with the worst tempers. [2]

He began his monastic life in Advent, received his new name – Frater Louis, and within days was clothed in his Oblate's habit, and clothed as a novice on the first Sunday in Lent. As the weeks went by, he learned more and more to recognise his old selfish appetites in their spiritual disguise:

> All my bad habits, disinfected, it is true, of formal sin, had sneaked into the monastery with me and had received the religious vesture along with me; spiritual gluttony, spiritual sensuality, spiritual pride . . . [3]

and yet he preserves a sense of humour in his descriptions. He was not the recipient of lights, voices, savours, unctions and the music of angelic choirs, and sometimes he experienced the 'vague disillusionment of the old days when I had paid down half a dollar for a bad movie . . .' He learned also that contemplation, which was in evidence in Gethsemani, was 'active contemplation', and that the monastery was not only a powerhouse of prayer but a powerhouse of work. And the work in which Merton would soon be involved was writing. But for the present he writes in lyrical praise of the labour of the fields, the heat of the summer and the praise of God. The heat of that first summer sent some novices away from the Abbey, as it did every year, but it only confirmed Frater Louis in his monastic resolutions. At the end of a long summer day, the sun is declining, the sky cool and the woods throwing off long blue shadows over the stubble fields where the golden shocks of wheat are standing. A clean smell of pine comes down from the woods on the breeze and mingles with the richness of the fields and of the harvest, and the undermaster claps his hands for the end of the work:

> And you take your rosary out of your pocket, and get in your place in the long file, and start swinging homeward along the road with your boots ringing on the asphalt and deep, deep peace in your heart! And on your lips, silently, over and over again, the name of the Queen of Heaven, the Queen also of this valley: 'Hail Mary, full of grace, the Lord is with thee . . .' and the Name of her Son, for whom all this was made in the first place, for whom all this was planned and intended, for whom the whole of creation was framed, to be His Kingdom. 'Blessed is the fruit of thy womb, Jesus!'[4]

There were to be days of tension and difficulty in the future, but the period of the noviciate was a time of knowing that he had found his place, and that there, and nowhere else, was where God wanted him to be.

One day in July, Thomas Merton's brother, John Paul, arrived at the monastery asking for baptism, but having had no instruction. As Merton describes those few days he reveals his profound understanding of a soul entering into faith. It was work much harder than the novices were doing in the fields, and much more exhausting in spirit. But he found an immediacy in his relationship with his brother, and an urgency in his brother's attitude that revealed the seriousness of the quest. He told him all that he himself had learned by experience, and all that he sensed John Paul wanted to know, commenting:

> He had not come here to find out a lot of abstract truths: that was clear enough. As soon as I had begun to talk to him, I had seen awaken in his eyes the thirst that was hiding within him, and that had brought him to Gethsemani – for he certainly had not come merely to see me. How well I recognized it, that insatiable thirst for peace, for salvation, for true happiness. There was no need of any elaborate argument: no need to try and be clever, or to hold his attention by tricks. He was my brother, and I could talk to him straight, in the words we both knew, and the charity that was between us would do the rest. [5]

The 'old days' with their confusion, their memories and their complications were all part of the conversation. The emptiness of a life lived apart from God, and the brothers' reaction against the world of materialism that brought no real happiness to their grandparents was recalled. The conversation went on:

> Once you have grace you are free. When you are baptized, there is no power in existence that can force you to commit sin – nothing that will be able to drive you to it against your own conscience. And if you merely will it, you will be free forever, because the strength will be given you, as much as you need, and as often as you ask, and as soon as you ask, and generally long before you ask for it, too. [6]

From that moment, John Paul's impatience to be baptised was intense. When Thomas had told him all that he knew, he stopped and was exhausted. 'Go on,' said John Paul, 'tell me some more.'

In five days it was all done, and John was on his way again.

Soon Merton was to hear the tragic circumstances of his death. On Easter Monday, 1943, he had received a letter which said that his brother had married and gone with his wife to the English Lakes for a week or so, and that he had immediately afterwards been put into the fighting in the RAF. He had been once or twice to bomb something, somewhere, but there was a tremendous change in his attitude towards the war and his part in it. He did not want to talk about it, and had nothing to say. He had come face to face with the world that he had helped to create, and the experience was an ugly one.

Merton wrote him a letter 'to cheer him up a little' on Easter Monday, but on Tuesday he was summoned to the Abbot's room and a telegram was read saying that Sergeant J. P. Merton had been reported missing in action ten days previously. Later Merton learned that on the night of Friday, 16th April, he had set out in his bomber with his crew for Mannheim. The plane came down in the North Sea, and badly hurt, yet supporting the dead pilot, he had been hauled aboard a rubber dinghy. He lay in the bottom of the dinghy in delirium, continually asking for water, but they had none. Merton writes of the experience that he could not forget:

> It did not last long. He had three hours of it, and then he died. Something of the three hours of the thirst of Christ who loved him, and died for him many centuries ago, and had been offered again on that very day, too, on many altars.
>
> His companions had more of it to suffer, but they were finally picked up and brought to safety. But that was some five days later. On the fourth day they had buried John Paul in the sea. [7]

As Merton closes his first autobiographical volume, he writes of the paradox that he is to himself. He was aware of his old, unspiritual self, now clothed in hypocritical spirituality, but also of the old 'writer' Thomas Merton who should have died, but who followed him into the cloister, more alive than ever.

He is constantly surrounded by contracts, reviews, page proofs, plans for books and articles, translation work . . . and says:

> Sometimes I am mortally afraid. There are days when there seems to be nothing left of my vocation – my contemplative vocation – but a few ashes. And everybody calmly tells me: 'Writing is your vocation.'[8]

And then there is the problem of his contemplative vocation seen within the context of the revival of Cistercian life in Gethsemani on a scale not known for ninety years. After a century of struggle and obscurity, Gethsemani was crowded with postulants and novices. On the Feast of St Joseph, 1944, when Merton made his simple profession, the names of those who were to form the first daughter house of Gethsemani were read out, and he speaks of four other houses which were emerging.

These things, together with the crowded guest house, and added publications, demanded more of the 'old' Thomas Merton. But it was not Merton the writer who was going to cause the greatest trouble, but Merton the religious, the 'early' Merton who had turned his back in puritan disgust upon the world to seek God in monastic seclusion.

Yet even in those days he knew St Thomas, St Bernard, St John of the Cross and other great mystics, who taught that the true comtemplative life is superior to the active – *Via contemplativa simpliciter est melior quam activa*, and yet that the mixed vocation can be superior to the contemplative if it is itself *more contemplative*. Merton expounds St Thomas:

> First comes the active life (practice of virtues, mortification, charity) which prepares us for contemplation. Contemplation means rest, suspension of activity, withdrawal into the mysterious interior solitude in which the soul is absorbed in the immense and fruitful silence of God and learns something of the secret of his perfections less by seeing than by fruitive love.

Yet to stop here would be to fall short of perfection. According to St Bernard of Clairvaux it is the comparatively weak soul that arrives at contemplation but does not overflow with a love that must communicate what it knows to other men. For all the great Christian mystics without exception, St Bernard, St Gregory, St Teresa, St John of the Cross, Blessed John Ruysbroeck, St Bonaventure, the peak of the mystical life is a marriage of the soul with God which gives the saints a miraculous power, a smooth and tireless energy in working for God and souls, which bears fruit in the sanctity of thousands, and changes the course of religious and even secular history.[9]

Then Merton looks into his own soul and wonders just what God is doing with him. The God who whispered 'Solitude, solitude' is the One who throws the whole world into his lap. He feels that half of New York is tied to his feet like a ball and chain, that his mind is making a noise like a bank, that he is stranded in a no-man's-land, or travelling and not knowing where he is going, and yet he can cry:

O my God, it is to You alone that I can talk, because nobody else will understand. I cannot bring any other man on this earth into the cloud where I dwell in Your light, that is Your darkness, where I am lost and abashed. I cannot explain to any other man the anguish which is Your joy nor the loss which is the possession of You, nor the distance from all things which is the arrival in You, nor the death which is the birth in You because I do not know anything about it myself and all I know is that I wish it were over – I wish it were begun.[10]

On the Feast of St Joseph, in 1948, at 33 years of age, Merton took his solemn vows. He had decided that he no longer was sure what a contemplative was, or what the contemplative vocation was, or what his vocation was, or what the Cistercian vocation was. All he knew was that God wanted him to take those particular vows in that particular house on that particular day for reasons best known to God himself . . . And God would eventually make things clear. 'That morning when I was lying on my face on the floor in the middle of the church, with Father Abbot praying over me,' he writes:

> I began to laugh, with my mouth in the dust, because without knowing how or why, I had actually done the right thing, and even an astounding thing. But what was astounding was not my work, but the work You worked in me.[11]

It is at this point, before the prophetic words with which Merton concludes *The Seven Storey Mountain*, that Merton's dialogue with God takes on a certain Zen-like quality which can be understood more perfectly by a retrospective look back from his later writings on Zen and Oriental thought. The whole concept of the 'direct grasp' of God, and of the 'awareness of full and spiritual reality, and therefore the realisation of the emptiness of all limited or particularized realities' is implicit within the passage that follows the above quotation. When Merton wrote later, 'Zen insight is not *our* awareness but Being's awareness of itself in us,' he was affirming something which caused him much struggle and turmoil in his 'early' days of limited Western and Thomistic thinking.[12]

The sorrow and joy of *The Seven Storey Mountain* is gathered up here in the realisation that Merton is aware that a new pilgrimage is beginning, which is a fulfilment of the first, and the prophetic words which he records are important in their forecast of solitude, pain, love, abandonment and ultimate fruitfulness:

> I hear You saying to me:
>   'I will give you what you desire. I will lead you into solitude. I will lead you by the way that you cannot possibly understand, because I want it to be the

quickest way. Therefore all things around you will be armed against you, to deny you, to hurt you, and therefore to reduce you to solitude. Because of your enmity, you will soon be left alone. They will forsake you and reject you and you will be alone. Everything that touches you shall burn you, and you will draw your hands away in pain, until you have withdrawn yourself from all things. Then you will be alone.

'You will be praised and it will be like burning at the stake. You will be loved and it will murder your heart and drive you into the desert. You will have gifts and they will break you with their burden. You will have pleasures of prayer, and they will sicken you and you will fly from them.

'And when you have been praised a little and loved a little I will take away all your gifts and all your love and all your praise and you will be utterly forgotten and abandoned and you will be nothing, a dead thing, a rejection. And in that day you shall begin to possess the solitude you have so long desired. And your solitude will bear immense fruit in the souls of men you will never see on earth.

'Do not ask when it will be or where it will be or how it will be; on a mountain or in a prison, in a desert or in a concentration camp or in a hospital or at Gethsemani. It does not matter. So do not ask Me, because I am not going to tell you. You will not know until you are in it.'[13]

The Merton we have followed up until his solemn vows did enter into an hitherto unknown experience, leading him into unknowing, and almost into despair. And yet we become aware that apart from the sentimentalism and a certain kind of immaturity manifested in his early writings, his profound, spiritual understanding and contemplative discernment is deepened and underlined when interpreted from the vantage point of his later writings.

His openness to Christians of other communions, to

mystical teachings of Oriental traditions and to all that is
human, could only have become possible and real as he
entered into the prophetic interior desolation with which his
first volume of autobiography concludes:

'But you shall taste the true solicitude of My anguish
and My poverty and I shall lead you into the high
places of my Joy and you shall die in Me and find all
things in My mercy which has created you for this and
brought you from Prades to Bermuda to St Antonin to
Oakham to London to Cambridge to Rome to New
York to Columbia to Corpus Christi, to St Bonaventure
to the Cistercian Abbey of the poor men who labour in
Gethsemani:

'That you may become the brother of God and learn
to know the Christ of the burnt men'
SIT FINIS LIBRI, NON FINIS QUAERENDI[14]

References

1 Merton, *SSM*, p. 372.
2 *ibid.*, p. 382.
3 *ibid.*, p. 387.
4 *ibid.*, p. 393.
5 *ibid.*, pp. 395f.
6 *ibid.*, p. 397.
7 *ibid.*, p. 403.
8 *ibid.*, p. 410.
9 *ibid.*, p. 415.
10 *ibid.*, pp. 419f.
11 *ibid.*, p. 421.
12 Merton's appreciation of Zen thinking is illustrated
   in the chapter on Zen in *MZM*, pp. 3-44.
13 Merton, *SSM*, p. 422.
14 *ibid.*, pp. 422f.

Part II: Evolution and Development

5: Continuing Conversion

Merton's autobiography, *The Seven Storey Mountain*, published in 1949, shot unexpectedly into the best-selling titles. This book, together with *The Sign of Jonas*, (1956), a kind of monastic journal, depicts a man who is constantly emerging, in the process of becoming. Yet the evolving pattern of Merton's life does not portray an intellectually or emotionally unstable man who cannot come to terms with himself or the world. In fact, his very vulnerabilities, as he records them, are moments of profound reflection, and his restlessness is understood as St Augustine would understand it – the restlessness and tumult of God within him.

But it is also true that he saw the psychological, intellectual and spiritual journey as all part of the great pilgrimage, in which he moved on to an ever greater appreciation of his inner experiences and outward circumstances, without the frustrating negations which belong to lesser men. Part of my own joy in reading and praying through Merton's life is that he enables me to see my own life in the mirror of his story.

His life was a microcosm, reflecting within his own experience the heights and depths of human life, the peace and tension, the joys and sorrows, the illumination and darkness that is part of our human lot. As A. M. Allchin wrote of him after his death:

> How much he was himself; how totally impossible to describe or define. He knew that each human person is unique and incomparable. He knew too that each one mysteriously contains the whole universe in himself. He not only knew this, but he lived it, and for this reason to meet him, whether in person or in his

writing, was liberating. It revealed something of the
true dimensions of human life, something of its strange
and unexpected goodness.[1]

What A. M. Allchin meant by the liberating experience
of Merton's influence was that his experience and teaching
was a liberation from the illusions of the world. The illusions
were subtler than Merton first expected, for they were inside,
as well as outside, the monastic walls – within religion, within
spirituality, within the search for holiness itself. And still he
went further. Merton traversed a long and arduous journey
from the young ardent idealist of the early years to the man
of wisdom, balance, humour and compassion of the later years.
He made the journey for himself and for others, as a pioneer
on the road where there were few guides. And he opened up
the way for others to follow. This long and arduous journey
can be traced in the *Mountain* and in the *Sign of Jonas*, and
in every piece of writing that came from his pen, right up
to the day of his death.

Fundamentally, Merton was a man of faith, a man of prayer
and of God. He had to realise that this involved an acceptance
and affirmation of his manhood, his humanness, his solidarity
with all mankind. But unless we understand that the inmost
centre, what he called *le point vierge*[2] of Merton's soul yearned
after God, and seek to understand him in his Christian and
monastic context, we shall be led to religious, sociological and
psychological conclusions which reflect only aspects of the truth
about the man, and neglect to affirm the fundamental and
basic meaning of his life. He loved God, he yearned for God,
he lived God.

Prior to the departure to his hermitage in 1965, he talked
to the novices at Gethsemani where he had been Master of
the Students and Master of Novices:

So I ask you to pray; and when you pray for me, all I
ask that you pray for is that above all I should
completely forget my own will and completely
surrender to the will of God, because that is just what

this pitch is all about and this is all I want to do. I don't want to go up there and just sit and learn a new form of prayer or something like that; it is a question of total surrender to God. And I in my turn will pray for you to do the same thing. And so may we all . . . The ambition of those Greek monks on Mount Athos is that you get to the point where you are kissed by God. There is a picture of a fellow, an Athonite hermit, in some old book, a beat-up, ragged old guy with a crow sitting on his shoulder, and the caption is: 'He was kissed by God.'[3]

Because Merton was a man whose mind and heart were set upon God, he appealed to and attracted many thousands of people with so many interests. His spiritual life overflowed into areas of aesthetic and artistic appreciation, sociological concern, political involvement and love for all men. He never professed to have arrived, but he never stood still. If he was a seeker, he was uniquely one who had found, and was forever finding and seeking and sharing in increasingly profound ways.

Many describe Father Merton as a searcher, and this is very exact. We are all searchers. The unique thing about Thomas Merton is that he was also a finder, a possessor, an enjoyer of that which he sought. For us, he is a symbol of hope that we, even we . . . can find God in contemplative prayer. As he had so obviously experienced the intimacies of mystical union, despite the fact that this is the twentieth century and not the fifteenth, he gives credence to our secretly cherished belief that deep union with the living God is actually attainable.[4]

The pilgrimage was a journey from the land of Egypt to the Promised Land in terms of his own personal salvation, but it was also a pilgrimage into the profound depths of the mystery of God. This involved interior darkness and wasteland, but every new understanding or perplexity broadened his horizons and deepened his commitment. From the beginning he understood his pilgrimage in this light:

> I know from my own experience that baptism was not the end of my conversion but only the beginning. I was baptized twelve years ago. I came to the font seeking what most people seek – faith, truth, life, peace. I found all that the first day, and yet I have continued to seek and have continued, also, to find. This seeking and finding goes on more and more. The pursuit becomes more ardent and more calm. The experience of discovery is something deeper and more vital every day.
>
> The faith, the love of God, the light of God's presence, the sense of rich and spiritual union with my brothers in God, all this grows and broadens with the ordinary joys and sufferings of life. You do not always have the sense that you are getting somewhere, and yet, whether you feel it or not, this expansion and deepening is always going on. The life of a Christian who does what he can to develop his Christian life is every day more serene and more profound.[5]

This is the kind of writing that makes an approach to Merton sheer joy. The pursuit is 'more ardent and more calm', it is 'more serene and more profound', as the pilgrimage continues. Sister Mary Seraphim, a Poor Clare, said after Merton's death that the proliferation of writings from the many-sided individual called Thomas Merton is excitingly bewildering. There is a tremendous variety of commitments, interests and evocations, some seemingly cancelling out others. She sees the reconciliating of his various phases a labour of love for some future genius, but she bears witness to the powerful secret at the heart of his being that the divine call to prayer and to love was his inmost centre, and that from that centre he communicates the divine call to all those who will follow such a path.[6]

The Belly of the Whale

The Sign of Jonas is an important book, for it is here that we begin to see the emergence of Merton as a man of deepening insights, profounder sympathies and growing compassion and understanding of God, of himself and of the world. It covers the period from December 1946 (five years after his entry into Gethsemani), to July 1952. It consists of personal notes and meditations which serve as a bridge between the early fervent convert monk on the *Mountain*, and the later more mature monk of genuinely catholic sympathies which were of ecumenical and international proportions.

Merton thought of Jonas, the Old Testament prophet, as a sign of paradox, if not contradiction. The whole ethos of *The Book of Jonas* appealed to him, for Jonas was an unwilling prophet, caught up both in the reality of his vocation and the struggle of his desires – the 'belly of the whale' being the place where the tensions and struggles were strangely resolved. Merton verbalises his Jonas-struggle:

> . . . for me the vow of stability has been the belly of the whale. I have always felt a great attraction to the life of perfect solitude. It is an attraction I shall probably never entirely lose. During my years as a student at Gethsemani, I often wondered if this attraction was not a genuine vocation to some other religious Order. It took me several years to find out that all contemplative Orders have much the same problems. Every man called to contemplation is called to some degree of solitude. God knows well enough how much each one needs. We need faith to let him decide how much we are to obtain. My own solution of this problem is the main theme of the present book. Like the prophet Jonas, whom God ordered to go to Nineveh, I found myself with an almost uncontrollable desire to go in the opposite direction. God pointed one way and all my 'ideals' pointed in the other. It was when Jonas was travelling as fast as he could away

from Nineveh toward Tharsis, that he was thrown
overboard, and swallowed by a whale who took him
where God wanted him to go.[7]

Merton could never have emerged as the mature, universal
man he later became without his early experiences of a certain
rejection of the world to find it again. There were times, in
later years, when he was exasperated with himself for his
former forthright rejection of the world as he became
sensitively aware of the respect, love and pity which welled
up within him by his coming into contact with ordinary men
and women. We have already noted his reaction on his first
journey outside the monastery in seven years in the streets
of Louisville, when he reflected: 'I went through the city
realizing for the first time in my life how good are all the people
in the world and how much value they have in the sight of
God.' And yet this amazing new awareness only deepened
his monastic commitment and interior solitude. In one of the
last books he wrote, he affirms both his humanity and his
vocation in such a way that reveals the necessity of the whole
pilgrimage which was the story of his life:

It is a glorious destiny to be a member of the human
race, though it is a race dedicated to many absurdities
and one which makes many terrible mistakes: yet, with
all that, God Himself gloried in becoming a member of
the human race. To think that such a commonplace
realization should suddenly seem like news that one
holds the winning ticket in a cosmic sweepstake.
    I have the immense joy of being *man*, a member of a
race in which God Himself became incarnate. As if the
sorrows and stupidities of the human condition could
overwhelm me, now I realize what we all are. And if
only everybody could realize this! But it cannot be
explained. There is no way of telling people that they
are all walking around shining like the sun.[8]

He goes on to say: 'This changes nothing in the sense and

value of my solitude', for it is the function of solitude, for
Merton, to make one realise such things with such a clarity that
would be impossible for anyone completely immersed in the
cares, illusions and automatisms of the tightly collective existence
that is so evident in contemporary society. But he also affirms
that this solitude is for all those with whom he finds such
profound solidarity. He enters into the depths of contemplative
prayer and solitude for them. The more he realises the simply
ordinariness of his own humanity, the more he feels that the
vocation to prayer and solitude comes from God, and re-echoed
within them. 'It is because I am one with them that I owe it
to them to be alone,' he says, 'and when I am alone they are
not "they" but my own self. There are no strangers.'

This is a mind-blowing dimension to solitude – it becomes
a necessity for some, so that all may live in love and joy.
'Thank God, thank God I *am* like other men,' says Merton
again, 'that I am only a man among others.' Experiences like
these deepened in Merton not only a sense of solidarity with
all humankind, but the certainty of the intrinsic value of every
human person, and that the destiny of all was a destiny of
love, through the incarnation of God in a human person –
Jesus Christ. As we glimpse where his solitude was taking him,
all the prophecies, innuendoes, yearnings and perplexities of
the *Mountain* begin to make sense on this larger canvas of ever-
deepening conversion.

Conversion as a Process

Conversion being a process, each stage therefore contains
within itself the fulness of the last. If there are things which
have to be unlearned, there is no loss, for there is positive
meaning in having learned, then learning to unlearn, in order
to learn again. His conversion is taken up into the larger
Benedictine vow to *conversio morum* which means the conversion
of the whole of life:

It is evident that the story of my life up to the day of
my baptism is hardly the adequate story of my

> 'conversion'. My conversion is still going on.
> Conversion is something that is prolonged over a
> whole lifetime. Its progress leads it over a succession of
> peaks and valleys, but normally the ascent is
> continuous in the sense that each new valley is higher
> than the last one.[10]

Baptism was certainly the initiating grace of his conversion,
but that was only the beginning. There is need for continuing
sanctifying grace which constantly imparts the life of Christ
to the believer. Christ nourishes us with the fruits of his
passion, says Merton, and enables us to participate in his risen
life. This spiritual life is increased and developed, ever deeper,
ever fuller, as we experience true mystical membership in the
Body of Christ.

This profound deepening of the concept of conversion made
Merton at the same time a more spiritual and a more worldly
man. I mean 'worldly' in the sense of *cosmic*, not in the sense
of *carnal*! The world as *cosmos* is indwelt by the immanent Spirit
of God, and all men, especially since the Incarnation, are
potentially redeemed. There was a shedding of the exclusiveness and puritanism of his early convert days, but there was
also a flowering of what had been a prophetic insight towards
contemplation found in both the *Mountain* and *The Sign of
Jonas*.[11] Writing of the sentimentality, immaturity and convert
mentality of parts of the *Mountain*, Merton says:

> I was still dealing in a crude theology that I had
> learned as a novice; a clean-cut division between the
> natural and supernatural, God and the world, sacred
> and secular, with boundary lines that were supposed to
> be quite evident. Since those days I have acquired a
> little experience, I think, and have read a few things,
> tried to help other people with their problems – life is
> not as simple as it once looked in The Seven Storey
> Mountain.[12]

Those are the words of a man of some maturity, and this

kind of humility is found throughout his writings. He later said that the world he was sore at on paper was sometimes a figment of his imagination, and that the attitude was a psychological game he had been playing since he was ten years old.[13] And yet, of course, he was continually critical in a constructive way of the world of pretence, avarice and violence that he saw quite clearly. He discerned, creatively, the difference between the world of the created order which God loves, and the world which is condemned by scripture:

> The real trouble with 'the world' in the bad sense which the Gospel condemns, is that it is a complete and systematic sham, and he who follows it ends not by living but by pretending he is alive, and justifying his pretence by an appeal to the general conspiracy of all the others who do the same.
>
> It is this pretence that must be vomited out in the desert. But when the monastery is only a way-station to the desert, when it remains permanently that and nothing else, then one is neither in the world nor out of it. One lives marginally, with one foot in the general sham. Too often the other foot is in a sham desert, and that is the worst of all.[14]

So although he affirms his monastic vocation, it is a vocation in which conversion, paradox and tension all have their place. He never became free of paradox and always felt the tension of what it meant to be in the prophetic tradition, of being somewhere on the borderland between the monastic state and life 'in the world'. This is what the sign of Jonas meant to him. And yet it is not only his sign – the prophetic task is that of every Christian.

For Merton, monks are the heirs of the prophets, for the prophet is a man whose whole life is a living witness of the providential action of God in the world. Every monk in whom Christ lives and in whom the great prophecies are therefore fulfilled, is a witness and a sign of the kingdom of God:

The sign Jesus promised to the generation that did not understand Him was the 'sign of Jonas the prophet', that is, the sign of His own resurrection. The life of every monk, of every priest, of every Christian is signed with the sign of Jonas, because we all live by the power of Christ's resurrection. But I feel that my own life is especially sealed with this great sign, which baptism and monastic profession and priestly ordination have burned into the roots of my being, because like Jonas himself I find myself travelling toward my destiny in the belly of a paradox.[15]

The sign of Jonas was never removed from Merton's life. He lived from the depths of his solitude and inner contemplation, but displayed a many-faceted activity, so that it became difficult for people to understand the underlying, integrated unity which bound it all together. This was especially the case when he took up new themes, new concerns, new enthusiasms without an obvious correlation of words and behaviour. This is reflectd in the homily preached by Father Flavian Burns, the Abbot of Gethsemani, on 11th December, 1968, the day after Merton's sudden death:

His life was far from silent, despite his hermit bent, since he was, in God's providence, an artful minister of the Word. The world knew him from his books, we know him from his spoken word. Few, if any, knew him in his secret prayer.

Still, he had a secret prayer and this is what gave the inner life to all he said and wrote. His secret was his secret to himself to a great extent, but he was a skilful reader of the secret of the souls that sought his help. It was because of this that although we laughed at him, and with him, as we would a younger Brother, still we respected him as the spiritual father of our souls.[16]

The matter is made explicit with great feeling in the *Letter from Gethsemani*, written on the day after the funeral by Fr Matthew Kelty, Merton's friend and brother in religion:

> The readings from the book of Jonah in the mass were not inappropriate! There was the whale (the coffin) in front of us with Fr Louis inside . . . I do not know how to summarize the man – the thought is not even decent! – except to say that he was a contradiction. He lived at the center of the cross, where the two arms meet. Maybe you could say, at the heart of life. And my guess is that at no other place is contradiction reconciled. He was a problem to many, here also, and this is the reason for the problem: I mean the terrifying tensions the man endured with a kind of courage that only the power of God made possible. I kept feeling when close to him: God is near. And to be near God is to be near something at once wonderful and terrible. Like fire. It burns. People were forever trying to get out of the spot made for them (by his simply being what he was) by putting him into some category or other and then making him stay there: about as good as bottling fog! For the task was impossible. They would decide he is a 'monk' and this is what a monk should be. Then they would expect him to be that. And he wouldn't, couldn't. Or hermit? Very well, this is what a hermit is: . . . And then they would see if he is being a good hermit. And he would not be!! And so on. In everything.[17]

Contemplative Yearning and Gregarious Communication

In the above quotation, Fr Matthew Kelty makes it clear that he loved Merton with all his contradictions, and Merton loved him. And it was a whole love, without qualifications, but with complete acceptance. But not everyone could treat Merton like that, especially his reading public. My own understanding of Merton's many-faceted personality took much time and thought, and the process involved led me to a greater self-

understanding of my own contradictions. He longed for the
solitude of the Face of God alone. And he longed for people,
for love, for communication. I remember how my heart was
stirred when I first read, in *The Sign of Jonas*: '. . . for myself,
I have only one desire and that is the desire for solitude – to
disappear into God, to be submerged in His peace, to be lost
in the secret of His Face.' People would understand such words
in a monastic, solitary and spiritual sense, and then find that
he was denouncing the evils of the Vietnam War with a
prophetic voice. And for them (though not for him), here was
contradiction.

There were constant demands upon his time and energies
for translating and writing within the monastery, together with
continual pressure from publishers outside the monastery. He
did eventually learn that he had to pray as he wrote his books
and that there were certain compensations in having to write,
not the least of which was solitude. But as time went on and
the overflow of his secret prayer and contemplative life
manifested itself in social concern, contacts with ancient
contemplative traditions of other Faiths and other matters
which did not explicitly indicate the Christian monastic life,
various rumours circulated which indicated that he had
forsaken his monastic tradition, broken his vows and lost his
vocation.

Such stories, were, of course, inevitable, and Merton
constantly denied them by his life, his words and his writings.
In fact, in all the twenty-seven years of his monastic life, apart
from his final (and fatal) trip to Asia in 1968, he only once
made an extended journey outside his monastery, and that
was in the company of his Abbot and Fr John Eudes
Bamberger to St John's Monastery. Fr Bamberger speaks of
his decision to comment on the situation in 1963 when Merton
wrote the preface to the Japanese edition of *The Seven Storey
Mountain*, quoting Merton:

> Many rumours have been disseminated about me since
> I came to the monastery. Most of them have assured
> people that I have left the monastery, that I had

returned to New York, that I was in South America or Asia, that I had become a hermit, that I was married, that I was drunk, that I was dead . . .

Certainly, I have never for a moment thought of changing the definitive decisions taken in the course of my life: to be a Christian, to be a monk, to be a priest. If anything, the decision to renounce and to depart from modern, secular society, a decision· repeated and reaffirmed many times, has finally become irrevocable . . . I am still in the monastery, and intend to stay there. I have never had any doubt whatsoever of my monastic vocation. If I have ever had a desire for change, it has been for a more solitary, and more 'monastic' way.[18]

Of course, there were many reasons in Merton's own temperament and behaviour which gave rise to such rumours. We have already noted that he was a most unusual monk, with his multitudinous interests and enthusiasms. It was difficult, if not impossible, for people to believe that such a man, with such a range of interests, could remain for twenty-seven years, to the very end of his life, in one monastic community. But if he did not go to people, they certainly came to him. Because of his spiritual, monastic, political, social and poetic writings, he was visited by, and gave counsel to, all kinds of people. Bamberger comments:

. . . there was a steady stream of persons of multifarious interests coming to speak with him from all over the world. He counted among his friends Vietnamese Buddhists, Hindu monks, Japanese Zen-masters, Sufi mystics, professors of religion and mysticism from Jerusalem's university, French philosophers, artists and poets from Europe, South America and the States, Arabic scholars, Mexican sociologists and many others. He was not only at home with all these men, he was on most friendly terms with each, and anyone who has been at the informal meetings he held with them over the years recognized how much pleasure he took in such company.[19]

Here is the 'sign of Jonas' again, the solitude he longed for and the constant stream of people (whom he loved). Here is another aspect of the paradox within himself which cried out for the silence of God, and for the men in whom God lived and moved. His heart went out to so many people, to so many circumstances, to so many things, and yet his heart was only and wholly set upon God. As long as we keep this in mind as we continue to share his pilgrimage, we shall be enabled to see his life in perspective. His life and writings seem filled with dialectical and paradoxical statements – and yet they are all 'true' and relevant at the time, in the sense and context in which they were experienced, spoken or written. As Bamberger puts it:

> Merton's writings teem with . . . contradictory statements. It is a regular feature of his style. This dialectical approach in dealing with life, where one assertion is negated by another, is more than a mere question of psychological ambivalence, though doubtless there was some of that in it. In contrast with psychological ambivalence, however, this feature was more in evidence as he grew more confident of himself, and appears with increasing frequency in his later writings. He came to surpass Emerson in his conviction that a man need not trouble himself overmuch about charges of inconsistency so long as he pursued, intuitively, his deepest truth in the confidence that the overall pattern of his life would witness to an ultimate authenticity and truth.[20]

Because of this, he spoke to the people in their own experience of contradiction, alienation and paradox. He experienced and expounded the human dilemma, explored the wasteland of his own being on behalf of the rest of us, and having diagnosed our contradictions, pointed to his own continuing experience of conversion and contemplation within the paradox of the mystery of God.

In the Preface to *A Thomas Merton Reader*, an anthology of twenty-five years of his writing, he speaks of the paradox of sharing restlessness and tranquillity:

> All life tends to grow like this, in mystery inscaped with paradox and contradiction, yet centered, in its very heart, on the divine mercy. Such is my philosophy, and it is more than philosophy – because it consists not in statements about a truth that cannot adequately be stated, but in grace, mercy, and the realization of the 'new life' that is in us who believe, by the gift of the Holy Spirit. Without this gift we would have no philosophy, for we could never experience such simplicity in the midst of contradiction. Without the grace of God there could be no unity, no simplicity in our lives: only contradiction. We can overlay the contradiction with statements and explanations, we can produce an illusory coherence, we can impose on life our intellectual systems and we can enforce upon our minds a certain strained and artificial peace. But this is not peace.[21]

References

1   A. M. Allchin, 'A Liberator, A Reconciler', *Continuum*, pp. 363f.
2   Merton, *CGB*, p. 142.
3   *Cistercian Studies*, Vol. V, 1970: 3, p. 226.
4   Sister Mary Seraphim, P. Cl., 'Thomas Merton: Who Was He?' *The Cord*, p. 261.
5   Merton, *Where I Found Christ*, (ed. John A O'Brien), p. 240.
6   Seraphim, *op. cit.*, pp. 259f.
7   Merton, *SJ*, p. 20.
8   Merton, *CGB*, pp. 141f.

82   *Soul Friends*

ibid.
10 O'Brien, *op. cit.*, p. 234.
11 Merton, *SJ*, p. 163.
12 Quoted by James Thomas Baker in *Continuum*, p. 260.
13 Merton, *SJ*, p. 163.
14 Merton, *CGB*, p. 310.
15 Merton, *SJ*, pp. 20f.
16 *Cistercian Studies*, Vol. III, 1968, p. 275.
17 *Monastic Exchange*, Vol. 1, Spring, 1969, p. 87 (Letters).
18 *Continuum*, p. 228.
19 John Eudes Bamberger, *Continuum*, p. 229.
20 *ibid.*, pp. 234f.
21 Thomas P McDonnell, (ed), *A Thomas Merton Reader*, p. xi.

6: *The Quest for Identity*

Merton never ceased to be a pilgrim. In his later, mature essays he wrote of the 'Identity Crisis' within contemporary monastic life,[1] but such a crisis among professed monks and novices of the post-Vatican II Church was rooted fundamentally for him in the personal quest for identity. And he saw this as every man's pilgrimage. In this respect too, my reading of Merton's evolving search has continually shed light upon my own tensions of the contrast between what I am and what I am meant to be. It is a question of attaining or realising, in Christ, the true identity to which I am called. 'Not to accept and love and do God's will,' says Merton, 'is to refuse the fulness of my existence.'

> If I never become what I am meant to be, but always remain what I am not, I shall spend eternity contradicting myself by being at once something and nothing, a life that wants to live and is dead, a death that wants to be dead and cannot quite achieve its own death because it still has to exist.[2]

This quest is no subjective flight into narcissistic fantasy. Merton is engaged on a dynamic journey which is intensely personal and powerfully corporate. Not to attain my true identity is worse than not to have been born. To exist simply in and for myself is to be an illusory, unreal individual. The first step towards liberation, freedom, salvation and the attaining of my true identity is the recognition of the human dilemma:

> To say I was born in sin is to say I came into the world with a false self. I was born in a mask. I came

into existence under a sign of contradiction, being
someone that I was never intended to be and therefore
a denial of what I am supposed to be. And thus I
came into existence and nonexistence at the same time
because from the very start I was something that I was
not.[3]

Merton is affirming the pilgrimage of identity, the journey
into becoming human, the making of our human nature. Not
to make such a journey is a denial of life, and to turn aside
from the true pilgrimage is to lapse into a caricature of what
it is to be human, and to become lost.

True Self and Pseudo-self

The secret of man's identity is hidden in the love and mercy
of God, and only in God can it be discovered and realised
in experience, so that God becomes the reason and fulfilment
of man's existence. 'Therefore,' says Merton, 'there is only
one problem on which all my existence, my peace and my
happiness depend: to discover myself in discovering God. If
I find Him I will find myself and if I find my true self I will
find Him.'[4]

For Merton himself, this led him to a contemplative
monastery, but also out into the dimensions of human
compassion, aesthetic appreciation, striving for social justice,
coupled with wise, humorous and mind-stretching writing that
challenges and excites at varying levels of the mind and heart.
He is not concerned with recruiting converts to the spiritual
hothouse of a contemplative monastery, but he is involved
in the invitation to participate in the fulness of human life.
John J Higgins, in *Merton's Theology of Prayer*, writes:

For Merton the problem of man's searching for his
union with God is basically a problem of man's finding
his true identity. For Merton describes identity as that
which 'you really are, your real self'. In actual fact,
the man who is seeking union with God is seeking to

recover possession of his deepest self – the self that is discovered after all other partial and exterior selves have been discarded as masks. Most simply, he is seeking to discover who he is in relation to God. And, when such a man draws near to God, he does not lose his identity; he becomes, rather, his real self, or his true self. However, if this transformation, which is ultimately accomplished by God's merciful love in man, is to be realized by man, then he must work together with God in creating his new identity in the sense that he must desire it and work to find it with God and in God.[5]

The early Merton seemed obsessed with religious questions, and the word 'salvation' had to do with the saving of one's soul. But the later and more mature Merton realised that salvation was the therapeutic wholeness which was God's love and grace invading the human life at every level. The more he experienced the forgiveness and the loving embrace of God, the more he felt the questions, the problems, the agony of human existence in the world. He is adamantly opposed to those who have never felt high ecstasy or black despair, but who smilingly concoct smooth religious answers or formulate firm, dogmatic propositions as answers to the agony and absurdity felt by men of integrity who recognise the human dilemma of contemporary existence. 'Indeed,' he says:

for the man who enters into the black depths of the *agonia*, religious problems become an unthinkable luxury. He has no time for such indulgences. He is fighting for his life. His being itself is a foundering ship, ready with each breath to plunge into nothingness and yet inexplicably remaining afloat on the void. Questions that have answers seem, at such a time, to be a cruel mockery of the helpless mind.[6]

These words occur in *The New Man*, published in 1962, which serves as a bridge or link between the early and later

Merton. It reveals a profound awareness of what Merton calls the *agonia* of contemporary man, which has to do not so much with questions and answers, but with being and nothingness, spirit and void. He is not only reflecting the mood of the atheist existentialist writers and novelists, but is voicing the pain and despair of suffering humanity over the world. In such exploration we become aware of the perplexing absurdities of our existence portrayed by Western atheistic existentialists, but also observe the kind of objective sociological criticism and commentary of which Merton is capable, together with spiritual insights from ancient contemplative traditions such as Buddhism, Hinduism and Sufism. And all this in the context of a Christian contemplative, in what he calls the exploration of 'the inner wastes of his own being as a solitary'.

I journey with him in *The New Man*. He does not chart autobiographic details or concrete historical experiences as in his former books, but invites to existential searching. I can feel the corporate sense of the human glory and dilemma as, with Merton, I become the *microcosmos* in which the experiences of humankind are reflected. A reviewer writes of this book:

> Fr Merton examines the restless unsatisfactory search of the uncommitted soul for God. The soul freeborn yet tied, created for God and made to his image and likeness, yet apart from him and for that reason lonely and desperate. Despite this picture, the overall theme is one of hope and trust. All men are created for God, and all men are called out of darkness by the darkness of Christ's death. There is hope yet for man. In his actualization by awareness and knowledge of God he arrives at the fullness of his life and so achieves his end. A salutary message for one who is searching for God. [7]

An Embracing Definition of Salvation

Merton finds any definition of salvation which does not embrace the *wholeness* of the human person as deficient, if not heretical! Salvation is the search for real and authentic identity, 'the peaceful integration of all man's powers into one perfect actuality which is his true self, that is to say, his spiritual self.' This definition redeems it from its hackneyed and despised use as a synonym for piety. 'Salvation,' he says, 'is something far beyond ethical propriety. God is concerned with the whole human person, for by the Incarnation he sees Christ is every man.' Yet it is not simply 'human nature' which is saved by the divine mercy, but above all, the human person. And God values every human being as precious:

> The object of salvation is that which is unique, irreplaceable, incommunicable – that which is myself alone. This true inner self must be drawn up like a jewel from the bottom of the sea, rescued from confusion, from indistinction, from immersion in the common, the nondescript, the trivial, the sordid, the evanescent. [8]

One of the ways in which Merton communicates this kind of salvation as the finding and affirming of one's identity in God, is to tell the story of Genesis, the story of 'the prodigal soul's journey back from the *regio dissimilitudinis*, (the land of unlikeness), to likeness to God'. The image of God in man is the summit of spiritual consciousness, the highest peak of self-realisation. He is not here speaking of some kind of platonic contemplation, but of real experience of God. 'No natural exercise can bring you into vital contact with him,' writes Merton. 'Unless he utters Himself within you, speaks His own name in the centre of your soul, you will no more know Him than a stone knows the ground upon which it rests in its inertia . . . We become contemplatives when God discovers Himself within us.'

In charting the journey of salvation, Merton is very much aware of the Western tradition, with its legalistic commercial and judicial analogies and interpretations of divine grace. He is much more enamoured with the understanding of the Eastern Fathers who speak more in terms of salvation as a participation of the soul in the life of God, which is God's ultimate intention for man. He puts it this way:

> Theological disputation about free will and grace, especially since the Reformation, has ended in many theologians unwittingly running off with the prodigal son. Once the question of grace and free will is reduced to a juridical matter, once witnesses line up with plaintiff or defendant and the jurors strive to determine who is entitled to what, we are inevitably tempted to act as if everything that was given to free will was taken from grace, and everything conceded to grace was withdrawn from our own liberty.[9]

Merton is not willing to side either with the Augustinians or the Pelagians in their soteriological disputes, for he sees them as placing man over against God. In such a case, divine grace becomes a foreign 'substance' which is injected into the soul of man, and this makes nonsense of the Gospel:

> Grace is not a strange, magic substance which is subtly filtered into our souls to act as a kind of spiritual penicillin. Grace is unity, oneness within ourselves, oneness with God. Grace is the peace of friendship with God . . . Grace means that *there is no opposition* between man and God, and that man is able to be sufficiently united within himself to live without opposition to God. Grace is friendship with God. And more – it is sonship. It makes us the 'beloved sons' of God in whom He is 'well pleased.'[10]

Merton's teaching represents a *synergism*, a *working together* of the Spirit of God within the spirit of man. It corresponds more closely to the Eastern gradualistic kind rather than the Augustinian suddenness kind which is a mark of the Western and post-reformation church. Merton himself did have a kind of evangelical conversion, yet it was within the context of the gradual unfolding of God's grace within him. In his lectures on St Bernard, Merton makes it clear that we do not jump suddenly right from fallen nature to the highest degree of supernatural life. Grace does not suddenly 'annihilate' fallen nature, inserting something totally new in its place. There is a restoration of lost balance, a return to the full integration within ourselves. We advance humbly and quietly one step at a time, the Holy Spirit slowly but carefully restoring the order he wills for our good. Otherwise, we live in illusion, for we imagine we are living a supernatural life when fallen nature is still operating under the cover of the inefficacious practices of religion with which we delude ourselves. Salvation is by grace, but it builds on nature.[11]

God's intention is that man might develop his freedom, extend his powers and capacities of willing and loving to an unbelievable breadth, and raise his mind to an unheard of vision and truth. Of course, this is beyond man's natural abilities, for Merton portrays man, apart from God, as caught up in a kind of 'schizophrenic self-alienation', lost in egocentric contradiction in which his life becomes meaningless.

But he also speaks of God adding to our natural gifts the gifts of grace which elevate and transfigure nature, healing nature's ills and expanding nature's hidden resources, developing them yet more by our mystical life in God. 'Is grace opposed to nature?' asks Merton. And he answers clearly:

Not at all. It is opposed only to the *limitations*, to the *deficiencies*, to the *weakness* of nature, and to the infections and illnesses nature has incurred through the misuse of its own judgement and the abuse of its own freedom. Is grace opposed to our own self-realization, to our perfection as persons? Far from it. Grace is given us for the precise purpose of enabling us to discover and actualize our deepest and truest self. Unless we discover this deep self, which is hidden with Christ in God, we will never really know ourselves as persons. Nor will we know God. For it is by the door of this deep self that we enter into the spiritual knowledge of God. (And indeed if we seek our true

selves it is not in order to contemplate ourselves, but
to pass beyond ourselves to find Him.)[12]

The 'self' to which grace is opposed, in this view, is not
only the passionate, disordered, confused self – the rambling
and dishevelled 'ego' – but also, and much more, the
tyrannical 'super-ego' which Merton understands as the rigid
and deformed conscience which is our secret god, 'and which
with an infinitely jealous resourcefulness, defends its throne
against the coming of Christ.'

Theosis: Participation in the Life of God

All this is part of the finding of our own identity in God. It
is the affirmation and experience within our own soul of the
redeeming work accomplished by Christ as the Second Adam.
Merton takes up the *recapitulation* idea of St Paul and St
Irenaeus, as he portrays Christ summing up within himself
and redeeming the old Adam in offering the obedience of his
life and death to the Father. As man finds his way back from
the *regio dissimilitudinis* through Christ the Second Adam, by
the inner illumination and power of the Holy Spirit, he thereby
affirms his identity in God, returning to the Edenic paradise.
He thus participates in the very life of God in which he
discovers his true self. Merton comments:

> It has been called by the Fathers of the Church the
> *divinization* (*theosis*) of man. It is the ultimate in man's
> self-realization, for when it is perfected, man not only
> discovers his true self, but finds himself to be
> mystically one with the God by Whom he has been
> elevated and transformed.[13]

He points out that the breath which God breathed into
Adam proceeded from the mysterious and intimate depths of
God's own being, and this gave actuality, existence and
movement to the first Adam. This is what is restored to us
in Christ, He shows the etymological relationship between

the words 'breath' and 'spirit' so that Adam's very existence was a continual 'inspiration' of God.

Following the early Fathers, Easten and Western, Merton makes much of the early chapters of Genesis, especially the paradise story and the Adam-Christ parallel. Here is enacted the story of mankind, reflecting its glory and pain. The pre-fallen Adam was the lowest in the order of spiritual beings, and the highest of those which had a place in material creation. Here is the pattern of what man is meant to be, for as he says:

> The early chapters of Genesis (far from being a pseudo-scientific account of the way the world was supposed to have come into being) are precisely a poetic and symbolic revelation, a completely *true*, though not literal, revelation of God's view of the universe and of His intentions for man.[14]

This kind of contemplative theology not only imparts significance, value and meaning for the life of man – he is of *value* to God and creation, but it also has dramatic implications for moral ethics, for the stewardship of animal creation and for ecology. Being the most exalted within the material order, Merton calls the Adam-figure the 'high priest of the universe', and being placed at the 'ontological centre of creation' he was the anointed mediator between God and the world.

God's intention was that Adam as the priest, should offer all things back to God without harming or destroying them, thus fulfilling his appointed function as a kind of creative cosmic mediator. The whole material world would justify its existence in being raised to the level of intelligibility and value in Adam, who would be continually transfigured by the presence of the creating and sanctifying Spirit of the Lord. The 'morning and evening knowledge of God' would be the contemplation and action which flowed from the Holy Spirit in the paradise which Adam was to tend.

For Merton, Adam is not only the representative of the solidarity of the human race, innocent and then fallen, but Adam is Thomas Merton, and in the reader's mind, Merton makes Adam to become the reader himself. When God said: 'Let us make mankind in our image and likeness'. Merton makes us feel that God's 'image' is our creativity, and God's 'likeness' is our ability to become the imitator and instrument of God in the world, bearing God's love to the rest of the created order and carrying the whole world to God in prayer, in intercession and in worship.

Merton says that the orientation towards contemplation is of the very structure of man's being, that man's true life and identity can only be found in reconciliation, in adoration and in contemplation of the beauty and holiness and sheer joy of God. He speaks of St Augustine seeking God 'in the most intimate depths of his own spirit', so that when God is sought and found in those depths, then love and illumination reveal the God who is enthroned in the very summit of the personal being – the *apex mentis* of the soul.

But Merton is also very aware that the *imago dei* has been damaged, broken, distorted. The 'fall' in the Genesis narrative has to be taken seriously, and the resultant 'natural man' is alienated in those very structures of his personal being where God should be enthroned and indwelling.

> . . . one's actual self may be far from 'real', since it may be profoundly alienated from one's own deep spiritual identity. To reach one's 'real self' one must, in fact, be delivered by grace, virtue and asceticism, from that illusory and false 'self' whom we have created by our habits of selfishness and by our constant flights from reality. In order to find God, Whom we can only find in and through the depths of our own soul, we must therefore 'return to ourselves', we must 'come to ourselves.'[15]

So on the one hand Merton cries out in wonder: 'Contemplation is a mystery in which God reveals Himself to us as the very centre of our own intimate self – *intimior intimo meo* as St Augustine said.' And on the other he bewails our fallen condition: 'The tragedy is that our consciousness is totally alienated from this inmost ground of our identity. And in Christian mystical tradition, this inner split and alienation is the real meaning of original sin. Merton goes on to define original sin as the perversion of man's active instincts, a turning of man's creativity away from God, to seek power and glory within the world which would then become an end in itself.

Sr John Oxenham says that the theme 'a return to the heart' is Merton's life-long quest, and she says:

> . . . if man is to turn his heart towards God, he must first of all *return* to his heart, from which he is so often absent. It was only after he had come back to his heart that the prodigal son could set out on the return journey to his Father. For man's true home is in the inmost depths of his heart.[16]

Merton, writing of the concept of 'the heart' in *Contemplative Prayer*, comments: 'It refers to the deepest psychological ground of one's personality, the inner sanctuary where self-awareness goes beyond analytical reflection and opens out into metaphysical and theological confrontation with the Abyss of the unknown yet present – one who is ''more intimate to us than we are to ourselves''.'

Merton is thus working with an interior dualism between the alienated self, the superficial ego which is proud, rebellious and fallen, and the true deep and contemplative self which is reconciled, forgiven and contemplative. When he added two important chapters to his *Seeds of Contemplation*, twelve years after its first appearance, he wrote:

> There is an irreducible opposition between the deep, transcendent self that awakens only in contemplation, and the superficial, external self which we commonly identify with the first person singular. We must remember that this superficial 'I' is not our real self. It is our 'individuality' and our 'empirical self' but it is not truly the hidden and mysterious person in whom

we subsist before the eyes of God. The 'I' that works
in the world, thinks about itself, observes its own
reactions and talks about itself is not the true 'I' that
has been united to God in Christ. It is at best the
vesture, the mask, the disguise of that mysterious and
unknown 'self' whom most of us never discover until
we are dead.*[17]

The asterisk draws attention to Merton's footnote which
reads: 'Hell can be described as a perpetual alienation from
our true being, our true self, which is God.'

The whole question of spiritual identity then is a matter
of man's spirit finding its rest and fulfilment in the Spirit of
God. This is what makes a man *spiritual*, *pneumatikos*, in the
New Testament sense. The *pneuma*, man's natural faculty,
the summit of man's nature is renewed and transformed,
acquiring an entirely new and different modality by the fact
that the Spirit of God is present within it. As Merton explains:

When a man prays 'in the spirit' it is he who prays
indeed, but it is also the Spirit of God who prays in
him, guiding him and showing how to commune with
God beyond language and understanding. The *pneuma*
is the spirit of man moved and directed by the Spirit
of God, liberated by deep faith and illumined by the
wisdom of God Himself.[18]

The New Adam and Contemplative Prayer

This mystical union of the spirit of man with the Spirit of
God is the *divinization*, *theosis*, referred to earlier and is what
Merton means when he speaks of a man 'finding himself in
God'. Locked and isolated in our own egocentric individualism
we cannot fully know ourselves. True identity only comes to
light when the Holy Spirit penetrates and enlightens our own
spirit from within ourselves. It is by his light and power that
we discover our true autonomy, our own identification.
Taking the pre-fallen Adam as the symbol of the believer's

contemplative life, Merton writes of his relationship with God in the Edenic paradise:

> Before the fall Adam, the prince of creation, conversed
> familiarly with God in the sense that he was constantly
> meeting Him in flashes of mystical intuition either in
> the existential reality of his own spiritual depths or in
> the reality of objective creation. He walked the earth,
> therefore, as one who had no master under God. He
> could be conscious of his own autonomy, under God,
> as the priest and king of all that God had made.
> Knowing no rebellion in the simplicity and order of his
> own being, he was also obeyed by all creatures. His
> mind had a perfect knowledge of himself and of the
> world around him and his will acted in perfect
> accordance with his vision of truth. This supreme
> harmony of all his powers flowed from their unity at
> the summit of Adam's being, in the pneuma, which
> was one with God.[19]

Therefore, to be oneself, to be truly human, is to have access to all the latent creative and healing powers of our rich human nature, in direct communication not only with the whole created order around, but also to be in direct, intimate and constant relationship with the indwelling Spirit of God. This is the point at which Merton relates the contemplative quest with the redemptive work of Christ as the Second Adam. What we lost in the fallen Adam, we recover with more besides in the Second and Last Adam. There is no by-passing the Christian scheme of redemption in Christ:

> All that has been said about man being made in the
> image and likeness of God and therefore being made
> for union with God is incomplete and indeed remains
> meaningless for a Christian until we see it in its proper
> orientation – to the Person of the Incarnate Word,
> Jesus Christ. The whole theology of the Redemption,
> of man's supernatural vocation as a son of God, is

summed up by St Paul in his parallel between Adam
and Christ: Adam the first man, the natural head of
the human race, and Christ the New Adam, the
spiritual head of regenerated and spiritualized
humanity.[20]

There is a special anguish that Merton sees in the biblical
view of man, in which the inner recesses of conscience, where
the image of God is 'branded' in the very depths of his being,
ceaselessly remind him that he is born for a far higher freedom,
and a far more spiritual fulfilment. There is no rest for him
save in God, and this divine restlessness is the pain and
groaning of creation. Following St Augustine's lead, though
avoiding his dark pessimism, Merton says that Adam's sin
was a double movement of introversion and extraversion. He
withdrew from God into himself, and being unable to remain
centred in himself, fell beneath himself into the multiplicity
and confusion of exterior things. 'Adam turned human nature
inside out,' says Merton, 'and passed it on in this condition
to all his children.' He does not subscribe to any platonic
notion of matter being evil in itself, but he does see Adam's
predicament, in which spirit becomes submerged in the flesh,
and therefore subject to, and dependent upon, matter:

Spirit that is immersed in matter which it cannot fully
control is therefore something like the captain of a ship
that has lost its rudder and is carried away by the
waves of a storm. The ship may well be a good ship,
but it is lost.[21]

This is the sense of lostness that Merton diagnoses as the
disease from which contemporary man suffers. It is a question
of loss of identity in God, and therefore the struggling to attain
an identity brought about by frenetic action, ambition,
commercial or political success, and the bid for power, money
and influence. The selfish and fleshly ego has replaced the
human spirit in union with the Divine Spirit. Thus, having
lost his true identity, man is literally 'dis-tracted' – pulled apart

by contradictory desires and guilt. 'No amount of business prosperity and luxury can hide the abomination of desolation within us,' says Merton, and he quotes one of the wisdom books to bear witness to the truth that men will rarely be honest enough to admit openly the interior emptiness: 'Therefore I loathed life, since for me the work that is done under the sun is evil: for all is vanity and a chase after wind. And I detested all the fruits of my labour under the sun.' And he comments:

> Those are terrible words, we will not listen to them because they sound too much like despair, and despair is precisely the spectre we would like to keep buried in oblivion by our ceaseless activity. For in fallen man action is the desperate anodyne, assuaging the pain of a soul that instinctively knows that it was made for contemplation – a soul that knows that action, which is itself necessary, is only a means to that end.[22]

He calls in the witness of modern psychoanalysis to underline the fact that there exists within man a tyranny of subconscious drives and compulsions in which man is so often governed by the blind needs and compulsive demands of passion. In his *Faith and Violence*, he writes on the psychological causes of war, treating spiritual alienation and perverted empirical individuality as among the psychological causes of personal and social destructive tendencies in our society.[23]

Here, then, is a personal and collective problem of immense proportions, with contemporary relevance to modern man's dilemma. It has social, ecological and international implications, and for Merton the reversal of this deadly pilgrimage is the same for nations as it is for individuals. The proud and rebellious journey of the First Adam is reversed by Christ, the last Adam, and it is the same journey for all.

Involved in such a journey is the reversal of pride of opinion and destructive lifestyle. This means *metanoia*, repentance, and the losing of one's life in order to save it. The pattern of such a repentant and converted life is the pattern of Jesus, the Last

Adam. It is the way of humility, compassion, material poverty and a laying down of one's life for others. This is an impossible prescription for unregenerate man, but Merton's diagnosis is of a fatal disease, and unless this prescription is applied by the Holy Spirit, then the prognosis is death.

Christ: Cosmic Mediator and Saviour

Merton is ultimately optimistic because he believes that not only is man as an individual a kind of *microcosmos*, a small world reflecting the *macrocosmos*, the whole world of men and nations – but Christ is the cosmic Mediator. This means that what Christ has done is an objective work in the reconciling of God and man. This holds good whatever man's attitude is, for God will not allow His work of redemption to be in vain. Ultimately, God will not permit the sin of man to blot his creation forever. The work of Christ as the Last Adam is objective, universal and cosmic. He represents the thinking of the Eastern Fathers, especially here reflecting a theology begun by St Paul in the Adam-Christ parallel, taken up by St Irenaeus in his theory of recapitulation, and re-echoed in such Eastern Fathers as St Maximus the Confessor. Merton moves freely and easily among such cosmic Eastern theologians.

His personal quest is caught up into the glory of the cosmic meaning of salvation for Jesus, the personal Saviour, is also the cosmic Lord and Mediator. This gives a corporate and universal sense to Merton's personal pilgrimage of salvation. It also gives social and political direction to his personal discipleship as a Christian.

After an intense theological exposition of Christ as the Last Adam in *The New Man*, he draws the thematic threads together in a mystical vision of regenerated humanity, in which his new identity is expressed on a personal and corporate level:

. . . we ourselves are 'the Second Adam' because we ourselves are Christ. In us the image or God, which is complete and entire in each individual soul, is also, in

all of us, 'the image of God'. The first Adam, 'who is
one man in all of us', is saved and transformed by the
action of Christ, and becomes, in us, the second
Adam. Thus, with something of the compenetrative
vision of the Fathers, we awaken to the deep and
mysterious presence within ourselves of the first man
and the last. We see that we ourselves are Adam, we
ourselves are Christ, and that we are all dwelling in
one another, by virtue of the unity of the divine image
reformed by grace, in a way that is analogous to the
circumincession of the Three Divine Persons in the
Holy Trinity. God Himself dwells in us and we in
Him. We are His new Paradise. And in the midst of
that Paradise stands Christ Himself, the Tree of Life.
From the base of the tree the four rivers of Eden flow
out to irrigate not only all the faculties of our soul and
body, filling them with grace and mystical light, but
also the whole world around us, by the invisible
radiation of the Spirit present within us. We are in the
world as Christ-bearers and temples of the Holy Spirit,
because our souls are filled with His grace.

This, then gives us a beginning of awareness of who
we are.[24]

References
1 Merton, *CWA*, pp. 56–82.
2 Merton, *SC*, p. 26.
3 *ibid.*, pp. 26f.
4 *ibid.*, p. 28.
5 See Higgins' chapter 'Union with God', pp. 1–24.
6 Merton, *NM*, p. 1.
7 DK, in *The Clergy Review*, July 1964, pp. 455f.
8 Merton, *SC*, pp. 29f.
9 Merton, *NM*, note especially pp. 25–30.
10 *ibid.*, p. 29.
11 Merton, *The Cistercian Fathers and their Monastic Theology*
    (unpublished 1963), p. 45.

12 Merton, *NM*, p. 30.
13 *ibid.*, p. 34.
14 Merton, *SC*, p. 225. See also *OB*, pp. 71f.
15 Merton, *NM*, p. 44.
16 *Cistercian Studies*, Vol. V, 1970: 1, p. 48.
17 Merton, *SC*, pp. 5f.
18 Merton, *NM*, p. 47.
19 *ibid.*, p. 51.
20 *ibid.*, p. 92.
21 *ibid.*, p. 81.
22 *ibid.*, p. 83.
23 See Merton, 'A note on the Psychological Causes of War',
       FV, pp. 111f.
24 Merton, *NM*, pp. 114f.

7: Merton as a Catholic Christian

The dynamic nature of Merton's pilgrimage reflected the emerging and enlarging awareness of himself as a Christian and as a human being. He was no ecclesiastic or church administrator, and my soul warmed to him for that very reason. He was not concerned with the kind of ecclesiastical politics which scored points or even 'in the best interests of the Church' imposed an artificial unity from above. His vision of unity was more basic. It was at the same time profoundly theological and more spiritual. He saw both the fallen Adam and the risen Christ in all men – that was a vision of theological clarity which ultimately meant universal salvation, without ignoring the massive destructive tendencies of fallen man. It was spiritual because he saw every man on a pilgrimage. His own pilgrimage was within the context of the Christian Church, and within the monastic tradition of the Roman Catholic communion. But as he travelled he related positively and enthusiastically to Christians of other traditions, to people of other Faiths, and the humanists and atheists of integrity. He was humble enough to learn from them all and compassionate enough to include them all in the same pilgrimage, the same salvation, and the same embracing love of God which held and sustained him. We shall note some of the tensions along the way – and the way he coped with them. For all these reasons I was infected with his joy, and continue to participate in his vision, though I must say that I share many of his tensions too.

Misunderstandings

First there were the rumours – about Merton himself and his relation to the Roman Catholic Church and monastic life.

`John Bamberger writes:

> He was somewhat sensitive on this point and not
> without reason. Over the years he had been
> alternatively vexed and amused at the persistent
> rumors that had him outside the monastery, the Order
> and even the priesthood. He knew that once he
> actually did travel for an extended period, there would
> be a plethora of such tales and a consequent
> misrepresentation of his whole aim and purpose in
> travelling to the East.
>
> Predictably, some journalistic accounts have spoken
> of him as having 'wandered back into the world' just
> as he had 'wandered into the monastery' in the first
> place, In reality, Merton was one of the most
> 'stabilised' monks in history. Until the last few years,
> when he visited physicians in town fairly often, he was
> almost constantly on the monastic grounds. When he
> did make a single trip in 1956 it was in order to go to
> St John's monastery and he went in the company of
> his abbot and a monk (myself). His travels in the last
> year of his life involved a couple of visits to
> monasteries. Hardly an exciting travelogue.[1]

His literary output was prolific, relating not only to theology
and spirituality, but to social criticism, current affairs, war
and peace, etc. He was an exciting, provocative and rebellious
writer. All this, coupled with his increasing interest and
openness to the great Oriental monastic traditions caused
perplexity in the minds of many 'Merton watchers'. The
rumours continued to the end of his life – rumours of a lost
vocation, a surrender of priesthood, a sense of disillusion, a
marriage, etc. In 1963, in the preface to the Japanese edition
of the *Mountain*, he commented on the situation:

> Many rumours have been disseminated about me since
> I came to the monastery. Most of them have assured
> people that I had left the monastery, that I had

returned to New York, that I was in Europe, that I
was in South America or Asia, that I had become a
hermit, that I was married, that I was drunk, that I
was dead . . .

Certainly I have never for a moment thought of
changing the definitive decisions taken in the course of
my life: to be a Christian, to be a monk, to be a
priest. If anything, the decision to renounce and to
depart from modern secular society, a decision
repeated and reaffirmed many times, has finally
become irrevocable.[2]

It was incredible to some people that Merton, being the
kind of man he was, with his impulsive, enthusiastic
temperament, what Jean Leclercq called *überschwenglich*, could
ever find in monastic life enough to keep him in the monastery
for long, let alone twenty-seven years. But as Merton affirmed
in 1963:

I am still in the monastery, and intend to stay there.
I have never had any doubt whatsoever of my
monastic vocation. If I have ever had a desire for
change, it has been for a more solitary, a more
'monastic' way.[3]

Certainly, in parts of his first autobiographical book he
portrays a narrow and exclusivist partisan catholicism, and
a negative and bigoted view of 'the world'. Retrospectively,
he was ashamed, irritated and amused by it in various ways.
There were jibes at protestant worship and his episcopalian
baptism, together with romantic and sentimental descriptions
of his call to the monastic life, the concept of such a life and
the liturgical worship at the Abbey of Gethsemani. Much
of this was reversed in later writings, but what remained was
a mature and positive evaluation of his relation to the Church
and the monastic life, with few illusions of his place within
it, together with a vital sense of fellowship and responsibility
within his own monastic community:

I am left with a sense of deep union with all the other
monks. I do not know what I expected to feel after my
profession. But afterwards I was left with a profoundly
clean conviction that I had done the right thing, and
that I had given myself as best I could to God. And
beyond that the nearest thing to sensible consolation
was a deep and warm realization that I was immersed
in my community. I am part of Gethsemani. I belong
to the family. It is a family about which I have no
illusions. And the most satisfying thing about this
sense of incorporation is that I am glad to belong to
this community, not another, and to be bred flesh and
bone into the same body as these brothers and not
other ones.[4]

Because Merton was creative, independent, energetic,
versatile, it was inevitable that he would find many difficulties
within community and within an institution. A fellow-monk
recalls after his death:

. . . his whole instinct made him keenly sensitive to all
forms of community life. Anything inauthentic he found
highly repellent. Not only in personal relations but
especially in 'the institution'. Though he had become
remarkably tolerant of human weaknesses of most
kinds, yet he did not suffer fools gladly and certain
rather common forms of human foolishness that many
of us take for granted grated upon him sharply . . .
However, the chief impression that Father Louis
made on his fellow monks was that he was a true
brother. In our community he was surely one of the
best loved of people. His whole manner was open and
outgoing and so constantly enthusiastic that he quickly
formed community. Many of us as young monks came
to feel that he was a friend and spiritual father. Behind
his criticism, his directness and independence there was
a great deal of obvious integrity and human affection.
He was moved by an immense elan for all that

pertained to the contemplative and monastic life.
Though he continually stressed solitude, silence, and
meditation, yet he did so in an atmosphere of human
warmth and wholesome insistence on the demands of
good relations among the brethren.[5]

Any discerning member of a religious community will smile
knowingly reading between the lines of the first paragraph
of the above quotation. Men of such integrity can be a pain
in the neck of ordinary mortals – and Merton must have been
such at times! He faced a lot of misunderstanding and adverse
criticism from some who were puzzled and sometimes annoyed
that he seemed no longer to be the 'holy monk' who had
confined his writings and opinions to contemplation, which
was a kind of religious exercise in monastic seclusion.

The broadening of his sympathies with the profound
understanding of the Church as a dynamic living organism,
the Body of Christ, in contrast to the triumphalism of
medievalism or the organised institutionalism which still exists,
is clearly seen in part of an answer to a critical priest recorded
in *Letters in a Time of Crisis*. Merton is speaking of Christian
optimism not as consisting of the wielding of worldly power
but of the mercy of God to man in Christ. He glories in the
proclamation of a total victory over evil, sin and death through
grace, not worldly power. Continuing the theme, he writes:

This victory reaches mankind of course through the
visible Church, but in actual fact there are no limits at
all upon the mercy of God, and no one can say
whether or not some people outside the visible Church
are not much more full of the Spirit than many of us
others. Consequently, it seems to me that the meaning
of the diaspora situation consists in recognizing this
fact and in realizing how true it is that the Christian
and the monk are actually in a position of working out
their own salvation and that of the world together with
the non-Christian and the non-monk, so that we
actually have much to learn from them, and must be

open to them, since it is always possible that life-giving grace may come to us through our encounter with them. This is what I mean by the Christian in the diaspora. I am for the diaspora. I prefer it to the closed medieval hegemony. It may offer much better chances of a real Christian life and brotherhood. Is this pessimism?[6]

Merton is writing as an evangelical Christian. His optimism is a positive evaluation of the Gospel of grace, and not salvation through the organisational structures of the institutional church. The mainspring of Merton's dynamism is the presence and experience of the Holy Spirit, and this is not a matter of human achievement or churchly power, nor a multiplication of superstitious ritual. To affirm true catholicity is to affirm the victory of Christ in the diaspora situation. He makes himself clear:

On the other hand I definitely eschew what seems to me to be a phoney and naive optimism, which consists, grossly speaking, of the following elements: an exaggerated and triumphalist view of the Church in her present, concrete and historical existence; she is regarded as having realized all perfection visibly, as being in her human elements beyond criticism because without spot or wrinkle. She knows all the answers thoroughly, not only the theological ones, but the answers to all social, economic, etc. problems. She has nothing to learn from anyone; she is just there to *tell* everyone. She is just about to go into high gear and 1) solve all these problems, 2) embrace mankind into the visible fold and this is to be done by stepping up our present activities, organizing them better, improving the system, polishing up the apparatus, better magazines, bigger and better schools, more impressive movements, etc. The optimism I distrust is an optimism that sees no further than this, and is content to believe that, with these means and a little more energy, the solution to all problems is just around the corner. That we are very soon going to have a big, happy, well-organized, entirely Christian world. This would be reducing Christian optimism to a rotarian cult of success and visible results, and would leave us with the spurious radiance of clerical Babbits . . . it has got to be Christian hope, hope in the Cross and Victory of Christ, not hope in Catholic organizations.[7]

Merton had written against pre-Vatican II triumphalism and about the Christian in the diaspora situation, following the theologian Karl Rahner, and had received from a cleric the comments that he had produced an expression of defeatism, withdrawal and evasion. The above paragraphs are part of Merton's published reply.

War and Peace

Merton adopted a critical and negative attitude toward the kind of ecclesiastical organisation that trusted in human ingenuity and machinery, but he remained committed to the Catholic Church in the world. Both these facts are illustrated in a single paragraph where he affirmed God's word through the Pope and criticised and opposed New York's Cardinal Spellman's attitude to the Vietnam War:

'War never again!' cried Pope Paul addressing the United Nations in October, 1965, and many who solemnly assented to his plea as reasonable and right, assented with equal solemnity a few weeks later when a retired Air Force General suggested that the way to bring peace to southeast Asia was to 'bomb North Vietnam back into the stone age.' It was in this atmosphere that Cardinal Spellman, addressing troops in Vietnam, deplored the protest against the war articulated at home, and summed up his view with, 'My country right or wrong.' All of which goes to

prove that when war is actually being waged,
emotional cliches come easier than creative thinking.[8]

Merton himself was not an unqualified pacifist, but he
certainly saw the Christian and the Church as instruments
of reconciliation in a world of violence. He was adamantly
opposed to the Vietnam War as unjust, and was behind such
people as the Berrigan brothers, Dorothy Day and the Catholic
Worker Movement in their civil disobedience and draft card
burning.

That such a contemplative monastic theologian as Merton
could apply his spiritual and theological perspective to the
situation of war and peace in such a biblical and reasonable
manner was a source of joy to me. His pacific stance, coupled
with a willingness to civil disobedience when the Gospel way
was trampled in the dust by the Church and the world, was
a validation of his contemplative teaching. He does not issue
ambiguous statements or engage in time-serving attitudes
when the world looks to the Church for a lead in the matters
of war and peace.

The Church's ambivalent attitude to violence and war
pushes Merton to a powerful affirmation of the reconciling
Gospel of forgiving love over the sometimes violent
triumphalism and justification of war on the part of Church
leaders. In a moving and penetrating essay on Franz
Jägerstätter, an Austrian Catholic conscientious objector,
Merton shows how Church and state combined to dissuade
the latter from his convictions. Thousands of Catholics were
serving in the Second World War under Hitler, including
many priests, Jägerstätter was told – and he should not try
to be 'more Catholic than the Church'. Merton makes his
point clear:

He was even reminded that the bishops had not
protested against this war, and in fact not only his
pastor but even his bishop tried to persuade him to
give up his resistance because it was 'futile'. One
priest represented to him that he would have

innumerable opportunities to practice Christian virtue and exercise an 'apostolate of good example' in the armed forces. All these are very familiar arguments frequently met with in our present situation, and they are still assumed to be so conclusive that few Catholics dare to risk the disapproval they would incur by conscientious objection and dissent.[9]

Merton then quotes Jägerstätter, showing that he was a man of genuine conviction who, with simplicity and clarity, knew where he stood and why, and revealing the man's loyalty to the Church as a witness and a prophetic voice:

The situation in which we Christians of Germany find ourselves today is much more bewildering than that faced by the Christians in the early centuries at the time of their bloodiest persecution . . . We are not dealing with a small matter, but the great (apocalyptic) life-and-death struggle has already begun. Yet in the midst of it there are many who still go on living their lives as though nothing had changed . . . That we Catholics must make ourselves tools of the worst and most dangerous anti-Christian power that has ever existed is something that I cannot and never will believe . . . Many actually believe quite simply that things have to be the way they are. If this should happen to mean that they are obliged to commit injustice, then they believe that others are responsible . . . I am convinced that it is best that I speak the truth even though it costs me my life. For you will not find it written in any of the commandments of God or of the Church that a man is obliged under pain of sin to take an oath committing him to obey whatever may be commanded him by his secular ruler. We need no rifles or pistols for our battle, but instead spiritual weapons – and the foremost of these is prayer.[10]

The whole tenor of this essay entitled 'An Enemy of the State', is that the Church authorities were those in error, and the lone prophet was the man who protested in the name of God and conscience against the Church authorities. After a negative reference to the Bishop of Linz in this affair, Merton concluded the essay:

> The real question raised by the Jägerstätter story is not merely that of the individual Catholic's right to conscientious objection (admitted in practice even by those who completely disagreed with Jägerstätter) but the question of the Church's own mission of protest and prophecy in the gravest spiritual crisis man has ever known.[11]

Despite the fact that Merton inveighs against the Church authorities and individual bishops, he does not include the Church as such under criticism and condemnation. The reverse is true. He speaks of the direction in which the Second Vatican Council in its 'Constitution on the Church in the Modern World', moved towards a sympathetic understanding and appropriate course of action in such a case as Jägerstätter's.

I was drawn to Merton, primarily, as a contemplative monk and writer of spirtuality and theology of a mystical bent. He endeared himself to me not only as a classic catholic contemplative, but also as an evangelical enthusiast. But as I followed his mystical theology, his spiritual pilgrimage, and his evolving progression into ever deepening experience of God and prayer, I was confronted with prophetic power and social awareness that both confirmed me in the way I had travelled thus far, and gave direction for the future. When I came across his *Seeds of Destruction*, I was bowled over by his clear vision of contemporary political movements, and by his fearless prophetic denunciation of social and political evils. It is ironic that the earliest of my two editions contains an Imprimatur by Francis Cardinal Spellman. This was before Merton's attitudes and writings took concrete form and particular relevance to Spellman's activities! The first part of the book is devoted to *Black Revolution* and is anti-apartheid in character. The second section *The Diaspora* is devoted to the Church and its attitude to war and peace, with a beautiful and powerful essay which is *A Tribute to Gandhi* – writing like this makes me want to dance and sing for joy. There are more important passages than the following in this essay, but you'll see why I appreciate this one:

> I remember arguing about Gandhi in my school dormitory: chiefly against the football captain, then head prefect, who had come to turn out the flickering gaslight, and who stood with one hand in his pocket and a frown on his face that was not illuminated with understanding. I insisted that Gandhi was right, that India was, with perfect justice, demanding that the British withdraw peacefully and go home; that the millions of people who lived in India had a perfect right to run their own country. Such sentiments were of course beyond comprehension. How could Gandhi be right when he was *odd*? And how could I be right if I was on the side of someone who had the wrong kind of skin, and left altogether too much of it exposed?
>
> A counter argument was offered but it was not an argument. It was a basic and sweeping assumption that the people of India were political and moral infants, incapable of taking care of themselves, backward people, primitive, uncivilized, benighted, pagan, who could not survive without the English to do their thinking and planning for them. The British Raj was, in fact, a purely benevolent, civilizing enterprise for which the Indians were not suitably grateful . . .
>
> Infuriated at the complacent idiocy of this argument, I tried to sleep and failed.[12]

Merton's writings, pilgrimage, and the implications of his life have often kept me awake too. But for different reasons.

The last section of the book incorporates thirty-five letters under the heading *Letters in a Time of Crisis*, and they indicate the breadth of Merton's sympathies and the depth of his compassionate understanding. They are only the tip of an iceberg, for there are 3,500 Merton letters lodged at the Thomas Merton Studies Center at Bellarmine College in Louisville, Kentucky. The scope and variety of his correspondents are amazing, revealing the true meaning of being a catholic Christian. The first volume of four containing nearly 700 pages of Merton's letters is entitled *The Hidden Ground of Love* – letters on religious experience and social concerns. They contain such names as Martin Luther King, Dom Helder Camara, Cardinal Jean Danielou, Pope John XXIII, Pope Paul VI, Karl Rahner, President Lyndon Johnson, John F. Kennedy, Shinzo Hamai (Mayor of Hiroshima), the Dalai Lama and countless others.

They are a patchwork of style, for he writes mind to mind, and heart to heart. Therefore the exciting dynamic of his letters involves the reader in slang, humour, grief, perplexity, outrage, cynicism and vitality. But always there is constructive counsel and criticism. And whether Merton is involved in solid theological writing or literary criticism, his humanity bursts forth, for in his letters he is not writing to order, but expressing himself in a disciplined spontaneity which catches the reader up into the mood of the moment, and in appreciation of Merton's many-faceted personality.

All this from a contemplative monk and potential hermit! Who can doubt the catholicity of Merton's faith as he writes to poets, heads of states, to popes, bishops, priests, religious and lay people; to monks, rabbis, Zen masters; to Catholics, Protestants, Orthodox, Baptists, Anglicans; to Buddhists, Jews, Hindus, Sufis, and to humanitarian agnostics and atheists.

If the accusation of passive inertia is made against men of contemplative prayer, here is Merton's clear rebuttal in *Seeds of Destruction*:

The contemplative life is not, and cannot be, a mere withdrawal, a pure negation, a turning of one's back on the world with its sufferings, its crises, its

confusions and its errors. First of all, the attempt itself
would be illusory. No man can withdraw competely
from the society of his fellow men; and the monastic
community is deeply implicated, for better or worse, in
the economic, political and social structures of the
contemporary world. To forget or to ignore this does
not absolve the monk from responsibility for
participation in events in which his very silence and
'not knowing' may constitute a form of complicity.
The mere fact of 'ignoring' what goes on can become
a political decision.[13]

He is not, of course, advocating partisan commitment, for
he says that the monk should be free of the confusions and
falsities of partisan dispute. 'The last thing in the world I would
want is a clerical or monastic movement in politics.' What
Merton intends is that the Christian, lay, clerical or monastic,
should develop a life of contemplative prayer, and should bring
the principles of Christian theology and spirituality down to
the marketplace and live them with courage and compassion.
This would have clear implications for apartheid, nuclear
weapons, economic policy, territorial power and political
aggrandisement. It would be the life of Christ incarnate in
the world – love of God and of neighbour – though the prisons
may be full of Christians, and the state declare war on the
Church! Poverty, chastity and obedience to the will of God
is the name of the game for all Christians. And that is
revolution.

Concern for Humankind

Because Merton thinks of the Church as a living organism,
the Body of Christ, it is self-evident that there is an overflow
of compassion for all that is human. If this is not true, then
the Church cannot be catholic, for as he wrote to a Professor
of Humanities, 'The "Catholic" who is the aggressive speci-
men of a ghetto Catholic culture, limited, rigid, prejudiced,
negative, is precisely a non-Catholic'.

The whole world is God's loving concern because he created it and sustains it; it is doubly so because he has become incarnate in it and redeems it. Exclusivism has always dogged the steps of the people of God from Old Testament times, and the Church has often forgotten the object of God's love in its obsession with itself or with its theology. It is when these legitimate concerns become a primary obsession that the Church sins against the image of God in humanity. In *Redeeming the Time*, another book on fire with 'the godless world' and 'beloved humanity', Merton puts it positively:

> In the earliest ecumenical councils the problems
> confronted were purely theological, and they concerned
> chiefly the divine and human natures of Christ, the
> divine Persons of the Word and of the Holy Spirit.
> The councils of the Middle Ages, the Renaissance and
> the nineteenth century were concerned with the life of
> the Church, with faith, grace and the sacraments. The
> Second Vatican Council, while continuing to develop
> and clarify the theology of the Church, manifested a
> wholly new concern – *man himself*. If one reflects on the
> historical and theological continuity of the Councils, it
> is rather awe-inspiring to see that a basic and
> permanent problem that once presented itself as a
> theoretical denial of the humanity of Christ now
> presents itself as a practical, concrete and existential
> denial of *man*. Thus the Council now found itself not
> merely affirming that in Christ God was made man in
> order that man might by grace attain to the freedom of
> the sons of God, but that man himself had a right to
> be man and to enjoy the elementary freedom and
> dignity due to the existential human person in his
> world of matter, in his everyday struggle to exist.[14]

Of course, Merton was not saying that the Church's concern with humankind is an entirely new insight. he constantly affirms in all his writings that the Church which says it loves God and does not love humankind is simply lying and hypocritical – and he is hard upon such a Church. But he is saying that one of the new and basic insights of the Second Vatican Council is the *attitude* of the Church to the world. And it is not so much in what is *said* but the *way* in which it is said. The Church now *feels* itself committed in love to the world. And the Church had to decide again in its own heart how it looked at the world. As Merton puts it:

> Was the world an object entirely separate from herself? Was the world simply to be seen again as her traditional enemy, as the realm of the devil? Or was the Church herself not only 'friendly towards' the world but even part of it, identified with it?
>
> The Council adopted a midway position. The Church, the People of God, is not simply identified with the whole world of man. She is ontologically separate from the world in which she is on pilgrimage. But she identified herself with the world by love and compassion.[15]

These are important words – ontologically separate but compassionately identified. They mean that the world should be holy *and* compassionate, separate *and* involved, redeemed *and* redeeming.

This is the kind of way that Merton loves to do theology – I find it native to me too, and exciting. Merton points me both to contemplative prayer in solitude, *and* to courageous witnessing in the marketplace. The witnessing is not 'spiritual evangelism' in the old evangelical and catholic sense of 'saving souls', but an application of the *whole* of the redeeming Gospel to the *whole* of the human person. This means the manifestation of divine and human love at every level – as Jesus demonstrated it. It involves repentance, forgiveness, new birth, reconciliation to God and man, then a life of gospel compassion and integrity, and the application of gospel principles to human rights, justice and freedom, equality and non-discrimination. It means living together within the whole variety of human colour, culture, language, religion, with

tolerance, understanding and compassion. It means a
realisation that the world is evil as system, and good as
humankind. It means a mature acceptance of the implications
of living like this as an individual, a family, a nation and a
species. It means the possibility of persecution for such radical
and revolutionary gospel views, and it may mean imprisonment and death.

In such thinking, Merton seems to have come to terms with
the radical difference which seems to be at the bottom of
Augustine's classical antithesis between the two cities, the City
of God, of peace and love, and the City of man, of conflict
and hate. He calls to mind the visit of Pope Paul VI to New
York, to address the United Nations, there to speak of man's
urgent need for peace and justice, calling on the nations of
the world to abolish war and eliminate poverty. That is where
he makes the reference to the few weeks later, when a General
of the US Air Force declared that the United States ought
to bomb North Vietnam back into the Stone Age.

But far from opting for a radical difference between sacred
and secular, Merton points out that the world is not simply
the realm of the irreligious and the Kingdom of God is not
simply the kingdom of religious piety. 'The distinction between
the world and the Kingdom is a distinction between self-
seeking and selfless love, not between the temporal and eternal
or the material and spiritual only.' He clarifies the situation
by showing that the bible and the Church use the term *world*
in different ways, summarising thus:

When the Council speaks of the Church in the world,
three possible senses of the 'world' must therefore be
kept in mind: one in which the world is simply God's
creation, and as such manifests the wisdom of the
Creator; another in which the wold is 'fallen' and
'dark' due to the self-idolatry of godless man and his
society; and a third in which the world is loved,
redeemed and saved by God, and destined to be
'recapitulated', summed up, perfected and completed
in Christ (Eph. 1: 9–12). The world is all these three

things at the same time: it is God's creation, it is the arena of a struggle between God's love and the evil which manifests itself in sin, rebellion against love, and ultimate death, and it is also God's Kingdom in which Christ already reigns and in which history is pointing to its final conclusion in him.[16]

That is a biblical and powerful statement. It is the context in which a full-blooded Christian faith is to be lived out by all Christians. In its light it is possible to see how Merton stood *for* all that is good and loving and reconciling in the Church and the world, and how he stood *against* exclusivist, hypocritical pandering to naked power and profit in the Church and the world. Thus, the Church and the world are both spheres of his activity. He sees the true catholicity of the Church being taken seriously by the Church itself since the Second Vatican Council, reaching out in love and compassion to the world which is itself the object of God's love, yet standing against the dark powers pervading the present world scene. Towards the end of *Redeeming the Time*, he speaks of this two-fold attitude:

> . . . one of the great problems confronted by the . . . Church in the modern world is this: the ideally scientific humanism of modern civilization tends to become a gross and destructive anti-humanism when science is taken over by men of power. (We need only to refer here to the pseudo-scientific theories behind Hitler's determination to wipe out the Jews).
> In the apocalyptic and destructive anti-humanism which we see to be so prevalent in our society we recognize the 'dark' aspect of the world condemned without ambiguity in the New Testament – the second of the three senses of the world which we considered at the beginning of this study. This is *not* the 'Modern World' to which the Council speaks, with encouragment and approval. It is the world which is the enemy of Christ and of man, a dark world of cruelty, cynicism

and hate to which the Council has said 'No' and said it unmistakably, while at the same time saying 'Yes' to all the legitimate hopes of modern man.[17]

It is clear, then, that Merton was totally committed to the Church and to the world, and when it is realised that such of the above writing, and much more, was published after he had taken to his hermitage in 1965, it makes such a double commitment even more powerfully influential and explosive.

References

1 John Eudes Bamberger, *Continuum*, pp. 227f.
2 Quoted in *ibid.*, p. 228.
3 *Loc. cit.*
4 Merton, *SJ*, pp. 39f.
5 *Continuum*, pp. 231f.
6 Merton, *SoD*, p. 220.
7 *ibid.*, pp. 220f.
8 Merton, *FV*, p. 40.
9 *ibid.*, p. 70.
10 *ibid.*, p. 72.
11 *ibid.*, p. 75.
12 Merton, *SoD*, pp. 222f.
13 *ibid.*, pp. xiiif.
14 Merton, *RT*, p. 7.
15 *ibid.*, p. 10.
16 *ibid.*, p. 17.
17 *ibid.*, p. 90.

Part III: The Contemplative Dimension

8: Contemplation in the World

Being Contemplative is Being Human

Merton did not so much change his mind as deepen his perspective. The early Merton found it necessary to reject certain of the world's standards and to radically change his manner of life. *Conversio morum* (conversion of lifestyle) was part of his monastic vow, though he did interpret it rather narrowly during the first years of his monastic life. Those parts of *The Seven Storey Mountain* which embarrassed him later were the elitist passages in which there was an implicit separation of nature and grace, and in which the contemplative monk was a special person with an unworldly vocation. Experience showed him not only that contemplation is for all, but that it is a manifestation of our simple and basic humanity.

The rejection of contemplation in contemporary technological society is the basic reason for its frustration and alienation. To reject the dimension of contemplation is to reject part of the basic structure of humanity – and ultimately that spells death, for it is going against the grain of one's nature. When Merton entered more profoundly into the dimension of contemplative prayer he found that he was affirming his true humanity, and that nature and grace complemented the fulness of humanity. Theologically, he maintained that the fount and source of all creativity, goodness and truth resided in the mystery of the Godhead. All the creative energies of God were manifested in the world by the indwelling Spirit and the eternal Logos – and that Logos became incarnate in the human life of Jesus. In Jesus, therefore, a completely human existence reveals the nature of the mysterious Godhead. This is not only an orthodox Catholic theology, but it is an inclusive one. The doctrine of the Incarnation for Thomas Merton meant that all men are included, and included at every level of their being:

> To a Christian who believes in the mystery of the Incarnation, that belief means something more than a pious theory without real humanistic implications. Since the Word was made Flesh, God is in man. God is in *all men*. All men are to be seen and treated as Christ. Failure to do this, the Lord tells us, involves condemnation for disloyalty to the most fundamental of revealed truths. 'I was thirsty and you gave me not to drink. I was hungry and you gave me not to eat . . .' (Matthew 25:24). This could be extended, all over the entire area of human needs, not only for bread, for work, for liberty, for health, but also for truth, for belief, for love, for acceptance, for fellowship and understanding.[1]

The sad thing, as Merton understands it, is that much of our contemporary world, especially in the West, has denied this basic truth of contemplation in frantic pursuit of materialism and transient pleasure; in lust for power and the political and ideological manipulation of others. Therefore it is all the more important that the contemplative life be maintained not only as a witness to the truth, but as the offer of an alternative way to all who will be open enough to listen. Contemplation is not alien or foreign to any human person who has not become totally corrupt. The very frustrating restlessness and discontent of our society is evidence of its lack and need. Merton speaks of contemplation as the vibrant life-force that moves through heart and mind, and through inanimate creation, from its deep source in God. Contemplation, he says, is the highest expression of man's intellectual and spiritual life. Alienated man's rejection of it only makes its reality and importance more urgent, and he goes on to define it:

It is that life itself, fully awake, fully active, fully
aware that it is alive. It is spiritual wonder. It is
spontaneous awe at the sacredness of life, of being. It
is a vivid realization of the fact that life and being in
us proceed from an invisible, transcendent and
infinitely abundant Source. Contemplation is, above
all, awareness of the reality of that Source. It *knows* the
Source, obscurely, inexplicably, but with a certitude
that goes beyond reasons and beyond simple faith.[2]

In Merton's view, if our technological inventiveness were
imbued with such contemplative awareness it would give rise
to such compassion in the sense of the sacredness of life that
there would arise a fundamental objection to the creation of
weapons of mass warfare. That negative objection would be
the logical outcome of a positive attitude to the worth of our
common humanity. And in turn, this would mean the end
of such 'collective monstrosities' as political totalitarianisms
of the extreme right or the extreme left.

In an essay, 'The Contemplative Life in the Modern
World',[3] Merton points out that not only is contemplation
absolutely necessary in the affirmation of our true humanity,
but that we know this within the depths of our own souls. He
says that man has an instinctive need for harmony and peace,
for tranquillity, order and meaning, but these do not seem
to be the salient characteristics of our modern society.

Contemplative monastic life is therefore a sign to man of
the way of his ancestors, which sometimes awakens the hope
of recovering the inner vision, so that glimpses of that life may
be imparted by such a witness.

But with this there awakens, too, in Western man, a
reaction of 'despair, disgust, rejection of the dream, and
commitment to total activism'. Our modern way of life has
become alien to modern man. He is restless, active, filling
his life with distractions in movement, speech, news,
communication, recreation. In all this he imagines a certain
dynamism, he creates for himself some foreign meaning,
foreign to that for which he is made. This is a substitute

meaning from an external source, but that source is society engaged in a gigantic effort to raise man above himself. This expounds the truth of Augustine's dictum that God has made us for himself, and that our heart is restless until it rests in him. Man's dilemma brings about inner confusion, for continual activity with no interior peace, a contrived dynamism with no inner dynamic, creates both tension and confusion. Merton diagnoses that:

> . . . the reason for the inner confusion of Western man
> is that our technological society has no longer any
> place in it for wisdom that seeks truth for its own sake,
> that seeks the fulness of being, that seeks to rest in an
> intuition of the very ground of all being.[4]

What he means by that last sentence is that for those who will listen, there is an intuitive sense of God's loving presence in the heart of every man. And he means this in a corporate as well as a personal sense. The contemplative attitude is the fruit of an openness to this basic intuition of love at the heart of all things. That there has been a wholesale denial of this truth he does not dispute, but that is the reason for his powerful affirmation of its demonstrative existence in *some* so that its potential existence in *all* may be given honest and reasonable attention.

It is a basic premise of the scriptures of the Old and New Testaments that man is made for God, and God is the fulfilment of every level of man's contingent being. Man rests naturally and supernaturally in God, as does the created order. When this is interrupted or frustrated it is called by many names, including sin, pride, ignorance, and results in rebellion and negative independence which in turn leads to estrangement and alienation in personal being and in social and spiritual relationships. This is the place at which the intuitive wisdom of God's loving presence is lost.

There was always place in ancient and traditional societies of Asia and the West for 'the way' of the wise, manifested not only in monastic life, but in art, in philosophy and in the way in which wisdom was applied to daily personal and corporate life. Far from being a contemplative escape from the harsh realities of life, it is a return to reality. It is setting one's foot upon the way to understanding the inner meaning of being. As Merton says:

> Once a man has set his foot on this way, there is no excuse for abandoning it, for to be actually on the way is to recognize without doubt or hesitation that only the way is fully real and that everything else is deception except insofar as it may in some secret and hidden manner be connected with 'the way'. [5]

In New Testament days, the disciples of Jesus were called 'followers of the Way', but Merton is affirming something wider than exclusivist Christianity here – it is the universal soil in which Christianity, as well as other Faiths have taken root and grown. He is describing an awareness that has taken hold on man universally, and seems only to have been missed or rejected by modern Western man in his foolish pursuit of materialistic values, which deny the profound spiritual values apprehended by all the great Faiths. He goes on to speak of this awareness of 'the Way' in terms of a journey, a mountainous climb, a pilgrimage, involving dangers, difficulties and solitariness, but a way which brings with it its own justification, joy and peace:

> This journey without maps leads him into rugged mountainous country where there are often mists and storms and where he is more and more alone. Yet at the same time, ascending the slopes in darkness, feeling more and more keenly his own emptiness, and with the winter wind blowing through his now tattered garments, he meets at times other travellers on the way, poor pilgrims as he is, and as solitary as he, belonging perhaps to other lands and other traditions. There are, of course, great differences between them, and yet they have much in common. Indeed, the

Western contemplative can say that he feels himself
much closer to the Zen monks of ancient Japan than to
the busy and impatient men of the West, of his own
country, who think in terms of money, power,
publicity, machines, business, political advantage,
military strategy – who seek, in a word, the triumphant
affirmation of their own will, their own power,
considered as the end for which they exist. Is not this
perhaps the most foolish of all dreams, the most
tenacious and damaging of illusions?[6]

The pursuit of such materialistic goals in Japan and China
destroys the awareness of 'the Way' in their Buddhist, Taoist
or Confucian traditions just as its pursuit in America or the
modern West destroys it in the Christian tradition. Merton
is saying that 'the real world' of the grasping, materialistic
man is an illusion, and if that is the 'end' for which he strives,
it will certainly come to an end – in disintegration, without
goal, meaning or purpose.

Wisdom and Sanity

For Merton, the way of wisdom was the way of sanity. But
all truly wise men were thought to be fools, including Jesus,
and St Paul in their turn. Both the Christian Gospel, and
the ancient Asian wisdom turned the wisdom of this ungodly
world-system onto its head. To be wise and sane in the world
means the acquisition of money, power, territory and the
pursuit of ambition without regard to compassion. It does
not *have* to be like that, but it invariably is, especially in
the confrontation of nations. Reading Hannah Arendt's *The
Human Condition*, and Shirer's *The Rise and Fall of the Third
Reich* devasted Merton in his consideration of wisdom and
sanity. This is the occasion of an ironic and penetrating
essay, 'A Devout Meditation in Memory of Adolf Eichmann'
which opens: 'One of the most disturbing facts that came
out in the Eichmann trial was that a psychiatrist examined
him and pronounced him *perfectly sane*. I do not doubt it

at all, and that is precisely why I find it disturbing.'⁷

Without the contemplative wisdom of which Merton has been speaking, he believes that there is an immense danger of an appeal to the reasonableness and sanity of a world-system dedicated to the pursuit of power, which ultimately denies human freedom and human love.

He says that if all the Nazis had been psychotics, as some of their leaders probably were, then their appalling cruelty could, in some senses, have been understood. But to consider Eichmann, a calm, well-balanced, unperturbed official conscientiously going about his task, which happened to be the supervision of mass murder, is totally perplexing. 'He was thoughtful, orderly, unimaginative,' says Merton. 'He had a profound respect for system, for law and order. He was obedient, loyal, a faithful officer of a great state. He served his government very well.'

He apparently slept well, did not develop any psychosomatic illness, and was not bothered much by guilt, and he had a good appetite! When he visited Auschwitz, the Camp Commandant, Hoess, tried to tease and scare the boss with some of the sights. And he was disturbed – merely disturbed. Auschwitz was no accident, says Merton; just the routine unpleasantness of the daily task.

> One must shoulder the burden of daily monotonous work for the Fatherland. Yes, one must suffer discomfort and even nausea from unpleasant sights and sounds. It all comes under the heading of duty, self-sacrifice, and obedience. Eichmann was devoted to duty, and proud of his job.⁸

This is the kind of sanity that Merton finds disturbing and frightening. Sanity should be equated with a sense of justice, humaneness, prudence, with the ability to love and understand other people. The sane people of the world should be the guardians of compassion and freedom, preserving it from barbarism, madness, destruction. But perhaps it is the sane ones who are the most dangerous! Then Merton writes these chilling words:

It is the sane ones, the well-adapted ones, who can without qualms and without nausea aim the missiles and press the buttons that will initiate the great festival of destruction that they, *the sane ones*, have prepared. What makes us so sure, after all, that the danger comes from a psychotic getting into a position to fire the first shot in a nuclear war? Psychotics will be suspect. The sane ones will keep them far from the button. No one suspects the sane, and the sane ones will have *perfectly good reasons*, logical, well-adjusted reasons, for firing the shot. They will be obeying sane orders that have come sanely down the chain of command. And because of their sanity they will have no qualms at all. When the missiles take off, then, *it will be no mistake*.[9]

The contemplative orientation holds a totally different view of reality from that which inspires the political world systems which are dedicated to the pursuit of power. They enlist men and women in a conscripted system of collective power which traps them and robs them of personal freedom and social conscience. It is aggressive, self-assertive, possessive and dominative. At the centre of this view of reality is the individual self with its bodily form, its feelings and emotions, its appetites, loves and hates. On an individual level, everything else is referred to itself, and the world is seen as a multiplicity of separate, conflicting, limited beings,

all enclosed in the prisons of their own individuality, all therefore complete in a permanent and vulnerable incompleteness, all seeking to find a certain completeness by asserting themselves at the expense of others, dominating and using others.[10]

The result of this, in Merton's view, is that victory goes to the strong, and the weak must submit to him in order to share his power. The solidarity and unity of mankind that the contemplative attitude affirms in compassion and love is

denied, and this power struggle displays a *functional* unity which
is the opposite of a unity of love. This is a 'collective
monstrosity' because it has only its existence in exploitation,
alienation and total subjection. This collective unity destroys
men's inmost need and capacity for contemplation, and
shrivels the springs of compassion and understanding. 'It
perverts the creative genius and destroys the innocent vision
that is proper to man in communion with nature.'

Now what is Merton's practical reaction to such a world
as this? The sanity of such a godless world is contained in
a logic which preserves one's own power and invades and
enslaves others. It is the policy and practice of Machiavelli.
That kind of sanity is insanity to the wise man:

> We can no longer assume that because a man is 'sane'
> he is therefore in his 'right mind'. The whole concept
> of sanity in a society where spiritual values have lost
> their meaning is itself meaningless. A man can be
> 'sane' in the limited sense that he is not impeded by
> his disordered emotions from acting in a cool, orderly
> manner, according to the needs and dictates of the
> social situation in which he finds himself. He can be
> perfectly 'adjusted'. God knows, perhaps such people
> can be perfectly adjusted even in hell itself.[11]

Religion without Wisdom

The way of wisdom does not *evade* such a world system, but
renounces it. And this is a witness in itself. Concern, compassion
and involvement in the world of humanity is the mark of a
contemplative, not withdrawal into a realm of narcissism and
abstraction. It means facing the world with a totally different
viewpoint. And perhaps being persecuted for it – and perhaps
killed!

Sometimes the persecution comes from religionists who are
not part of the way of wisdom, for it was such people, using
the arm of the state, who were responsible for the crucifixion
of Jesus. And it is not only worldly religionists that Merton

has in mind, but the monastic communities who can become deeply implicated, for better or worse, in the economic, political and social structures of their own culture. Sounding a note of warning, he says:

> Too often it has happened that the contemplative communities in Europe, whose individual members were absorbed in other-worldly recollection, have officially and publicly given support to totalitarian movements. In such cases it can ultimately be said that the monk in his liturgy, in his study or in his contemplation is actually participating in those things he congratulates himself on having renounced.[12]

For as Merton says, silence and 'not knowing' may constitute a form of complicity, and the mere fact of 'ignoring' what goes on can become a political decision.

He is not advocating either partisan political commitment and certainly not violent action – this would be a surrender to the world system which he is witnessing against. And anyway, the monk should be free from the confusions and falsities of partisan dispute. But he should be aware of his own commitment, and of the commitment of his monastic Order and tradition. Michael Mott, in his exhaustive and official biography of Thomas Merton indicates the tensions within Merton's own thinking on the question of monastic obedience in the light of our present discussion.[13] Personal integrity and obedience to one's own conscience are important factors in Merton's thinking.

And that is the kind of sanity that Merton envisages – one of personal and corporate integrity, in which the 'way of wisdom' is demonstrated and witnessed to in the midst of an unbelieving world. Sanity cannot exclude love or destroy our capacity to love and sympathise with other human beings, whoever they may be. His irony comes to the surface again when he says:

> The worst error is to imagine that a Christian must try to be 'sane' like everybody else, that we *belong* in our

kind of *society*. That we must be 'realistic' about it. We must develop a *sane* Christianity: and there have been plenty of sane Christians in the past. Torture is nothing new, is it? We ought to be able to rationalize a little brain-washing, and genocide, and find a place for nuclear war, or at least for napalm bombs, in our moral theology. Certainly some of us are doing our best along those lines already. There are hopes! Even Christians can shake off their sentimental prejudices about charity, and become sane like Eichmann. They can even cling to a certain set of Christian formulas, and fit them into a Totalist Ideology. Let them talk about justice, charity, love and the rest. These words have not stopped some sane men from acting very sanely and cleverly in the past . . . [14]

Merton sees the same demonic powers which were at work in the sanity of Eichmann inspiring the American aggression in Vietnam, with religious and moral approval and encouragement from Cardinal Spellman whose name appears under the 'Imprimatur' impression on some of Merton's own books! Merton's irony rebounds!

The point he is making is that the demonic power of enslaving totalitarian regimes and ungodly world systems are apt to appear anywhere, in any age, and religion and politics may go hand-in-hand to further their own ends, thereby destroying the contemplative dimension of love and compassion. Eichmann was sane. The generals and fighters of both sides in the Second World War, the ones who carried out the total destruction of entire cities, these were the sane ones.

Those who have invented and developed atomic bombs, thermonuclear bombs, missiles; who have planned the strategy of the next war; who have evaluated the various possibilities of using bacterial and chemical agents: these are not the crazy people, they are the *sane* people. The ones who coolly estimate how

many millions of victims can be considered expendable
in a nuclear war, I presume they do all right with the
Rorschach ink blots too. On the other hand, you will
probably find that the pacifists and the ban-the-bomb
people are, quite seriously, just as we read in *Time*, a
little crazy.[15]

Who Represents Wisdom?

So Merton does not identify the Way of Wisdom with the
professing Church. Nor yet with the Asian or other religious
traditions. It is to be found everywhere, wherever there
are people whose hearts have been moved with compassion,
who are in touch with their deepest selves, and who listen
to the depths of their own humanity. Because in his 'natural'
state man seems alienated and trapped in the illusions of
his own cultural or political ideology as well as his own
selifishness and pride, he acknowledges that God must take
the initiative, and stir up the contemplative dimension which
is his gift to humankind. This is represented in all the great
religious and wisdom traditions of the world, and for
Merton, uniquely so in the Incarnation and Redemption
which is in Christ.

This means that the monastic tradition of which Merton
is part, *can* be a contemporary and an eschatological witness
to the contemplative life. This means that the monk should
not only demonstrate by his contemplative life of prayer,
but also by his incarnate life of compassion and simplicity,
that he is part of this Way of Wisdom. Because it is
universal, the monk can be open to all men, everywhere.
This makes the monastic tradition subversive to some
political minds, and dangerous to any form of totalitarianism, and this becomes quite clear in any part of the
world where the authorities feel they must persecute the
religious groups in their midst. Tertullian said that the blood
of the martyrs is the seed of the Church. Merton puts it
humorously:

> . . . the two Macarii, both men of God,
> Going to visit a brother
> Took the boat that crosses the river.
>
> The boat was full of officers, rich brass,
> With horses, boys and guards.
>
> One tribune saw the monks like a pair of sacks
> Lying in the stern, ragged bums, having nothing.
> Free men.
>
> 'You' he said, 'are the happy ones.
> You laugh at life. You need nothing from the world
> But a few rags, a crust of bread.'
>
> And one Macarius, replied: 'It is true,
> We follow God. We laugh at life.
> And we are sorry life laughs at you.'
>
> Then the officer saw himself as he was.
> He gave away all that he had
> And enlisted in the desert army.[16]

Of course this is over-simplification. Merton certainly does not imply that one has to opt for celibacy, poverty and a monastic obedience. The officer in the desert story had to do that, and the reader may be called to do that, but the contemplative call is universal, and it is a call to live out prayer and compassion in a simple and human life, both personally and corporately just where you are at present.

Merton had to work it out his own way, and we must do it in ours. But he is a stimulus and catalyst for all who seek to live out the values of the Kingdom of God in this world.

In this book I have been more concerned with Merton as a man of prayer than as a social or political critic, but it is clear that he does not separate the two. His essay 'Christianity and Totalitarianism'[17] is a model of prayer and action, of loving compassion and prophetic insight. It is a product of his contemplative life, and he answers the activist critics of the contemplative life by out-thinking and out-living them with both enthusiasm and compassion. He is able to criticise the

the fanatic by being enthusiastic, and to call the Church back
to personal and gospel simplicity and humanness by a
trenchant evaluation of Marxism.

Merton maintains that the Kingdom of God is ultimately
spiritual and eschatological (of the age to come), but that is
all the more reason why it must be concretely manifested in
the here and now by practical compassion. Social justice,
political honesty and human equality are basic requisites for
the Kingdom of God. Man is not a pure spirit and his life
in the world is a bodily life. Therefore, Merton reasons, he
needs food, shelter, protection, freedom, friendship and work,
as a member of a visible society. His interior spiritual life – his
salvation – is involved in his being able to find basic standards
of living for himself and his family, taking part freely in the
social, artistic and intellectual life of his community, and above
all to serve and love God.

He is not here talking of the rare courage of the great
contemplative saints, but of the ordinary human beings whom
God loves and calls to simple gospel contemplation. He echoes
the epistle of St James in calling for basics so that the spiritual
quest can be undertaken by all. Merton knows that only in
the fertile soil of political freedom and compassion affirmed
by the Church can the same Church proclaim the spiritual
and intellectual quest with honesty. Such thinking condemns
any form of totalitarianism by the power of love and simplicity.

Totalitarianism in Church or state leads to fanaticism, says
Merton, and he is well aware of the hypocrisy and violence
perpetrated by the Church in pursuit of a 'holy war' whether
that war is against the Orthodox Churches of Constantinople
by Western Crusaders or against communist aggression in
Asia or elsewhere. Merton's contemplative life enables him
to see clearly the need for gospel principles to undergird and
sustain Christian discipleship both personally and corporately,
for close and living adherence to Christ is the only real and
lasting answer to human need, and against all forms of
totalitarianism.

Merton's affirmation in this socio-political essay is that of
the saving Gospel of Christ and our personal and corporate

participation in it. It is God's Kingdom and we cannot usher it in either by our works or our prayers. It is a sheer gift of grace. That Kingdom must be rooted in our hearts and we must be born again into it. We must apply its gospel principles of compassion at the level of daily and social life, and we must not lose sight of the eternal aspect of the Kingdom in the life beyond.

This is a full-orbed gospel and a balanced perspective. It has evangelistic fervour without fanaticism; it has social cutting edge with profound compassion. Merton says we must not be proselytisers but apostles, and his gospel and social perspective is spelled out: 'The true apostle is not preaching a doctrine or leading a movement or recruiting for an organization: he is preaching Christ because he loves other men and knows that thus he can bring them happiness, and bring meaning to their lives.' And after contrasting the differences between proselytisers and apostles, he says: 'Proselytism, not being rooted and grounded in charity (Ephesians 3:17) but springing rather from a hidden anxiety for domination and power, is over-anxious to imitate the techniques and the policies of politicians and business men.'

In all this, I find Merton a man of humanness and compassion; not afraid to reveal his powerful prophetic spirit, but also not afraid to be humorous about the lovable absurdity of humankind. This lends objectivity to his perspective, for although, in much of his social criticism, he castigates the United States for its triumphalism and tyrannical political policies, and although he acknowledges the insight of the 'sharp instrument of Marxian criticism', he takes a firm Christian stand against atheistic Marxist totalitarianism:

Where has man's spirit ever reached such a pitch of alienation as in the mass movements of the twentieth century, and especially in the Soviet Union? The intellectual, spiritual, artistic and religious life of the Soviet citizen has been systematically drained at its source by communist indoctrination. The pseudo-scientific 'organization' of man's life in all its

departments, not for his benefit but for the benefit of
the 'revolution' (that is for the heads of the communist
Party) has completely emptied man's life of personal
meaning and enterprise. . . . The most ironical fact
about the twentieth century is that Atheistic
Communism has finally realized, in its ultimate
perfection, the economic alienation of man which Karl
Marx ascribed in part to religion.[18]

Merton's contemplative writing has practical and political
overtones. In certain contexts it would lead to persecution,
imprisonment and martyrdom. But this is the kind of writing
that has helped me to keep the two poles of gospel concern
alive in my thinking and devotion. I am totally committed
to the saving Gospel of Christ within the context of contemplative prayer on the one hand, and I am as committed to
gospel simplicity and sharing in the political realities of the
world on the other. In a world dominated by money, power
and violence, full of inequalities and discrimination that is
no easy task. But it is one which Merton continually keeps
before my mind and heart.

For Merton, Christ is the prototype for all humanity in the
manner in which life should be lived, and it is well to
remember that Jesus was a member of a minority nation which
was dominated by the powerful, politically organised Roman
Empire. And in the midst of that he lived simply to glorify
God.

Sister Mary Seraphim, from her own Franciscan tradition,
sees Merton as a contemplative representative of suffering
humanity, destined to unite the divergencies of human
yearnings in Christ, both intellectual and spiritual. She thinks
of such a vocation as indispensable to our contemparary world:

And this is the vocation of the contemplative: to be the
eyes, the ears of humanity, open to the springs of the
Spirit. (Merton) described contemplatives as sentinels
on the world's frontier, living on the outposts of the
reaches of the spirit, naked and burnt in the desert.

They are the ones who seek the world's gain in 'an unthinkable experience.' They are the exiles, the listeners heralding the distant, unmistakable, coming of the Lord.[19]

References
1 Merton, *ESF*, pp. 78f.
2 Merton, *SC*, p. 1.
3 Merton, *FV*, pp. 217ff.
4 *ibid.*, p. 217.
5 *ibid.*, pp. 218f.
6 *ibid.*, p. 219.
7 Merton, *RU*, pp. 29ff.
8 *ibid.*, p. 30.
9 *ibid.*, pp. 30f.
10 Merton, *FV*, p. 220.
11 Merton, *RU*, p. 31.
12 Merton, *SoD*, pp. xiiif.
13 See *The Seven Mountains of Thomas Merton*, pp. 396f., 404f.
14 Merton, *RU*, p. 31f.
15 *ibid.*, p. 33.
16 Merton, *ESF*, p. 19.
17 Merton, *PML*, pp. 130–151.
18 *ibid.*, pp. 149f.
19 Seraphim, *op. cit.*, pp. 262f.

9: *Contemplation and the Gospel*

In spite of the deadness of ecclesiastical institutions, in spite of the polarisation of exclusivist views, in spite of the lack of understanding and charity found in various parts of the Church – there is a revival of living faith, openness of mind, theological excitement and immense love. Applauding both sections of the Church, I can say that I am a child of the evangelical tradition, continuing to grow in catholic maturity. And this is where the best thought and experiential life style is taking place today. I owe to Thomas Merton so much of the stimulus and experience that has given me joy and stability in my pilgrimage, not least in the two areas that constitute the theme of this chapter – *Contemplation*, and the *Gospel*.

It took Merton many years to move out of the early 'convert' exclusivism of a pre-Vatican II Catholicism, but though the pilgrimage was long in the making, it consisted of an increasingly clear understanding of the evangelical nature of the Faith of Christ, which led towards a contemplative depth. And only when he was aware of the experience of both these dimensions, could he speak of true catholicity. There was then less emphasis on the polarisation, and more concentration on the unity of the Gospel. In my own mind and pilgrimage I needed to understand and experience the particularity of both emphases quite clearly, before I could embrace the unity of a catholic stance that embraces the fulness of the Gospel.

I find it sometimes amusing, but sometimes sad, that because I am heard to preach with evangelical zeal and fervour in a warm and enthusiastic appreciation of the saving Gospel of Christ, some fundamentalist friends will say approvingly: 'Oh, you haven't changed at all'. This is good news if they mean that my enthusiasm and proclamation of Jesus has lost none of its fire and verve. But I'm afraid that these words often express the hope that I haven't moved from my early exclusivism and insularity. This applies as much to catholic fundamentalism as to evangelical fundamentalism. Such friends really believe that the proof of 'evangelical apostasy' is the loss, not only of gospel assurance, but also of zeal, enthusiasm and the desire to let Christ be known.

Nothing could be further from the truth. And Merton's life and writings enabled me to keep the two themes together in a unity which compromised neither, but enabled me to move into a deeper appreciation and a more profound dimension of faith.

The contemplative dimension of faith is present at the heart of the evangelical experience. St Augustine's conversion in the garden in Milan, St Francis' hearing the crucified Christ in San Damiano and John Wesley's evangelical experience in Aldersgate Street, London, in 1738 are of a piece with St Paul's Damascus Road confrontation with the risen Christ. Christ's call was not only to forgiveness and assurance, but to discipleship, to sanctification, to participation in the new humanity of compassion and love. This was the pattern of Thomas Merton's conversion, for at his baptism, describing the moment of his first communion, as he was drawn into trinitarian fellowship with the fulness of God, he wrote the sentence which has haunted me from the first moment that I read it: 'And He called out to me from His own immense depths'.

This is both a gospel word and a contemplative word. The whole of Merton's life from that moment was a gradual unfolding of these words, and much misunderstanding will be avoided if both the evangelical and the contemplative poles are held together in any evaluation of Merton's writings or experiences. He is not always explicit concerning the evangelical nature of his faith when he is in dialogue with other contemplative traditions, but it is the foundation from which he lives. Because he did not always wear his monastic habit does not mean that he was in any way denying his Cistercian

Order – though some people were threatened by his pioneering freedom in exploration.

Merton maintained a firm trinitarian faith which held to the universality of the divine Love and the mystery of the divine Being, a high Christology expressed in the cosmic Lordship of Christ, and a pneumalology which experienced the Holy Spirit at the heart of the created order and in the redeeming and reconciling work of Christ. Eleven years after his conversion he writes in his journal of contemplative prayer:

> Contemplative prayer is the recognition that we are the Sons of God, an experience of Who He is, and His love for us, flowing from the operation of that love in us. Contemplative prayer is the voice of the Spirit crying out in us, 'Abba, Pater'. In all valid prayer it is the Holy Ghost who prays in us: but in the graces of contemplation He makes us *realize* at least obscurely that it is He who is praying in us with a love too deep and too secret for us to comprehend. And we exult in the union of our voice with His voice, and our soul springs up to the Father, through the Son, having become one flame with the Flame of their Spirit.[1]

It is understandable that Merton was a source of puzzlement and perplexity to some people who did not move with him. He would not be straitjacketed into any theological or contemplative category to satisfy either conservative fundamentalists or radical reductionists. His freedom was the fruit of his stability, and because of his own monastic tradition, rooting him as an ancient tree, he had the freedom to climb out onto a limb-branch without fear of uprooting the venerable tree! Clear evidence for this statement is found in a consideration of his later monastic and Asian writings – for instance the table of contents in his *Mystics and Zen Masters*. Here is an exposition and a synthesis of various spiritual traditions in a series of diverse interpretive essays.

Why Have You Come Here?

Eight years after the publication of the autobiographical *Mountain*, Merton wrote his *Basic Principles of Monastic Spirituality*, particularly for novices and postulants of the Cistercian tradition, especially in the Abbey of Gethsemani. Throughout, he keeps in mind the true end and goal of the monastic life, which is the life, light and glory of Christ. Monks must be careful not to confuse external observance of religious rules and regulations with life in Christ:

> Christ is the centre of monastic living. He is its source
> and its end. He is the way of the monk as well as his
> goal. Monastic rules and observances, the practices of
> monastic asceticism and prayer, must always be
> integrated in this higher reality. They must always be
> seen as part of a living reality, as manifestations of a
> divine life rather than as elements in a system, as
> manifestations of duty alone. [2]

His concern is to keep the evangelical and contemplative nature of the Gospel together, and not to confuse them with ecclesiastical or monastic rules which may or may not be helpful, but which may trap a legalistic mind or system into making a 'pseudo-gospel' of ascetic or ritualistic regulations. The only reason for the existence of the monastic tradition, for Merton, is that the individual and the corporate body of monks grow into the image of God and become compassionate intercessors for the world. The pattern of the monastic life is the incarnation, redemption and resurrection of Christ. The fact that the monk is found within the monastic life means that he is there to seek God, and the life of the contemplative is one which is totally abandoned to the Holy Spirit. It is a life of obedience, humility, solitude and prayer, in which selfish desires are renounced in order to live in the liberty of the sons of God under the guidance of the Holy Spirit. And the monastery provides the context. But what applies to the monk applies to every Christian:

The question 'Why have you come here?' is then the
question Jesus asked in the Garden of the agony;
'Whom do you seek?' We seek Jesus of Nazareth,
Christ, the Son of the Living God, who descended
from heaven for the love of us, who died on the Cross
and rose from the dead and sits, alive, at the right
hand of God the Father, filling us with His life and
directing us by His Spirit, so that He lives and
breathes and works and acts and loves in us. Our
purpose in life is then to grow in our union with the
risen Christ, to live more and more deeply the life of
His Body, the Church, to continue on earth the
Incarnation which manifests the love of God for men,
so that we may share the glory of God with Christ in
heaven.[3]

Merton is saying that because of the Incarnation, God is
actually to be found within the world. For he has entered and
sanctified material things. Not only is the visible creation called
into, and held in being, by the eternal Word or Logos, but
the Word Himself has entered into the material creation to
be its crown and glory. If the monk therefore seeks Jesus the
Word, He may be found in the world of nature and creatures.
And because the Incarnation confirmed the divine approval
of creation, the Church uses material things in her liturgy
because they speak eloquently of God: lights, vestments,
colours, incense, music. Above all, material things are used
not only as symbols, but as means by which the grace of God
is directly applied to our souls in the sacraments. We must
be careful not to repudiate or despise the material world like
the pagan mystics, but see the material creation elevated
through the Incarnation.

Salvation and Asceticism

These things are said by Merton under the heading *Verbum
Caro Factum Est*, (the Word was made flesh), but he does not
stop there. He goes on to speak of the *Verbum Crucis*, (the Word

of the Cross), moving from creation, through incarnation to redemption. The world is fallen, and man is fallen. Therefore salvation is not possible by following our natural instincts or merely making use of created things. 'Man and the world were enslaved by the prince of darkness and plunged into error,' says Merton. 'Sin made it impossible for man to find his way back to God.' Then with an appeal to the Epistle to the Romans, he warns against any merely human asceticism or religiosity which places man at the centre of things. He is specific:

> Everywhere the New Testament puts us on our guard against the folly of a purely human kind of contemplation and a purely human asceticism, which produce an illusion of holiness and wisdom, but cannot unite us with God or reconcile us with Him. Human ascetic and mystical techniques cannot save us from our sins. They keep us far from God, and take us further from Him because their illusion engenders in us a false confidence and pride. They are centered in man, not on God, they tend to glorify man, not God.[4]

Merton is making the point that Christ is not only the Creator and Exemplar of all things, but the Redeemer, the Saviour of the world. He answers the great question of Anselm, *Cur Deus Homo?* (Why did God become Man?) by saying: 'The Word was made flesh in order to die on the Cross for the sins of mankind, and to reconcile fallen man to God.'

This means that man is not saved by asceticism, by ritualistic ceremonies, by acts of contrition, by forms of religion or moral and ethical duties, not by contemplation or any form of human effort or merit – but solely and entirely by Christ, the crucified and risen Lord. It is then, and only then, that asceticism is a result of the salvation of Christ and the sanctifying work of the Holy Spirit. The good works of man are the result, not the cause, of salvation. We are not even saved by our faith, but by grace alone. Then asceticism is the result of the Spirit's work within us:

There is only one true asceticism; that which is guided
not by our own spirit but by the Spirit of God. The
spirit of man must first subject itself to grace and then
it can bring the flesh in subjection both to grace and to
itself. 'If by the Spirit you mortify the deeds of the
flesh, you shall live.' (Romans 8:13).[5]

He never tires of making the point. Christ alone is our
salvation, and our works (monastic or otherwise) flow out of
the life of the risen Christ – or they are dead. He wrote to
a brother monk: 'At root we are men of very little faith; and
though we claim to believe in the Risen Saviour, at heart we
have more faith in forms and formulas and systems.'

This does not make salvation something individualistic and
exclusive. The Gospel does not consist in any individual's
subjective participation in it, but leads to an objective and
experiential participation in the Church as the Mystical Body
of Christ. 'Here then is our situation,' says Merton:

Without Christ, we are entirely cut off from God, we
have no access to Him, except in rites of natural
religion which cannot save our souls of themselves (but
we know that by the merits of the Passion of Christ
God will give His grace to everyone who does what he
can to live according to the light of his conscience).
With and *in* Christ, all our lives are transformed and
sanctified, and the smallest acts of love have their
value as propitiation for sin. We need a Saviour in
whom we will be born again to a new life, and ascend
into heaven. God so loved the world that He has given
us His Son to be our Saviour. The more we appreciate
this fact the greater our gratitude and trust, the more
will we enter into the knowledge of God in Christ and
serve Him with all our hearts.[6]

Merton is at pains to show that the saving Gospel is not
at variance with true monastic life, and that where monastic
life is not a manifestation and an overflow of the Gospel of

God's redeeming love, then it is false and dead and dangerous.

In a discerning essay, *Ecumenism and Renewal*, Merton castigates the kind of monastic religion which evades the Gospel. He applauds the evangelical discovery of Martin Luther but believes that his schismatic answer was not the right solution, and he goes on to say: '. . . Luther's challenge now has a definite relevance for Catholic monks who are anxious to renew their monastic lives and to test the seriousness and authenticity of that renewal.' His understanding of the true centre of the Reformation is made clear:

> Before Vatican II it was still possible for monks to ignore the Reformation with its serious charge that the vowed life of the monk, lived under traditional disciplines and devoted to a complex system of pious works, was in fact an evasion of the basic call to discipleship. Instead of responding to the summons of Christ in faith, placing his entire trust in the word and promises of the Risen Saviour, seeking salvation, grace and light in the community of those called to confide entirely in the all-merciful Redeemer, the monk took refuge in vows and rites which (in the context of the late Middle Ages) could seriously be seen as a system of more or less superstitious fictions. In Reformation thought, monastic obedience became an abdication of mature responsibility and an escape from freedom which could, in extreme cases, turn the monk into a blind instrument of the most nefarious kind of power politics. Poverty became a mere hypocritical formality which enabled one to enjoy the goods and comforts of the world without even having to do an honest job of work to get them. Chastity was a fruitless evasion of the duty of marriage, corrupted perhaps by the most shameful kind of failures. [7]

Together with this appreciation of reformation insight is a profound appreciation of the 'highly successful Protestant monastic experiment of Taizé . . . as a paradigm for Catholic

monastic renewal.' The kind of renewal that Merton has in
mind is not ecclesiastical schism or the proliferation of
divergent sects; neither is it a matter of tinkering with
reformative legislative procedures, but life in the Spirit. As
he says: 'It has to be a kind of miracle of water in the desert.'

Merton does not set the Epistle to the Romans in opposition
to the Epistle of St James. It is not 'faith alone' or 'works
alone', but a living faith born of the Holy Spirit in the believing
heart, evidenced and confirmed by compassion and asceticism
which is the fruit of the Gospel. He is determined to emphasise
the primary gospel facts of human need and divine grace.
Christ is the Saviour for poor sinners, who brings us in
Himself, forgiveness, new life, transformation and sanctification. In Christ we seek and find God as our Creator, our
Father and our Redeemer. And this is what the monk is truly
seeking in the monastery. Merton warns against the Pelagian
heresy of seeing Christ crucified merely as a moral challenge
and inspiration for living, and affirms the atoning work of
Christ in his cross and resurrection as the basis of our
redemption, our strength, our wisdom and life in God. Against
Pelagianism, he says:

> Christ is not just a sublime hero whom we must strive
> every nerve to imitate – He is a loving Saviour who
> has come down to our level to give us His strength.
> He willed to identify Himself with our weakness in
> Gethsemane and on the Cross. [8]

Personal Faith and Cosmic Salvation

It is refreshing to find Merton evaluating, appreciating and
validating the work and insights of Luther, as other Roman
Catholic theologians are writing positive evaluations of Calvin,
Melanchton, and the reformed theologian who died on the
same day as Thomas Merton – Karl Barth. There is now
unqualified cross-fertilisation taking place across the denomi-
national board, and this can only be to the good of
contemporary ecumenical theology. But it is Merton who has

the ability to combine theological truth with psychological insights in a spirituality for the contemporary Christian which is both personal and corporate.

His appreciation of personal and evangelical experience does not become individual and subjective, but is lived out in the community of faith, and extends to the salvation of mankind in a cosmic dimension. This is what he understands by true catholicity. We have noted his use of the Adam-Christ parallel and his recourse to the Irenaean concept of *Recapitulation* in expounding his view of Christ as the 'Spiritual Head of regenerated and spiritualized Humanity'. And like the Eastern Fathers, he is not enunciating a scholastic or academic theological concept, but expounding the content of his experienced spirituality. He actually participates in what his theology proclaims.

Here it is that Merton puts his evangelical theology into contemplative context. He is not satisfied to formulate a catechism of theological doctrines, but invites us to participate in the reality behind such formulations. This is the tradition in which Athanasius could say: 'God became Man in order that man might become God'. It is *theosis*, divinisation – an actual participation in the divine nature, made possible by divine grace.

Far from evading an orthodox theology in the cause of vague mystical contemplation, Merton affirms that true Christian contemplation must enter into the riches of an orthodox theological foundation. His teaching runs something like this: Even if Christ had not become incarnate, he would be, as the Eternal Logos, the archetypal image of each human soul created in the image of God. But by his Incarnation he has become the cosmic Mediator in whom all things were made, all things are sustained and in whom all are redeemed. The resurrection of Christ completed and perfected his passion, and by the communication of his incorruptible life we become part of his mystical Body, the Church. As the work of redemption in Christ is of one piece, from creation to the consummation of all things, so our life in Christ is one in the mighty reversal of all that our solidarity in the first Adam brought about in sin. The implication that Merton sees in Irenaeus's concept of *Recapitulation* is one of universal dimensions, as he states clearly: 'The recapitulation of all men in Christ implies the mystical union of all in Him, in one perfect image, one love, one freedom.'[9] He takes great delight in the succinct statement of Irenaeus to this effect: 'The Word . . . by whom all things were made, in the fullness of time, to recapitulate and contain all things became man in order to destroy death, to manifest life, and to restore the union between God and man.' If such a concept is to fulfil its intention, the implication is that it must be universal, cosmic in its scope.

Merton freely acknowledges his debt to the Eastern Fathers in following this line of thought, especially in taking together St Paul's Adam-Christ parallel and Irenaeus's *Recapitulation* teaching, leading us into the experience of the alienation and desolation of the first Adam, and into the redeeming and liberating experience of the last Adam who is Christ – indicating with St Paul that all that is lost in Adam is restored in Christ – and projecting that into a cosmic vision of the great consummation of all things.

In order for this theology to come to life, to become exciting – and even dangerous (as God is dangerous), it is necessary for it to be *applied*. And if you follow the maturing writings and experience of Thomas Merton, it is clear that he actually walked (sometimes most painfully) this pilgrimage of contemplative experience. As Merton says, it is not enough to have *left* Egypt, contemplatives are called upon to *enter* the promised land, and not with the feet alone, but with the heart. I remember coming to Merton's *Contemplative Prayer*, and being persuaded that Merton actually lived what he wrote, for only a man who had trodden the places of desolation and ecstasy could write about them like that. As Douglas Steere the Quaker says in his preface to the same book:

> Nor is Thomas Merton afraid of the insights of those deepest voices that the monk has left behind. He has no hesitation in calling Baudelaire and Rimbaud

'Christians turned inside out'. He is quite as ready to
call attention to the fact that Existentialists like
Heidegger and Camus and Sartre have looked into the
face of death, have plumbed the abyss of man's
nothingness, have probed man's inauthenticity, and
have cried out for his liberation. He is prepared to
praise their withering power to strip man bare and to
insist that for one who dares to move on through the
stages of prayer, there can be no evading these ruthless
disclosures of man's existential situation.[10]

As Merton understands St Paul and Irenaeus, they are not
scholastic theologians but pilgrims of prayer and spirituality,
and their theology was an existential wrestling with the nature
and Being of God, as Jacob wrestled with the mysterious Being
all night at the brook Jabbok. If Christ recapitulated the
wholeness of man's being, it meant a descent into hell as well
as an ascent into glory, and as we follow Christ, it means
sharing in his Gethsemane and Calvary suffering, in order
to enter into the realms of ecstatic bliss and union. And as
Christ entered into his passion and glory for others, so the
contemplative lives the Gospel life in all its stages of darkness
and light for the salvation of the whole race. Douglas Steere
comments on Merton's existential journey again in
Contemplative Prayer:

Perhaps the deepest insight in the whole book comes in
the guidance that is given as to how to get dislodged
from the cowardice of complacency and how to move
on into the presence of the God who is a consuming
fire. For Blake knew well enough what a long and
costly business it was to learn to *bear* the 'beams of
love'. If it is true that the deepest prayer at its nub is
a perpetual surrender to God, then all meditation and
specific acts of prayer might be seen as preparations
and purifications to ready us for this never-ending
yielding. Yet what is so often concealed is that there is
a terrible dread that sweeps over me in the face of

such an expectation. If I am what I think myself to be and God is as I have pictured him to be, then perhaps I could bear to risk it. But what if he should turn out to be other than I have pictured him, and what if, in his piercing presence, whole layers of what I have known myself to be should dissolve away and an utterly unpredictable encounter should take place? Now we begin to face human dread – the dread that cloaks the unknown encounter of death – the dread that in miniature so often creates a crisis in a betrothal.

Thomas Merton continues quietly: 'We should let ourselves be brought naked and defenceless into the center of that dread where we stand alone before God in our nothingness without explanation, without theories, completely dependent upon his providential care, in dire need of the gift of his grace, his mercy, and the light of faith . . . (for) true contemplation is not a psychological trick but a theological grace.'[11]

These themes run together in this chapter – the evangelical nature of the Gospel and the contemplative soil in which the Gospel is planted and rooted, and also the personal nature of such a salvation along with the corporate awareness and participation which delivers from subjectivity and illusion. But as we have seen, the personal pilgrimage of faith in Merton is for and on behalf of others, and the corporate nature of the mystical Body of Christ heralds the cosmic salvation of all mankind.

The fact that Merton takes sin and redemption so seriously delivers him from the accusation of universalism in the 'larger hope' manner of some of the nineteenth century liberal theologians. He is not, in that sense, a universalist, but he does espouse the ancient tradition of *apokatastasis* (universal restoration) found in certain of the Eastern Fathers.[12]

Merton's universal and cosmic vision is not incompatible with his understanding of biblical particularity in which the Gospel appears to be clothed. In fact, the universal reconciling work of Christ, especially in terms of the Pauline and Irenaean concepts, are rooted in the very particularity of the Gospel, and in the understanding of the eternal Christ as the final and ultimate revelation of the Father.

This produces certain tensions, of course, for Merton wants to take seriously the biblical teaching on sin and judgement *and* the biblical affirmation of the total victory of Christ and the ultimate universal and cosmic reign of the divine Love. It is not either/or, but both/and! If I say that he finds himself less and less at home with the Augustinian and judicial framework and much more able to express himself within existential and ontological categories that is another way of saying that he is doing for New Testament theology what the Johannine tradition does within the New Testament itself. For instance, he says in *Seeds of Contemplation* that 'Hell can be described as a perpetual alienation from our true being, our true self, which is God.' And in the same book he uses existential categories to indicate a 'mere existence' which denies true life and identity:

> If I never become what I am meant to be, but always
> remain what I am not, I shall spend eternity
> contradicting myself by being at once something and
> nothing, a life that wants to live and is dead, a death
> that wants to be dead and cannot quite achieve its own
> death because it still has to exist.[13]

Now in a peculiar way this illustrates the tensions of Merton's theological vision. On the one hand Merton cannot deny the terrible seriousness of the human dilemma, with the awful possibility of alienation and separation which persists beyond the frontiers of this life into eternity. On the other hand, his trinitarian understanding of the nature of the Gospel underlines the universal scope of the redeeming work of God in Christ. The doctrine of the Holy Trinity is an eternal circle of universal love, and as Merton contemplates the divine Being in the cosmos and in himself, he must affirm the ultimate victory of love.

Such a contemplative dimension leaves no room for an

eternal dualism in which alienation, rebellion and sin co-exist
forever with the divine Love. If sin, death and hell are not
vanquished completely, then God's love can never be
ultimately victorious, and God will never be 'all in all'.

An Eschatological Secret

Eschatology has to do with the last things – traditionally they
are death, judgement, heaven and hell. It is the Gospel that
has caused Merton to move from an early exclusivism to a
universal love, and it is the Gospel that causes him to look for
what the Greek Fathers called *apokatastasis* – a reconciliation of
all things.

Merton is not here talking about the nineteenth century liberal
theologians who spoke of 'the larger hope' – the kind of universalism which is possible because sin is not taken seriously,
or because God is simply sentimental. Merton does not set aside
the teaching of the Church on the reality of judgement against
sin, but neither does he subscribe to some doctrine of everlasting
conscious torment for the damned. He comes to certain conclusions which indicate that death and judgement, retribution
and hell will be swallowed up within the greatness of the divine
Love, and that the nature of this amazing act of divine grace
is 'an eschatological secret' – because in our present state we
are unable to comprehend the heights and depths of such grace.

All Merton's thinking led him to such eschatology, for he
cannot think of the divine Love being in vain. He cannot think
that God would elect to damn the majority of his creatures,
or that somehow the pains of the damned in hell would give
glory to the God and Father of our Lord Jesus Christ. So when
he discovers perplexity over this matter in a fourteenth century
English recluse of Norwich, he rejoices over her conclusions,
and describes them as 'an eschatological secret'.

Lady Julian of Norwich

When a twentieth century American Trappist monk joyfully
appreciates the contemplative theology of a fourteenth century

English recluse and mystic, the result is a powerful witness
to the universal Gospel. Merton thinks of Julian as the greatest
of the English mystics, and a theologian in the ancient sense
of the word; 'He who really prays is a theologian and he who
is a theologian really prays.'[14] Writing of her mystical and
intuitive theological approach he says:

> She is a true theologian with great . . . clarity, depth
> and order: she really elaborates, theologically, the
> content of her revelations. She first experienced, then
> thought, and the thoughtful deepening of her
> experience worked it back into her life, deeper and
> deeper, until her whole life as a recluse at Norwich
> was simply a matter of getting completely saturated in
> the light she had received all at once, in the
> 'shewings', when she thought she was about to die.[15]

Merton is excited about Julian's theology because it adheres
to the catholicity of the Church, and yet is fresh and original
because it is born of personal, immediate experience and vision
of God. It is not only God's word from a fourteenth century
mystic for today – but God's word concerning the eschatological future and concerning the whole cosmos caught up in
the light, glory and revelation of universal love. No wonder
Merton enthuses!

> The theology of Lady Julian is a theology of the all-
> embracing totality and fullness of the divine love. This
> is, for her, the ultimate Reality, in the light of which
> all created being and all the vicissitudes of life and
> history fade into unimportance. Not that the world and
> time, the cosmos and history are unreal: but their
> reality is only a revelation of love.[16]

And although her meditations and visions are concrete and
simple, they are profound in their implications. She meditates
upon a hazel nut in her hand, and it teaches her about the
whole cosmic order, resting within the sustaining love of God.

The nut is willed by God, held in being by him, and therefore infinitely precious to him, becoming itself a revelation of his infinite compassion:

> It lasts and ever shall last for God loveth it. And even so hath everything being – by the love of God. In this little thing I saw three properties. The first that God made it: the second that God loveth it; the third that God keepeth it. And what behold I in this? Truly the Maker, the Lover and the Keeper.[17]

After dealing with some of her particular insights, Merton then turns to what he believes is the most profound intuition of her divine 'shewings' – the affirmation that 'everything will be made right', and it is an affirmation that has to do with the secret counsel of God. Julian confronts evil in the light of the divine mercy, and he, with her, cannot conceive of the failure of the mercy of God. As she says: 'Sin must needs be, but all shall be well. All shall be well; and all manner of thing shall be well.'

Lady Julian does not bolster up an optimistic and subjective explanation of redemption by minimising sin. She sees sin in all its tragedy in the horror and evil of the crucifixion of Christ, and of the persistence of sin and evil in the world. She sees also the sufferings of the just and the crushing humiliations of those who strive to love Christ; their pain and anguish, their descent into the abyss of near despair. The *eschatological secret* which breaks into the darkness of the mystery of iniquity is what stirs Merton with the light of the divine love, convincing him that Julian intuits the secret of God's loving heart for his creation:

> One of her most telling and central convictions is her orientation to what one might call an *eschatological secret*, the hidden dynamism which is at work already and by which 'all manner of thing shall be well.' This 'secret', this act which the Lord keeps hidden, is really the full fruit of the Parousia. It is not just that 'He comes',

but that He comes with this secret to reveal, He comes with this final answer to all the world's anguish, this answer which is already decided, but which we cannot discover, and which (since we think we have reasoned it all out anyway), we have stopped trying to discover. Actually, her life was lived in the belief in this 'secret', the 'great deed' that the Lord will do on the Last Day, not a deed of destruction and revenge, but of mercy and of life, all partial expectations will be exploded and *everything* will be made right. It is the great deed of 'the end' which is still secret, but already fully at work in the world, in spite of all its sorrow, the great deed 'ordained by Our Lord from without beginning'.[18]

Lady Julian's distinction between the mystery of sin and redemption as proposed 'openly' by the Church, and her personal conviction that this also implies 'secretly' something that has never been revealed and which no-one will know until the end of time – this is what Merton takes up and makes his own. He paraphrases Lady Julian's words:

. . . though there is great evil in the world, though there are devils and a hell, with the damned in it, and though the Church shall be attacked and shaken in a great storm, yet the Lord assures her: 'I *may* make all things well and I *will* make all things well: and *thou shalt see thyself* that all manner of things shall be well.'[19]

The breakthrough comes at this point. This is not a *solution* to evil as Merton understands it – it is even an admission that there exists no satisfactory intellectual solution. It is, even in spite of the revelation in scripture and in the Church, a problem which has not been and cannot be solved until the end of time when Christ himself will make known something which has never been revealed before. This is the 'secret' which God alone knows, which not even the blessed in heaven have yet seen because it is not necessary for our salvation.

Perhaps Merton is also drawn towards Julian *because* of the
seeming inconsistencies and contradictions involved in her
faithfulness to scripture and Church, and yet affirming, even
more firmly, that 'the word of Christ shall be saved in all
things' and 'all manner of thing shall be well'.

Here, for them both, is the heart of theology – the vision
of the unity of all things in the divine Love. Such an understanding does not solve the contradiction, but remains in the
midst of it, in peace, knowing that it *is* fully solved, but that
the solution is the eschatological secret, and cannot be
fathomed until it is revealed.

Nevertheless, Merton, like Lady Julian, participates in the
glory of such an eschatological understanding here and now.
He began his exposition of Lady Julian in the context of a
prayer for a wise heart, and he concludes:

> To have a 'wise heart', it seems to me, is to live
> centered on this dynamism and this secret hope – this
> hoped-for secret. It is the key to our life, but as long
> as we are alive, we must see that we do not have this
> key: it is not at our disposal, Christ has it, in us, for
> us. We have the key in so far as we believe in Him,
> and are one with Him. So this is it: the 'wise heart'
> remains in hope and in contradiction, in sorrow and in
> joy, fixed on the secret and the 'great deed' which
> alone gives Christian life its true scope and
> dimensions!
>
> The wise heart lives in Christ.[20]

Universal Salvation

Now I am not saying simply that either Julian or Merton were
universalists in the generally understood sense. But I am
saying that, for me, Merton's reading of Julian, and Merton's
understanding both of creation and redemption fills him with
universal joy and universal love. When I first read these
sections of Merton's writings on Julian I was reminded
particularly of the Wesleyan understanding of 'pure, universal

Love', and especially the hymns of Charles Wesley which say such things as:

> Oh, that the world might taste and see
> The riches of His grace;
> The arms of love that compass me
> Would all mankind embrace.

Merton does not systematise his eschatology, but he is so saturated with the Gospel of redeeming grace, with the universality of God's love and with the contemplative vision for all creation, that his heart bounded for joy when he read Lady Julian's *Revelations of Divine Love.*[21] And my heart bounds for joy as I read before me objectively the same secret that is buried in the contemplative depths of my own heart.

References

1 Merton, *SJ*, p. 284.
2 Merton, *SPMS*, p. 8.
3 *ibid.*, pp. 7f.
4 *ibid.*, p. 25.
5 Merton, *NMI*, p. 89.
6 Merton, *BPMS*, p. 28.
7 Merton, *CWA*, pp. 184f.
8 Merton, *BPMS*, pp. 29f.
9 See 'The Second Adam', in Merton, *NM*, pp. 92ff.
10 Merton, *CP*, pp. 10f.
11 *ibid.*, p. 13.
12 Clement of Alexandria, Irenaeus, the Cappadocian Fathers, *et al.*
13 Merton, *SC*, p. 26.
14 Merton, *MZM*, pp. 140ff.
15 Merton, *CGB*, p. 207.
16 Merton, *MZM*, p. 141.
17 *ibid.*, p. 142.
18 Merton, *CGB*, p. 208.

19 Merton, *MZM*, p. 144.
20 Merton, *CGB*, p. 208.
21 Julian of Norwich, *Revelations of Divine Love*, (trans. Clifton Wolters), (modern translation).

10: Contemplation and the Cosmos

The Cosmic Dimension of Prayer

One of the exhilarating and satisfying things about Merton's teaching on prayer is that it is to be experienced at every level of one's being. Prayer is experience of God, and that experience comes through the medium of the created order. God is present in other people, God is present in all creative impulses, God is present in the arts, in the sciences, in literature, poetry, music and all aesthetic aspiration. God is at the heart of the created order – there is a cosmic dimension to the experience of prayer.

So really, there is nothing – sin apart – in which God may not and does not manifest his presence, and at the level of body, mind or spirit, he is there manifesting his presence, and waiting, as it were, to be 'enjoyed'.

Of course, such enjoyment of God is only for those who are prepared, receptive, cleansed and open to his love. Otherwise, the experience of God comes as challenge, as confrontation, as numinous awe or unbidden terror. Enjoyment is to enter into the joy of his presence and being. Terror is the blinding, fearful invasion of his judgement. Merton is well aware of both poles of divine manifestation, for both are within his experience of the living God, and he has charted enough of the pilgrimage to indicate ecstasy and despair in the presence of the living God.

Merton mirrored, for me, the presence of God in the created order, and it was with great joy that I traced the theme of a contemplative perspective within the created order itself. The Western church has always been somewhat fearful of the doctrine of the immanence of God – fears of pantheism seem always to lurk in the Western mind and heart. Perhaps that is why there has been grave suspicions of mystical theology, and the teaching and charted experience of prayer in the lives and writings of the mystics. Merton's understanding of immanence can more be described as *panentheism*. The being of God is not exhausted by the created order, is transcendently 'high and lifted up' from all eternity. Nevertheless, he is intimately present at the heart of the created order, and he lives and moves in all creaturely beings and in the material world. Merton does not render worship and adoration to sun, moon and stars, for they are of the created order, but he does see and feel and respond to the manifestation of God's glory and life mediated in and through their existence.

Part of the beauty of all this is that the whole of man's being is drawn into holy communion with the glory and splendour of God. At the level of the physical God can be intuited and loved. I have always felt God's dynamic and rhythmic presence in my body and in the material world, and I have always responded at the level of worship and adoration at the glory of sunrise and sunset, at the reverberating thudding of the Atlantic Ocean around the rocky coastline of my home, and felt his living presence in the earth, the trees and in numerous living creatures. It is a source of ceaseless wonder to me, though not of complete surprise, that God should become incarnate in a body like mine – for I feel its potential, its glory, its promise and hope.

There is, of course, the other side to it – I feel its finitude, its mortality, and its vulnerability with increasing age, and its many imperfections brought about by mortal weakness or human sin. Yet in the light of redemption I know the springing up of hope and immortality reflected in the transfiguration and resurrection stories of the gospels. But let me get back to Thomas Merton.

Following the description of his conversion and baptism, he takes up the Deuteronomic picture of deliverance from the land of Egypt into Canaan, the land flowing with milk and honey, to represent the spiritual pilgrimage of his present and future experiences. He has left the carnal country of Egyptian bondage and is a stranger and pilgrim in the wilderness with his face and heart towards the heavenly Canaan. The aridity, the fertility, the watered land, the early and latter rains – all these and other pictures from the Deuteronomic passage speak to him of the darkness and glory of the spiritual life:

> How beautiful and how terrible are the words with which God speaks to the soul of those He has called to Himself, and to the Promised Land which is participation in His own life – that lovely and fertile country which is the life of grace and glory, the interior life, the mystical life. They are words lovely to those who hear and obey them: but what are they to those who hear them without understanding or response?[1]

Merton follows the Eastern Fathers in such intuitive exposition of the Old Testament. The theology of the Land or the People of God is spiritualised and contemporarised. Merton is part of the New Israel in which the warnings and blessings of the ancient people of God are existentialised into the present, and the theology is a theology of the material cosmos yielding its mystical meaning:

> I had come, like the Jews, through the Red Sea of Baptism. I was entering into a desert – a terribly easy and convenient desert, with all the trials tempered to my weakness – where I would have a chance to give God great glory by simply trusting and obeying Him, and walking in the way that was not according to my own nature or my own judgement. And it would lead me to a land I could not imagine or understand. It would be a land that was not like the land of Egypt from which I had come out: the land of human nature blinded and fettered by perversity and sin. It would be a land in which the work of man's hands and man's ingenuity counted for little or nothing: but where God would direct all things, and where I would be expected

to act so much and so closely under His guidance that
it would be as if He thought with my mind, as if He
willed with my will. It was to this that I was called. It
was for this that I had been created. It was for this
that Christ had died on the Cross, and for this that I
was now baptized, and had within me the living
Christ, melting me into Himself in the fires of His
love.[2]

You see how wonderfully geography had become theology
for Merton, as he traced in the experience of the ancient people
of God a holy history of salvation – what theologians call
Heilsgeschichte. But this is precisely what the old black slaves
used to do when Jesus became their Saviour and Deliverer
as Moses had redeemed the ancient people out of the bondage
of Egypt. Well Merton remembered the distasteful days of
his own Egypt, his former days and nights of emptiness and
intolerable boredom in both study and leisure, with the stale
satiety of the social roundabout and the constant awareness
of his lack of real freedom and joy.

Transformation of the World

His conversion experience had given him a glimpse of the way
in which the world can be transformed in the light of Christ,
and his spiritual pilgrimage would lead him more and more
to see the whole world ablaze with the glory of God – the vision
hidden from the eyes of the carnal man of Egypt.

The contemplation of the glory of God in Christ led Merton
into the world of nature, and the world of nature led him to
an ever-deepening understanding of the glory of God. Until
he entered into a knowledge of God in Christ, the natural
world not only did not bring him joy, it brought him pain.
In his former life he had denied not only the God who created
him, but in such denial, the end for which he was created.
He merely 'used' things for the enjoyment of his false self,
and thus lived a frustrated existence, with his deepest yearnings
unsatisfied. He puts it:

The only true joy on earth is to escape from the prison
of our own false self, and enter by love into union with
the Life who dwells and sings within the essence of
every creature and in the core of our own souls. In
His love we possess all things and enjoy fruition of
them, finding Him in them all. And thus as we go
about the world, everything we meet and everything
we see and hear and touch, far from defiling, purifies
us and plants in us something more of contemplation
and of heaven.

Short of this perfection, created things do not bring
us joy but pain. Until we love God perfectly,
everything in the world will be able to hurt us. And
the greatest misfortune is to be dead to the pain they
inflict on us, and not to realize what it is.[3]

This was and is certainly true of my own experience. If one
merely uses another in creaturely or sensual gratification
without consideration for the fragility and preciousness of
human relationship, it turns to dust. If one holds onto any
created thing, of beauty or harmony or pleasurable experience,
treating it as an end in itself, it does not yield peace and
tranquillity, but brings one to frustration or tears. And even
those moments and hours of creative sharing, of loving service,
of poetic and musical pleasure, or of work done for sheer joy
of creativity – even these hold greater promise than they are
able to yield – if they are ends in themselves.

Merton says that until we love God perfectly, his world is
full of contradictions, for the very things he has created to
draw us to him are the things which keep us away from him
if we continue to live on a superficial level, according to the
false self, the ego of self-love which we have created.

We become alienated in ourselves, and therefore from the
cosmos of which we are part. In all created things, therefore,
because we are what we are, we find the reflection of both
heaven and hell. There is blessedness because all created things
partake of the life of God and belong to God; there is anguish
because we treat them as ends in themselves for our own selfish

purposes, and this yields emptiness and frustration because they are not capable of fulfilling our desires.

This false self of which Merton speaks is not to be identified wih the body; for the body is neither evil or unreal. It has a reality which is given it by God and is called symbolically the 'temple of God'. The false self is rather our denial of our true self. We are at liberty to be real or unreal, and we may take the way of superficiality and falsity if we will. Or we may take the way which leads to discovery of our true self in Christ. As Merton says: 'For me to be a saint means to be myself. Therefore the problem of sanctity and salvation is in fact the problem of finding out who I am and of discovering my true self.' In this sense, we have a responsibility and a possibility that the world of nature does not have. Making the distinction clear, Merton says:

> A tree gives glory to God by being a tree. For in being what God means it to be it is obeying Him. It 'consents', so to speak, to His creative love. It is expressing an idea which is in God and which is not distinct from the essence of God, and therefore a tree imitates God by being a tree.
> The more a tree is like itself, the more it is like Him. If it tried to be something else which it was never intended to be, it would be less like God and therefore it would give Him less glory.[4]

This is the kind of theology which must be experienced. It is lifeless if left as a statement in a book on spirituality. My friend, the chestnut tree, stands in the field outside my room beyond the laurel hedge. I wrote about it in *Fulness of Joy* in the winter of last year, and you can see how a theology of creation such as Merton envisages comes to life in the experience of connatural relationship with, in this case, my friend the chestnut tree. I was writing about the shadow of death as it falls over our finitude and I look to the tree analogy to affirm gospel-hope:

I write today before an upstairs window of the
monastery at Glasshampton on a clear, crisp December
day. There is a beautiful chestnut tree before me in
the field beyond the laurel hedge. It stands stark and
bare under the grey winter sky, with the ragged
remnants of crisp, dried leaves clinging here and there,
its branches moving rhythmically in the gentle wind.
And I know that it contains a great secret within its
centre, and that unseen, the root-network reaches deep
down into the profound mystery of humus and
darkness below. I know that it will maintain its silent
and naked witness throughout the coming months of
frost, ice and cold. It will be shaken by the winds,
soaked by the rains, and stand a sentinel in the falling
snow. I've seen it before. But I also know that the
secret of springtime is locked within its being, and that
when the time is right the ground will soften, the year
will turn, the warmth will come, the sun will shine.
Then the sap will rise, unknown, unsuspected to the
faithless eyes, and the glory of resurrection will fulfil
its yearly cycle and all the world will sing again.[5]

The time is right just now. It is the month of April, and
the year has turned, the ground is soft, the warmth has come,
the sun is shining. The first cuckoo of the year sang from its
branches at 5.30 am this morning, and now a blackbird is
singing its full-throated song from the topmost boughs and
through my open window. After the first twelve feet of trunk
there is a threefold division, and the hundreds of branches
are bearing thousands of buds. The sap has risen, and the
tree itself is almost bursting into song. I not only observe it,
but I feel it! I have lived with it through those months of cold
winds and wintry rain, and I rejoice with the tree in its
anticipation of foliage, blossom and fruitfulness.

This chestnut tree stimulates in me theological reflection,
devotion and an experience of the immanence of God in the
world. That is what Thomas Merton was constantly finding,
pointing out and celebrating. And that is what engages me

in his life and writings. But he is no nature mystic, no
pantheist, for he goes on to enunciate clear moral implications:

> Unlike the animals and trees, it is not enough for us to
> be what our nature intends. It is not enough for us to
> be individual men. For us, holiness is more than
> humanity. If we are never anything but men, never
> anything but people, we will not be saints and we will
> not be able to offer to God the worship of our
> imitation, which is sanctity.
>
> It is true to say that for me sanctity consists in being
> myself, and for you sanctity consists in being *your* self
> and that, in the last analysis, your sanctity will never
> be mine and mine will never be yours, except in the
> communion of charity and grace.[6]

Merton was well aware of the kind of hippy-philosophy
of the 1960s and 1970s which was a manifestation of pseudo-
Zen and subscribed to such sentiments as 'If it feels good,
do it'. Some of this trendy feeling appealed to a sentimental
nature mysticism, laying great store by the emotional 'high'
that accompanied such experiences. Merton will have none
of this. An excellent antidote to such emotional ferment
is a concentrated perusal of *Seeds of Contemplation* where
discipline and spontaneity move together, and where the
intellect is not alienated from the emotions. Speaking of
merely sensual response, even when it appeals to religious
emotion, he says:

> . . . these things mean very little or nothing at all.
> They are a kind of sensible intoxication produced by
> some pleasure or other, and there is only an accidental
> difference between them and the tears that children
> sometimes shed when they go to the movies. . . . This
> blaze flares up and burns out in a few moments, or a
> half an hour. Whilst it lasts, you taste an intense
> pleasure which is sometimes deceptively lofty. But this
> joy occasionally betrays itself by a certain heaviness

that belongs to the sensual level and marks it for what
it is: crude emotion[7]

I have found Merton particularly valuable at this point,
and I would certainly commend to charismatic Christians,
both catholic and protestant, his chapter entitled 'The Wrong
Flame', where he clearly differentiates between emotional
religious ferment which is a manifestation of lusting after crude
experience and true mystical contemplation in both the natural
and the supernatural order. I find myself continually ministering to such charismatics who are constantly seeking more
and more religious 'highs' and seem to be hooked on religious
emotionalism – and they even come to a monastery hoping
that the silence and solitude will provide another fix! They
are soon disillusioned! And the disillusion is salutary! You
can imagine the shock which is administered to such people
by the following Merton paragraph:

> . . . Many of those who seem to be so superior to
> the *sensible* element in religion show, by their
> devotions, their taste for sentimental pictures and
> sticky music and mushy spiritual reading, that their
> whole interior life is a concentrated campaign for
> 'lights' and 'consolations' and 'tears of compunction',
> if not 'interior words' with, perhaps, the faintly
> disguised hope of a vision or two and, eventually, the
> stigmata.[8]

Such a taste for 'experience' can be a dangerous obstacle
even to those having a genuine call to a contemplative life
of prayer. 'It is the rock on which many who might have
become contemplatives have ended in shipwreck', writes
Merton, and that reflects some of his own bitter experience
which he records in his autobiographical *The Sign of Jonas*. He
affirms that emotion is part of the wholeness of faith, and
experience is integral to a true theological quest, but the wrong
flame which savours of sensuality is to be discerned and
avoided. Of such feelings he says:

Withdraw your consent from anything that may be
inordinate about them, and leave the rest to God,
waiting for the hour of your deliverance into the real
joys, the purely spiritual joys of a contemplation in
which your nature and your emotions and your own
selfhood no longer run riot, but in which you are
absorbed and immersed, not in this staggering
drunkenness of the senses but in the clean, intensely
pure intoxication of a spirit liberated in God.[9]

This is reminiscent of the way in which Christ commanded
the emotional, inebriated and wildly mystical Jacopone da
Todi, the thirteenth century Franciscan friar, to 'order his
love'. His conversion had been so dramatic, his emotional
feelings and love for Christ so intense, and the flame of his
fervour so radiantly hot, that it was like a river in flood which
overflowed its banks. Jacopone's poetical fervour abounds in
analogies to describe his experience of the divine Love. Christ
has stolen his heart, he complains ardently, and how can his
love be ordered in such fervour? He is hardly his own any
longer for Christ has laid hold on him, and the experience
is like the sky's shining gold at sunrise, like an iron which
glows white-hot in love's flame, like one who has been 'dipped
and clothed in Love':

Christ, Who hast stolen my heart, Thou biddest me
In Order fair my trembling mind to set;
But am I still mine own, though one with Thee?
 – Never was such a bargain driven yet!
As skies at sunrise shining lucently,
Or iron that the piercing flame hath met,
Their native form forget,
In wondrous change,
 – So I, O strange!
Am dipped and clothed in Love.[10]

That stanza is taken from a long and beautiful poem from
Jacopone da Todi's *Laude*. It is one of more than thirty stanzas

which swings from pain to ecstasy in the torment of divine
Love. There is no evidence that Merton read this powerful
and emotional Franciscan mystic, but I would have liked to
have heard his comments on this particular *Lauda* – for it is
entitled *How the Soul Complains to God of the Over-ardent Love
Infused in Her*. I find discipline and spontaneity manifested
in both Jacopone and Merton. But I do realise that the
excitement and inebriation which Jacopone stimulates in me
is corrected by these cautionary words of Merton:

> Passion and emotion certainly have their place in the
> life of prayer – but they must be purified, ordered,
> brought into submission to the highest love. Then they
> too can share in the spirit's joy and even, in their own
> small way, contribute to it. But until they are
> spiritually mature the passions must be treated firmly
> and with reserve, even in the 'consolations' of prayer.
> When are they spiritually mature? When they are
> pure, clean, gentle, quiet, nonviolent, forgetful of
> themselves, detached and above all when they are
> humble and obedient to reason and to grace.[11]

Perhaps here we have portrayed the different emphases
found in a white-hot, Italian Franciscan mysticism, and a
controlled, disciplined, well-ordered and reasoned Cistercian
spirituality. I find the Merton in me ministering to the
Jacopone, representing the two poles of my own spiritual
experience and theology. And this applies both in my
awareness of God in nature and in grace.

Thomas Merton in Camera

At this point, keeping in mind what we have said about
Merton's experiential awareness of God in the created order,
and his warnings about pseudo-mysticism, I want to show how
he actually applies and works out his theology in a practical
manner.

John Howard Griffin was Merton's official biographer

before his premature death prevented him completing the task. In the late 1950s, Griffin visited Gethsemani with his camera (he was a professional photographer), and Merton showed a childlike and absorbing interest in it, and Griffin's photography. Griffin was so impressed by Merton's attitude and results that he presented him with a camera 'on extended loan', and in Merton's hands it became a contemplative instrument, discovering and communicating 'the love of Christ which hides itself mysteriously in the inner logoi of created things'.

In a book published after Merton's death, John Howard Griffin expounds his way of looking at things, his awareness of relationship to the created order, by means of photographs and commentary. The book is entitled: *A Hidden Wholeness: The Visual World of Thomas Merton*, and consists of photography by Merton and Griffin, and text by Griffin. Throughout this beautiful volume, Griffin demonstrates how Merton was philosophically and experientially involved in his relationship with the natural world by means of his contemplative orientation through photography. It is a modern and contemporary expression of the ancient contemplative attitude, manifesting one of the ways in which the contemplative life invades all aspects of human existence and experience. [1 2]

In Merton's hands, his photography was a reflection of, and a way to, God. His camera, no less than his typewriter, caught and communicated the divine presence to the person whose mind and heart were open to receive it. He approached the natural objects of his contemplative attention, respecting the way in which such objects gave themselve to him. He did not impose himself or his subjective patterns upon them, but allowed them to be, to communicate, to reveal the immanence of the divine Love. As Griffin says:

> Thomas Merton's approach to photography, and one
> of the reasons his photography is truly personal, lay in
> his use of his lenses primarily as contemplative
> instruments. He photographed the things he
> contemplated; his 'serious work' as he called it, is a

meditation. He did not seek to capture or possess, and
certainly not to arrange the objects he photographed.
He lent his vision and his lenses to them in a real way;
he was there and he did the mechanical things –
focusing, composing – but he allowed the objects to
remain true to themselves, and he trusted that the
connections would somehow be made.[13]

These words call to mind the notion of what the Greek
Fathers called *Theoria Physike*, which Merton paraphrased as
Contemplation of the Cosmos in presenting it to his novices and
scholastics when he was Master of Novices at Gethsemani in
the 1960s. Quoting St Maximus, the father of Byzantine
mysticism, whom he calls 'the great doctor of *Theoria Physike*,
he writes:

The love of Christ hides itself mysteriously in the inner
logoi of created things . . . totally and with all his
plenitude . . . In all that is varied lies hidden He who is
One and eternally identical, in all composite things. He
who is simple and without parts, in those which have a
beginning, in all the visible He who is invisible.[14]

This contemplative orientation, the perceiving of the inner
logoi of created things, is what God intends for all men.
Theologically, for Merton, the *Logos* is the Eternal Word, the
Second Person of the Holy Trinity, by whom all things were
created, and who indwells all creatures and creation by right
of their creaturehood – this is what is meant by the inner *logoi*.
Such a contemplation of nature is inseparable from loving
attention to the sophianic depths of man's own nature. This
is an exciting theology of nature and grace, as Merton
envisages the regenerated and purified man transfiguring
material things by his very contemplation of them. Grace
informs and builds upon nature as the hidden and mysterious
presence of the living God communicates itself from the bosom
of his creation. Writing of such a *synergism* (working together)
of nature and grace, Merton says:

The world is no longer seen as merely material, hence as an obstacle that has to be grudgingly put up with. It is spiritual through and through. But grace has to work in and through us to enable us to carry out this real transformation. Things are not fully spiritual in themselves, they have to be spiritualized by our knowledge and love in our use of them. Hence it is impossible for one who is not purified to 'transfigure' material things; on the contrary, the *logoi* will remain hidden, and he himself will be captivated by the sensible attractions of these things.[15]

This means that it is spiritual to be truly human, and the experience of being truly human is a work of the Holy Spirit. A basic, existential understanding of holiness is a pre-requisite for the revelation of the hidden *logoi* at the heart of the created cosmos. Humanity and holiness go together as is clear in Griffin's evaluation of Merton's contemplative attitude:

Merton did not believe that man came to God through the truncation of his humanity but through the wholeness of humanity. All of the senses were valued in his contemplative and creative life. Never content with externals, he sought, in the phrase of Herakleitos, 'to look into the essence of things'. As novice-master, he warned his novices against the 'vice' of insensibility that men sometimes cultivate as a means of detachment. 'The body is good,' he said, 'listen to what it tells you.' He esteemed the senses and what they could teach, especially the senses of sound and sight. His writings are filled with striking visual images. His drawings, his calligraphy and his photography express the visual growth of his vocation.[16]

Because it comes from the hand of God, Merton grew in his awareness of the inherent and fundamental intelligibility and rationality of the created order. And this is the attitude we find exemplified in his contemplative writings as well as his photographic studies. Such an awareness and response did not only embrace inanimate and animate nature, but spilled over into the dimension of personal relationships:

> This concept: going out to the thing and giving oneself to it, allowing it to communicate its essence, allowing it to say what it will, reveal what it will, rather than trying to bring it into the confines of self, altering and changing it by the presentation of it, was one of Thomas Merton's profoundest orientations. It was reflected in his relations with people. He so thoroughly gave himself in focusing on the other person that nothing seemed to be held back, and yet he left the person free to be himself, never sought to alter the person to fit his concepts, never possessed the person. [17]

This is the basic and fundamental test of a theology – that it is translated into love, into compassion, into relationships which produce joy, dialogue and openness. It meant that Merton would accept things as they were, he would not alter them to suit himself, he would not impose his own logic or pattern or read into them that which was not *inherent* within their own potentialities. For Merton it was not what you did to the objects that presented themselves to you, but what you allowed to be done to yourself. He worked at producing photographic images which, when viewed in quietness and openness of heart, would accomplish the secret work of communicating 'a hidden wholeness', revealing some hint of that wordless gentleness that flows out from the unseen roots of all created being. It was Griffin, who gave him his first camera, who taught him all he knew concerning the art of photography. Writing of Merton as a photographer he says:

> From the beginning, then, in his photography, he focused on the images of his contemplation, as they were and not as he wanted them to be. He took his

camera on his walks and with his special way of
seeing, photographed what moved or excited
him – whatever responded in some mysterious way to
that inner orientation.

All of his culture, his high poetic sensitivity, his
training in the arts, his spiritual and intellectual being
formed the filter through which he viewed these things,
but his view was not imprisoned by his culture, not
limited. He believed in the 'gradual growth' and
trusted the 'connections'.

As a result his concept of aesthetic beauty differed
from that of most men. Most would pass by dead tree
roots in search of a rose. Merton photographed the
dead tree root or the texture of wood or whatever
crossed his path. In these works he photographed the
natural, unarranged, unpossessed objects of his
contemplation, seeking not to alter their life but to
preserve it in its emulsions.[18]

As I write these words, glancing out of the window past
the chestnut tree of which I wrote earlier, I see one of our
guests in the distance, returning from a contemplative walk.
Perhaps he has been practising an actual 'walking meditation'
or perhaps it is a walk in the beauty of this spring day after
a morning of prayer and study. He is a busy lecturer in one
of our large theological colleges, and has just returned from
an exceptionally busy time of communication and seminars
at the *Spring Harvest* celebration. I shall show him Merton's
words when we meet for interview tomorrow, and share our
thoughts on the presence of God in the created order, Merton's
'special way of seeing', and its relation to openness and
compassion in human relationships.

Merton not only waited upon nature for an understanding
of its own message and beauty, but he was able to capture
and communicate it in his pictures and words. 'We don't have
to run after it,' he says, 'it was there all the time, and if we
give it time, it will make itself known to us.'

Commenting on Merton's photography after his death, a

fellow-monk points out the sensitivity and implications inherent in his approach:

> It is indeed striking to consider the beauty which Merton could capture in such simple things as an old railway stage which is now abandoned; three old paint buckets; a pair of sawhorses; a gate in the fields of the monastery. These are the things which modern man completely fails to view with any sense of the sacred which is present within. Man is too concerned with the 'use' of creation to take time to view it objectively, to *listen* to its inner voice. Merton said: 'To begin to realise the *logoi* of creatures we must always be conscious of their mute appeal to us and find and rescue the glory of God which has been hidden in them and veiled by sin.
>
> Because man cannot hear this appeal he views an old paint bucket simply as something to be discarded in the quickest possible way. It is this which is now leading to the ecological crisis facing man. This is diametrically opposed to that reverence with which St Benedict says that the monk should use the tools of the monastery 'as if they were the sacred vessels of the altar'. [19]

If I think of Thomas Merton as a soul-friend, it is not because I accept all he says, or would endorse all he did – he would laugh at such an attitude. Rather it is because he is the kind of man who knew, felt and could communicate a theology and spirituality of grace and nature that has been the theme of this chapter, He evokes and stimulates in me that contemplative spirit that he believed was the inheritance of every man, and he was on the pilgrimage of the integration of all his faculties of body, mind and spirit that are inherent in his understanding of *salvation* – wholeness of the human person. He once wrote some beautiful words on *Hagia Sophia*, (Holy Wisdom) which are found on the fly-leaf of the book we have been considering – *A Hidden Wholeness*:

There is, in all visible things an invisible fecundity, a
dimmed light, a meek namelessness, a hidden
wholeness. This mystery, unity and integrity is
Wisdom, the Mother of all, *Natura naturans*.

There is in all things an inexhaustible sweetness and
purity, a silence that is a fount of action and of joy. It
rises up in the wordless gentleness and flows out to me
from the unseen roots of all created being.

One thing remains in this chapter – that is to draw out
another aspect of the *Theoria Physike* concept of St Maximus
that Merton saw and used in his contemplation of the
cosmos – and that is the created order as the 'game of God'.

Creation as the Game of God

Let's first define our terms. Merton's use of St Maximus's
concept of 'game' is not to be understood in the sense of a
jest, a contest, a competitive round of skill, strength, fortune,
or with innuendoes of a trick or dodge. Rather it is meant
in the sense of play, dance and inter-related movement. God
does not 'play chess' with his creation – rather he dances in
and through it, and all participate in the *diversion* of
diversification into unity, or of *a-muse-ment* in the sense that
the muse is the author of creative thought and word. The
cosmos is the 'game of God' in which we all participate. The
words of St Maximus which Merton takes up are these:

The whole world is a GAME OF GOD. As one
amuses children with flowers and bright colored clothes
and then gets them later used to more serious games,
literary studies, so God raises us up first of all by the
great game of nature, then by the Scriptures (with
their poetic symbols). Beyond the symbols of Scripture
is the Word . . .[10]

The reason why Merton takes up St Maximus is the same
reason why I am drawn to Merton – because I already intuit

and experience the mystical theology which Merton expounds, as Merton already understands the potential and experience of St Maximus's concept. The last chapter of Merton's *Seeds of Contemplation* is called 'The General Dance', where he views the world as a temple, a garden, a paradise in which God takes delight. He writes:

> The Lord made His world not in order to judge it, not in order merely to dominate it, to make it obey the dictates of an inscrutable and all-powerful will, not in order to find pleasure or displeasure in the way it worked: such was not the reason for the creation either of the world or of man. The Lord made the world and made man in order that He Himself might descend into the world, that He Himself might become Man. When He regarded the world He was about to make He saw His wisdom, as a manchild, 'playing in the world, playing before Him at all times'. And He reflected, 'My delights are to be with the children of men.'[21]

For Merton, the presence of God in the world was two-fold. He was immanent in it by his Holy Spirit, at the heart of the created order, and He became incarnate in it in the Incarnation of the eternal *Logos*:

> The Lord God would not only love His creation as a Father, but He would enter into His creation, emptying Himself, hiding Himself, as if He were not God but a creature. Why should He do this? Because He loved His creatures, and because He could not bear that His creatures should merely adore Him as distant, remote, transcendent and all-powerful. This was not the glory that He sought.[22]

Merton calls upon us not to subjugate, to impose our will or endeavour to mould creation to our own egotistical desires, but to open our eyes, to intuit and experience the reality of things, to actually feel our participation in the creative play of the cosmos. If we do impose our own will, it will not ultimately alter the reality of things, but we shall bear the loss of it, and perhaps lose our part in such cosmic participation. God intends our participation, which is a game, a dance, a rhythm of the general glory of things which will turn our natural values upside down. He describes the game:

> What in God might appear to us as 'play' is perhaps what He Himself takes most seriously. At any rate the Lord plays and diverts Himself in the garden of His creation, and if we could let go of our own obsession with what we think is the meaning of it all, we might be able to hear His call and follow Him in His mysterious, cosmic dance. We do not have to go very far to catch echoes of that game, and of that dancing. When we are alone on a starlit night; when by chance we see the migrating birds in autumn descending on a grove of junipers to rest and eat; when we see children in a moment when they are really children; when we know love in our own hearts; . . . – at such times the awakening, the turning inside out of all values, the 'newness', the emptiness and the purity of vision that make themselves evident, provide a glimpse of the cosmic dance.[2][3]

This cosmic dance is not an appeal to the natural instinct in its alienation (remember Merton's warning against the *Wrong Flame*?). It is not any kind of religious or pagan rhythm that accompanies the sensual throbbing of a pagan fertility cult. It is rather an experience of being drawn into the rhythm of the heartbeat at the centre of the cosmos. It is the rhythm and pulsation of the world which is the mind and heart of its Creator and Redeemer. It is heard in silence, and yet in all things that glorify God in the created order. And only those who strive for purity of vision in contemplation truly participate in such a dance. The redeeming love and grace of God in Jesus Christ, applied by the power of the Holy Spirit, is the foundation upon which the contemplative life is built. There is no dance, no celebration of joy, no liberty or music apart from the redeeming and reconciling grace of God. But because the Creator is also the Redeemer, celebration of the cosmic dance is the only appropriate attitude for Merton:

> For the world and time are the dance of the Lord in emptiness. The silence of the spheres is the music of a wedding feast. The more we persist in misunderstanding the phenomena of life, the more we analyse them out into the strange finalities and complex purposes of our own, (so) the more we involve ourselves in sadness, absurdity and despair. But it does not matter much, because no despair of ours can alter the reality of things, or stain the joy of the cosmic dance which is always there. Indeed we are in the midst of it, and it is in the midst of us, for it beats in our very blood, whether we want it to or not.
>
> Yet the fact remains that we are invited to forget ourselves on purpose, cast our awful solemnity to the winds and join in the general dance.[24]

Now what does all this mean for us? Well for me it meant that Merton invited me to allow my eyes to be opened, my heart to be touched, my body to be embraced by the creative reality by which I am surrounded – the cosmos itself. Merton's intuitive feel for the created order caused him to affirm the dynamic presence of God at the heart of creation. It caused him to look, to listen, to feel, to appropriate and then to participate willingly, joyfully and creatively in the cosmic dance.

Such an attitude of passive openness and active dialogue regulated his relations with other people, and the integration of his bodily and mental faculites in such participation persuaded him of the inherent intelligence and reasonableness of creation, which implies ultimate meaning and purpose in the cosmos.

All this is seen from the perspective of a redeemed and

purified man – a man of contemplative prayer. And as I heard
and accepted an invitation to the pilgrimage, I found myself
a participant in the cosmic dance.

He brings both the immanence of God in creation and the
incarnation of God in Christ together as part of that invitation:

> The presence of God in His world as Creator depends
> on no one but Him. His presence in the world as Man
> depends, in some measure, upon men. Not that we
> can do anything to change the mystery of the
> Incarnation in itself: but we are able to decide whether
> we ourselves, and that portion of the world which is
> ours, shall become *aware* of His presence, consecrated
> by it, and transfigured in its light.[25]

References

1 Merton, *SSM*, p. 148.
2 *ibid.*, pp. 148f.
3 Merton, *SC*, p. 20.
4 *ibid.*, p. 24.
5 Ramon *SSF*, *Fulness of Joy*, p. 194.
6 Merton, *SC*, pp. 24f.
7 *ibid.*, pp. 190f.
8 *ibid.*, p. 191.
9 *ibid.*, pp. 192f.
10 Jacopone da Todi, *Lauda XC*.
11 Merton, *SC*, p. 193.
12 The 'ancient contemplative attitude' is based upon the
    Theoria Physike (contemplation of nature) notion of the
    Greek Fathers.
13 John Howard Griffin, *A Hidden Wholeness*, pp. 3f.
14 Merton, *Ascetical and Mystical Theology*, (unpublished),
    p. 58.
15 *ibid.*, p. 59.
16 Griffin, *op. cit.*, p. 2.
17 *ibid.*, p. 50.

18 *Loc. cit.*

19 Tarcisius Conner, review of *A Hidden Wholeness* in *Monastic Exchange*, Vol. II, No. 3.

20 Merton, *Ascetical and Mystical Theology*, p. 63.

21 Merton, *SC*, p. 225.

22 *ibid.*, p. 227.

23 *ibid.*, p. 230.

24 *Loc. cit.*

25 *ibid.*, pp. 228f.

Part IV: Wider Horizons

11: The Eastern Contemplative Traditions

I call Thomas Merton 'soul friend' because of the amazing rapport we share, and because of the particular light he sheds on my own pilgrimage which, like his, is dynamic and evolving continually. When I first discovered Merton, I looked to him for a way of contemplative spirituality, not as a systematic theologian (which he was not anyway). But because his journey was a beckoning invitation to me, it was not long before I began to read the Eastern contemplative texts which he referred me to, and participated, in spirit, in his dialogue with eastern spirituality in its Taoist, Buddhist, Hindu and Sufi forms.

This did not only call for an openness of mind and spirit on my part, but also a radical rethinking of my faith in terms of theism, christology and soteriology – the Being of God, the uniqueness of Christ and the way and experience of salvation in revelation to the great world Faiths.

Merton's own journey involved him in many changes of opinion and attitude, for you cannot enter into real dialogue and friendship with men of other faiths and traditions without endeavouring to stand where they stand and to appreciate the insights, depth and sincerity of their convictions. As a result of this, and of a study of oriental texts as expounded by *their* representatives (and not as *interpreted* by exclusivist Christians), I followed Merton into an appreciation of the world Faiths in their own right and of my own Christian Faith from other perspectives and cultures. It has been, and is, an enriching experience, though one fraught with some pitfalls and calling for disciplined and honest thought.

Merton redefined his catholicism in universal, rather than exclusivist, terms, and admitted the validity of genuine spiritual experience outside the specifically Christian Church. He felt a rapport and closeness with many non-Christian contemplatives, but Christ continued to be the centre and sum of his life and proclamation. My favourite picture of Thomas Merton is one in which he stands in his Cistercian habit with the Dalai Lama just a month before his death, reproduced in the posthumous *Asian Journal*. On the morning of his death he addressed the Asian monastic leaders at Bangkok, and said:

> I believe that by openness to Buddhism, to Hinduism, and to these great Asian traditions, we stand a wonderful chance of learning more about the potentiality of our own traditions . . . The combination of the natural techniques and the graces and the other things that have been manifested in Asia, and the Christian liberty of the Gospel should bring us all at last to that full and transcendent liberty which is beyond mere cultural differences and mere externals . . .[1]

Conversion and Dialogue

It is at such a point that the life and witness of Merton became something of a stumbling-block to those who had categorised him and expected him to remain in the pre-Vatican II mould that was the mark of his early convert days. There was more to conversion than a change of opinion, than an affirmation of an exclusivist set of propositions which ruled others out rather than drew them in, and the regulating factor was love. Merton's understanding and practice was according to this stanza:

> He drew a circle that kept me out,
> Heretic, rebel, a thing to flout;
> But love and I had a wit to win –
> We drew a circle that brought him in.

There was an increasing desire to share the riches of the love and redeeming grace of Christ, and a high christology that affirmed the uniqueness of the incarnation of God in Christ. But he came to believe that the Church did not have a monopoly on Christ, but that the grace of God and the work of the Holy Spirit was manifest universally among all peoples, cultures and traditions. Not only did he seek to share the redeeming Christ with those who had not recognised him in the Christian tradition, but he also sought to find and learn of the hidden Christ in the oriental cultures which preserved a wisdom and love much needed in the West.

Conversion was high on his list, but it was the conversion of himself and of the Church as much as anyone else. He did not believe that the cause of truth was served by comparing and contrasting the worst of the non-Christian Faiths with the best of Christianity. Indeed, he often found that whereas the Christian tradition of 'holy war' could justify not only defence but attack, often the Buddhist and Hindu traditions sought the way of peace and non-violence. He believed that this was the way of Christ, and that therefore, they had understood the language of the Holy Spirit far more clearly than the Christian church in a Western capitalist society.

So he did not indulge in missionary proselytising, endeavouring to 'convert' men who already had an explicit contemplative life, to a Western, dogmatic and scholastic Christian faith. Rather he sought to share their contemplative perspective with them, allowing its light to illuminate his own faith. In the very act of such experienced participation, sharing and dialogue took place in profound silence and spiritual interchange.

This kind of dialogue sounds like compromise to many Catholic and Protestant ears, and I remember the extreme caution with which I followed Merton's pattern of spiritual dialogue, fearful for the uniqueness of Christ and the blurring of the Gospel's clarity, apprehensive lest the cutting edge of repentance and faith in Christ be blunted.

I had at least two problems in this respect. First, I had no Hindu, Buddhist or Moslem friends – no-one to dialogue with;

and second, I thought in my arrogance that I had to defend
and propagate the Gospel, arrogating to myself the charge
and work of the Holy Spirit. I had long left behind the idea
of cultivating friends in order to 'win them to Christ',
recognising that as spiritual blackmail, but I was still not
mature enough to enter into the openness of dialogue – a
learning process in which one shared in a mutual interchange
in which one commended one way of Christ which had become
precious, while learning of the ways of Christ and the Spirit
in the mystery of God which had not been part of one's own
tradition, or which had long been forgotten. It was really a
recognition of the fact that Christ, as the Eternal Logos
enlightens everyone who is open to his creative light.

One cannot live in London, Bradford, Birmingham,
Cardiff, or many other cities and towns of Britain without
coming into contact with people of non-christian traditions
which are as precious to them as our faith is to us. When I
say 'contact' it means some kind of a meeting. But some
Christians are still afraid to be open enough to be friendly
to neighbouring Sikhs, Moslems, Hindus or Buddhists. It is
not a matter of colour, for some of our best Christians are
certainly not white, and some of our white acquaintances are
quite likely to be following a Hindu or Buddhist path. The
time is long overdue for full and open friendships with no
strings attached. This is what Thomas Merton showed me,
and this is the way I continue to follow.

One of the best chapters in my *Deeper Into God* is entitled
'What People Say', and it is given over to what others have
said and written about making a retreat. One of the contributors
to that chapter, Roger, wrote of the immense value of retreat
in his personal and vocational life, for he works among people
of other faiths in Birmingham. I added my comment of a 'sting
in the tail' of a letter from Roger in which he wrote:

> Could one think of Buddhist monks visiting
> Glasshampton and the friars of Glasshampton visiting
> the Buddhists? To say more would be an impertinence,
> but to say less would be a betrayal, so I will shut up!

Well since that time, I have taken a group of novices, with Roger, to visit the Hindu temple, the Jewish synagogue, the Moslem mosque and the Sikh temple. We were received courteously and even with gratitude, and given some exotic things to eat. It was nothing new to *us* to remove our sandals at the door, or to sit in meditative posture and share silence and meditation, but it was a new experience for some of *them* to find that not only were these a group of Christians who showed reverence and courtesy to their religion, but who also had dimensions of contemplation and prayer akin to their own understanding. I must admit that we were 'evangelised' by a young Hindu guru who was visiting from the States, while the resident priest squirmed at such discourtesy and we smilingly listened, and added a few gentle comments at the end. But it was good to experience it this way round, for we were made aware of continual Christian insensitivity that they suffered day by day.

At the Sikh temple there was a wonderful atmosphere of openness and trust that grew from the first few minutes of strangeness and apprehension on both sides. This particular Sikh temple had a group of monks attached which is quite rare. We sat together on the carpeted floor and shared a token meal, and the novice-interpreter enabled their 'guardian' to have a conversation with me. Within a quarter of an hour we both felt an affinity of spirituality, and he was so happy to find such Christians, and we were showered with gifts as we came away in the pouring rain.

Since that time this group of Sikhs have come to visit us at Glasshampton, and in our meditative sharing we said the *Jesus Prayer* and they took up one or two themes which seemed to them to be shared in the Sikh and Franciscan traditions.

What does this accomplish? Well according to Merton it deepens our humanity, encourages a proper humility and illuminates faith. It is at the contemplative and not the dogmatic level that fellowship can grow, and that without compromise of precious doctrinal revelation. Such an attitude must lead to dialogue, as he says:

Not only must the Catholic respect these other
traditions and honestly evaluate the good contained in
them, but the Council adds that he must
'acknowledge, preserve and promote the spiritual and
moral goods found among these men as well as the
values in their society and culture.'[2]

Merton did not believe that any great syncretistic synthesis
would be brought about, and he didn't want such, but he did
work towards an interpenetration of understanding and reconciliation which would reveal the possibility of harmony which
itself would be a rebuke to the negative factors in Christianity
and the other faiths. The whole 'holy war' idea of Christianity,
Judaism and fundamentalist Islam is a misrepresentation of
faith and a grief to many believers.

Merton is very aware of the important differences between
the various traditions, but he also affirms the basic assumptions
which set the monk of any tradition apart from people
dedicated to lives which are what Merton calls 'aggressively
non-contemplative'.

The assumptions which the typical Western 'money-making
man' has of the Oriental traditions are usually caricatures of
a grossly pessimistic rejection of the material world, a desire
to escape into some spiritual realm of pure essences, and of
a path to annihilation in a negative void. But Merton points
out that the great contemplative traditions of both East and
West, while differing sometimes quite radically in their
formulation of aims and methods

agree in thinking that by spiritual disciplines a man
can radically change his life and attain to a deeper
meaning, a more perfect integration, a more complete
fulfillment, a more total liberty of spirit than are
possible in the routine of a purely active existence
centered on money-making. That there is more to
human life than just 'getting somewhere' in war,
politics, business – or 'the Church'. They all agree that
the highest ambition lies beyond ambition, in the

renunciation of that 'self' which seeks its own
aggrandizement in one way or another. And they
agree that a certain 'purification' of the will and
intelligence can open man's spirit to a higher and
more illuminated understanding of the meaning and
purpose of life, or indeed of the very nature of Being
itself. [3]

Merton was faced by two extremes as he thought and prayed
his way through to a deeper understanding of both conversion
and dialogue. The one denied validity to all non-Christian
religious experience, and the other affirmed all religious
traditions equally true and valid. These are both superficial,
he maintained, because neither of them involve themselves
in an objective study of the documents, and both lack the
dimension of contemplative *experience* with other traditions.
There must be sympathetic, informed and scholarly study,
together with a sharing of life, especially in the area of
contemplative prayer and meditation.

One of the problems is that neither Christian nor non-
Christian contemplatives are often found in the places of
ecumenical dialogue – they are devoted to a hidden and
solitary mode of life. They also often lack scholarly and
theological preparation, or are extremely reticent to speak of
their inner experience, knowing how publicity often abuses
and falsifies even those things which may be indicated in
human language.

Since Merton's death in 1968, much of this has been
reversed. There have been mystical theologians of the
Christian and non-Christian variety who have shared together,
and publicly. And there have been responsible people of
integrity in the mass media who have allowed such people
to speak for themselves, thus meeting the needs of an
increasing number of spiritually hungry and thirsty people
in our technological age.

In many ways Merton blazed the trail of such contemplative
seeking, for although he spent twenty-seven years at the Abbey
of Gethsemani (his only long journey being the occasion of

his death), within the last few years of his life there was a
continual flow of distinguished and qualified non-Christian
contemplatives visiting him. Speaking of such communication,
he writes:

> While on the level of philosophical and doctrinal
> formulations there may be tremendous obstacles to
> meet, it is often possible to come to a very frank,
> simple and totally satisfying understanding in
> comparing notes on the contemplative life, its
> disciplines, its vagaries and its rewards. Indeed, it is
> illuminating to the point of astonishment to talk to a
> Zen Buddhist from Japan and to find that you have
> much more in common with him than with those of
> your own compatriots who are little concerned with
> religion, or interested only in its external practice. [4]

And moving in the other direction, Christmas Humphreys
of the British Buddhist Society says of Thomas Merton:

> He was a remarkable man in that by the power of his
> enlightenment, however labelled, he formed a bridge
> between the Church of Rome and Zen Buddhism
> where alone such union can be made, at the highest
> level of each. For him the limitations and imperfections
> of both were no longer barriers to the light which, in
> pure experience, he found to be theirs in common. His
> was indeed a brilliantly illumined mind. [5]

With such 'contemplative men' Merton was able to enter
into a basic human relationship and, building upon that, there
was what he called a sharing of the 'natural metaphysical
intuition of being' as the foundation for a contemplative
attitude. By that he meant that the contemplative mind and
heart was open to that mysterious power which indwells all
particular beings, so that they 'know' and 'feel' that they are
enveloped in 'Being itself'. This experience may be, to
contemplatives of different traditions, a manifestation of the

Holy Spirit, of the Tao, of Brahma or of the Void, – many different words may be used in different traditions to indicate the same spiritual reality which is beyond language.

The Christian scriptures are supremely precious to Merton, but he cannot envisage the reality, presence and experience of God being limited or incarcerated within the covers of any book. So the grace, love and mercy of God is universal, and open to all who are sincere in their spiritual quest:

> Since in practice we must admit that God is in no way limited in His gifts, and since there is no reason to think that He cannot impart His light to other men without first consulting us, there can be no absolutely solid grounds for denying the possibility of supernatural (private) revelation and of supernatural mystical graces to individuals, no matter where they may be or what may be their religious tradition, provided that they sincerely seek God and His truth.[6]

The Johannine biblical tradition, because of its high christology, does not limit the grace of God to the historical Jesus. John is writing of the eternal Logos, and Merton reminds us that when his friend Dr John Wu translated the Gospel of John into Chinese, he wrote: 'In the beginning was the Tao . . .' So the Johannine saying of Jesus: 'I am the way, and the truth and the life; no one comes to the Father, but by me' – far from limiting salvation to the historical followers of the historical Jesus, includes and embraces not only the godly people of the Old Testament, but all who are indwelt and influenced by the universal Logos. The saying is not exclusive but inclusive, for it is not possible to respond to the eternal Father save through the eternal Son, for it was through the pre-incarnate eternal Son or Logos that God made the world. And of John Wu, Merton says:

> He is remarkable as a Catholic who has brought over into his fervent life of Christian faith all the humility, the sense of dependence on the unseen, and the

sapiential awareness of the hidden patterns of life which, in Taoism, foreshadowed their fulfilment in the Gospel of Christ.[7]

But Merton also realised that it was no use speaking of the unity of all men or even of the unity of the Church unless there was a personal integration and interior unity within oneself. He sought to avoid the heresy of individualism by an openness of heart and attitude to everyone who lived in truth and love. He makes it explicit:

I will be a better Catholic, not if I can *refute* every shade of Protestantism, but if I can affirm the truth in it and still go further.
So, too, with the Muslims, the Hindus, the Buddhists, etc. This does not mean syncretism, indifferentism, the vapid and careless friendliness that accepts everything by thinking of nothing. There is much that one cannot 'affirm' and 'accept', but first one must say 'yes' where one really can.
If I affirm myself as a Catholic merely by denying all that is Muslim, Jewish, Protestant, Hindu, Buddhist, etc., in the end I will find that there is not much left for me to affirm as a Catholic; and certainly no breath of the Spirit with which to affirm it.[8]

Merton realises that all the great Faiths, Christianity included, have become decadent in their cultural and official garb. But he also believes that the Holy Spirit is particularly at work in these ecumenical days within the faithful remnant of all the great Faiths, and that without falling into a naive and unrealistic syncretism, there is a convergence of spirit that builds on the basic human relationship and intuition of the creative Being of God. With such contemplative people, especially those of the Asian Faiths, he experienced a certain freedom from the 'inner confusion of Western man' in which technological society has 'no longer any place in it for wisdom that seeks truth for its own sake, that seeks the fulness of being, that seeks to rest in an intuition of the very ground of all being.' It was in the company of such men, in the Christian and non-Christian traditions, that he became a pilgrim of this simple, contemplative way. Of fellowship with such non-Christian contemplatives, he says:

> The Western contemplative can say that he feels
> himself much closer to the Zen monks of ancient Japan
> than to the busy and impatient men of the West, of his
> own country, who think in terms of money, power,
> publicity, machines, business, political advantage,
> military strategy – who seek, in a word, the triumphant
> affirmation of their own will, their own power,
> considered as the end for which they exist. Is not this
> perhaps the most foolish of all dreams, the most
> tenacious and damaging of illusions?[9]

He feels it to be particularly ironic that the 'world-negating' Buddhist and Hindu cultures are not those that have brought us to the edge and brink of cosmic nuclear catastrophe, but the so-called 'world-affirming' nations with their Judeo-Christian inheritance. The more Merton enters into contemplative dialogue with such Faiths, the more he recognises the true light of the pacific Christ who has been neglected or rejected by the impatient and violent men of the West referred to above.[10]

Mystical and Christian Faith

As I have followed Merton along this path, reading his writings, entering into a more contemplative understanding of the great contemplatives of our own and other Faiths, and meeting prayerful representatives of these Faiths, the more I have caught a glimpse of what Merton believes must be the Christian attitude in our contemporary world. And far from leading to a compromise or watering-down of the orthodoxy and uniqueness of the 'Faith once delivered to the saints', it sheds a profounder contemplative light upon the Christian tradition, and at the same time reveals the domestication of Christ and accommodation of the Gospel to bourgeois values of which we are guilty.

In Merton's mind, an exciting convergence was taking place in which the Holy Spirit was saying the same thing to men of faith universally, which was not good news to the political and totalitarian men of power in our increasingly bureaucratic and technological society – or rather that part of it dedicated to power and violence. The contemplative orientation demands a totally different view of reality from that which concentrates on the satisfying of the pseudo-self, the individualistic ego, or the collective will to power.

The contemplative way requires a renunciation of the obsession with the individual or collective power structures. The effect of such collective mass obsession is that it destroys in man the interior need and capacity for contemplation, drying up the springs of compassion and understanding. This pattern is seen in all totalitarianisms whether of a Soviet or capitalist kind, and that is why poets, musicians and creative artists suffer under such regimes – they are people of contemplation.

Another concern of Merton is that liberal theology and activist stance of the organised Church has hidden the contemplative depth of Christian Faith from the Asian world:

> So active, in fact, has been the face presented by Christianity to the Asian world that the hidden contemplative element of Christianity is often not even suspected at all by Asians. But without the deep root of wisdom and contemplation, Christian action would have no meaning and no purpose.[11]

Merton has no difficulty in showing that contemplation is at the heart of Christian Faith, and in doing so he develops the concept of the immanence of God which has been neglected but has always been a basic part of orthodox Christian teaching:

> The Christian is then not simply a man of goodwill, who commits himself to a certain set of beliefs, who has

a definite dogmatic conception of the universe, of man,
and of man's reason for existing. He is not simply one
who follows a moral code of brotherhood and
benevolence with strong emphasis on certain rewards
and punishments dealt out to the individual.
Underlying Christianity is not simply a set of doctrines
about God considered as dwelling remotely in heaven,
and man struggling on earth, far from heaven, trying to
appease a distant God by means of virtuous acts. On
the contrary Christians themselves too often fail to
realize that the infinite God is dwelling within them, so
that He is in them and they are in Him. They remain
unaware of the presence of the infinite source of being
right in the midst of the world and of men. True
Christian wisdom is therefore oriented to the experience
of the divine Light which is present in the world, the
Light in whom all things are, and which is nevertheless
unknown to the world because no mind can see or
grasp its infinity. 'He was in the world and the world
was made by Him and the world did not know Him.
He came unto His own and His own did not receive
Him.'[12]

This contemplative way is open to everyone; it is both simple
and profound. Contemplative wisdom is not an intellectual
extrapolation of dogmatic principles, but a 'living contact with
the infinite source of all being', in which there is a transcendent
union of consciousness in union with God. The prerequisite
for this path is not the monastic life, but the simple Christian
life and even ordinary humanity. That is why Merton is able
to share at the level of experienced involvement, though not
doctrinal agreement, with contemplatives of non-Christian
traditions:

One need not be a monk to turn this way. It is
sufficient to be a child of God, a human person. It is
enough that one has in oneself the instinct for truth, the
desire of that freedom from limitation and from

servitude to external things which St Paul calls 'the servitude of corruption' and which, in fact, holds the whole world of man in bondage by passion, greed, the lust for sensation and individual survival, as though one could become rich enough, powerful enough and clever enough to cheat death.[13]

Christian Activists and Eschatologists

Merton is aware of the objection lodged by the Christian activist who is at pains to prove that Christianity is active, dynamic, primarily concerned with the realisation of God in the world and with his 'epiphany in the society of men'. Dialogue with Eastern faiths are an anachronistic futility to such men. He is also aware of, and sympathetic towards, the Christian eschatologist who dismisses such contemplative dialogue as a dangerous compromise or a delusion. He expounds the eschatologist's view:

What is important is that the Word of God has broken through the structures of a collapsing world to establish a new aeon. Contemplation, with its abstraction and its resting within the self in expectation of a pure and gnostic light is only a refinement of the old and unregenerate aeon, and has nothing to do with the Kingdom of God. We are not called to 'purity of heart' or to the gifts of wisdom and understanding. We are not invited to that virginity of spirit which even now apprehends the 'light of the Transfiguration'. We are simply called to wait in patience for the second coming of the *Kyrios* and for the definite establishment of the Kingdom. Our 'contemplation' should take no other form than the song of praise and the pure and spotless sacrifice which we continue to offer in memory of the Lord 'until He comes'.[14]

Merton has stated the eschatologist's case – and shows that he understands the evangelical and catholic eschatologist. He also shows that the case not only can be answered, but that the eschatologist, like the activist, holds precious only *part* of the Faith of Christ. Without the contemplative dimension, there is no gospel, there is no ethic, and contemplation is the universal soil in which the Faith of Christ takes root. Merton handles his material superbly in his essay 'Contemplation and Dialogue' making it clear that the *fulness* of the Faith is his concern. I recognise the arguments of the eschatologist, for it was in that fundamentalist section of the Church that I was brought up. There is not only an impatience with the contemplative dimension (of which woefully little is known), but also a fear of that tradition. The fear is twofold; it has to do with the security of the fundamentalist position, (exclusivists *have* to be right!), but also with the suspicion in which contemplative prayer is held. Such is the fear of openness that I often wondered whether it was being said that the devil could enter an open mind sooner than the Lord!

The broader evangelical and catholic traditions are neither as fearful nor as exclusive as this, for there is an experienced awareness of the Christ-mysticism that lies at the heart of both the Pauline and the Johannine teachings. But there is genuine concern that the Gospel is not compromised by some pagan mysticism. Merton allays the fears:

> Christian contemplation is centered not upon a vague
> inner appreciation of the mystery of man's own
> spiritual essence but upon the Cross of Christ, which is
> the mystery of *kenosis*, the self-emptying of God, the
> sacrificial submission of the 'Suffering Servant' (Isaiah
> 53) who became obedient 'even unto death' (Philippians
> 2:5–10).[15]

In the mystery of the cross, Merton sees not only the evangelical and eschatological dimensions of faith, but also the mystical dialectic of 'fulness and emptiness' which appears at the heart of all the traditional forms of contemplative wisdom. In the emptying out of all forms of human wisdom which is the 'word of the cross' (1 Cor. 1:18–25), the light and power of God is one which is outside and beyond all human rationalisations. Merton develops the catholicity of the contemplative tradition from the basis of the Gospel, at the same time showing both the Christian activist and eschatologist that their concerns are not incompatible with his, but complementary to them. Referring to the scriptures, Ephesians 1:18–23; Isaiah 53; Philippians 2:5–10 and 1 Cor. 1:18–25, Merton says:

> Texts such as these, which have so often been invoked as having power triumphantly to destroy all 'pagan mysticisms', will then be seen as being, on the contrary, Christian answers to the profound questions raised by all these ancient traditions, which seem to have been grasping at the central truths in their own way. Thus, the full idea of Christian contemplation is a *theoria* (vision) that powerfully unites and fuses both 'incarnational' and 'eschatological' Christianity and then opens out into the highest mystery; the Trinity of Persons in one Nature, is not contemplated as 'object' but is celebrated in the hymn of the Spirit, 'Abba, Father!' which it is nevertheless not given to the tongue of man to utter in intelligible human speech. (Rom. 8:14–18; 2 Cor. 12:4).[16]

So Merton takes the very allegations which the eschatologist uses against contemplation and wields them against pseudo-contemplation – what he calls 'consecrated narcissism'. Christian contemplation that has its place within ecumenical dialogue must be true contemplation. It must be able to show the Protestant that the Catholic contemplative is nourished with the scriptures, strengthened by the Holy Spirit and filled with the love of Christ. It must be able to reveal itself, not as an esoteric and quasi-magical technique, but as God's gift to the simple through the Gospel, confounding all presumptuous, worldly and rational wisdom.

But Merton is quite as firm on the other side. The Christian contemplative must be able to show the Asian contemplative that he is aware of the religious dimensions of the Person and of the mystery of Being. Speaking of Christian contemplation he says:

> . . . it must show that the Christian does not confuse the person with the individual, and does not consider his relation to the ground of Being as a purely subject-object relationship – that he is not confined to the fussy and materialistic individualism of purely ethical and practical concerns. That he is, above all, dissociated from the crudeness and brutality of a society that seeks to thrive on purely material and scientific exploitation. It must also show modern man that Christianity is deeply aware of the power at work in history while at the same time defending him against the demonic illusion that comes from identifying the Church with the interests of this or that side in the inhuman struggle for political power.[17]

Some agenda! Under Merton's guidance, it became clear to me that neither the Asian traditions nor the Christian can measure up to such an immense task in their present state. Change in attitude is called for. In my first reading of Merton's works in the few years following his death in 1968 I saw him as a man before his time – a kind of contemplative pioneer blazing the trail for a future generation of theologians and contemplatives involved in ecumenical and inter-faith dialogue. He affirms priorities, lays down guidelines and indicates the difficulties which are inevitably involved. But the time of such dialogue is now upon us, and slowly spreading to different sections of the Church, calling for patience, openness and understanding.

I see my own quest and pilgrimage in this light, finding it theologically exciting and productive prayerfully to read and share with non-Christian contemplatives. It is a universal quest, and I believe that I am one of many responding to the Holy Spirit along the lines laid down by Thomas Merton.

To conclude this chapter I want to make reference to the

Zen Buddhist monk Thich Nhat Hanh who visited Merton
at Gethsemani in 1966. He lives in Paris at present and
continues to travel, speak and write on spirituality, meditation
and non-violence in politics and life. Merton felt such rapport
with him at the time of the Vietnam War when Nhat Hanh
was courageously pleading for peace and non-violence while
both sides were hostile to him, that he wrote a powerful and
compassionate plea for him in Jubilee magazine, entitled: *Nhat
Hanh Is My Brother.* [18]

After affirming compassionate brotherhood with the Zen
monk and referring to the inhumanity and atrocities of the
Vietnam War, Merton goes on to speak of the innocence and
humanity of Nhat Hanh who was not a 'political' Buddhist,
nor yet a communist. In Merton's eyes he represented the
common peasant people caught unwillingly in the political and
violent crossfire between America and the Vietcong in the
context of the war which ravaged his country. Merton acclaims
his innocence and courage, saying that Nhat Hanh may be
returning to imprisonment, torture or death. 'We cannot let
him go back to Saigon to be destroyed,' he wrote, 'while we
sit here, cherishing the warm humanitarian glow of good
intentions and worthy sentiments about the ongoing war.' He
portrays the monk as a free man, moved by compassion and
spiritual dynamic, representing the new ranks of youth who
in many nations are seeking through compassionate justice and
spiritual intuition to live in love with all men.

This compassionate plea of Merton's exemplifies the new,
yet ancient, attitude which fires my own mind and heart, clearly
expressed in the last paragraph of the article:

I have said Nhat Hanh is my brother, and it is true.
We are both monks, and we have lived the monastic
life about the same number of years . . . I have more
in common with Nhat Hanh than I have with many
Americans, and I do not hesitate to say it. It is vitally
important that such bonds be admitted. They are the
bonds of a new solidarity and a new brotherhood which
is beginning to be evident on all the five continents and

which cuts across all political, religious and cultural lines to unite young men and women in every country in something that is more concrete than an ideal and more alive than a program. This unity of the young is the only hope of the world. In its name I appeal for Nhat Hanh. Do what you can for him. If I mean something to you, then let me put it this way; do for Nhat Hanh whatever you would do for me if I were in his position. In many ways I wish I were.[19]

References

1   Merton, *AJ*, p. xxiv.
2   *Documents of Vatican* II., p. 661, quoted by Merton in *MZM*, p. viii.
4   *ibid.*, p. 209.
5   Merton, *ZR*, Foreword.
6   Merton, *MZM*, p. 207.
7   *ibid.*, p. 70.
8   Merton, *CGB*, p. 141.
9   Merton, *FV*, p. 219.
10   See Merton's essays, 'Nirvana' and 'Is Buddhism Life-Denying?' in *ZBA.*, and Merton's books *MZM* and *WChTzu, passim.*
11   Merton, *FV*, p. 222.
12   *Loc. cit*
13   *ibid.*, p. 224.
14   Merton, *MZM*, pp. 211f.
15   Merton, *MZM*, pp. 212.
16   *ibid.*, pp. 212f.
17   *ibid.*, p. 214.
18   Merton, *FV*, pp. 106ff.
19   *ibid.*, p. 108.

12: Intellect and Intuition

The Mind and the Heart

There was nothing irrational or unreasonable about Thomas Merton's faith and spirituality. His devotedness to scholarship, study, teaching and writing made him a first-class communicator engaging both mind and heart. But he did find, in the Western philosophical tradition which had invaded and permeated Christian thought, an emphasis on *ratio* and the cerebral aspects of intellect, that gave rise to arid scholasticism and led to intellectual legalism and dogmatic exclusiveness. He found this to be true both in the Catholic and Protestant world, and that is why he was drawn, right from the beginning, to the Christian mystical tradition, and to an appreciation of the Eastern contemplative traditions and faiths.

He was aware of a decadence in all the great faiths, including his own, and that made him selective and discerning in his appreciation – there is no wholesale acceptance of any religious package deal, but an inspired and informed critical assessment, and a commendation of universal, living spirituality in the context of its own time and culture. Take these commendatory and cautionary words about Taoism:

> The humour, the sophistication, the literary genius, and philosophical insight of Chuang Tzu are evident to anyone who samples his work. But before one can begin to understand even a little of his subtlety, one must situate him in his cultural and historical context. That is to say that one must see him against the background of the Confucianism which he did not hesitate to ridicule, along with all the other sedate and

accepted schools of Chinese thought, from that of Mo
Ti to that of Chuang's contemporary friend, and
constant opponent, the logician Hui Tzu. One must
also see him in relation to what followed him, because
it would be a great mistake to confuse the Taoism of
Chuang Tzu with the popular, degenerate amalgam of
superstition, alchemy, magic, and health culture which
Taoism later became.[1]

Merton did not write 'anthologies of spirituality' picking
crypto-Christian plums out of oriental pies for the inspiration
of pious Christians! His integrity of mind and intellect would
not allow him to compare and contrast the best of the oriental
tradition with the worst of the Christian in an avant-garde
syncretistic manner. But neither would he do the opposite in
a bigoted and exclusivist Christian manner. Both honesty and
integrity demanded an objective and reasonable attitude. But
what he did find so often in Eastern thought was the emphasis
on the intuitive without any surrender of the intellect. The
Second Vatican Council stimulated Merton's thought in the
direction of non-Christian faiths, and he took up such
questions as how other mystical traditions strive to penetrate
'that ultimate mystery which engulfs our being, and whence
we take our rise, and whither our journey leads us.' He goes
on, in *Mystics and Zen Masters*, to quote from the Council's
Declaration on Non-Christian Religions:

. . . the Catholic Church rejects nothing which is true
and holy in these religions. She looks with sincere
respect upon those ways of conduct and of life, those
rules and teachings which, though differing in many
particulars from what she holds and sets forth,
nevertheless often reflect a ray of that Truth which
enlightens all men.[2]

He goes on to say that the Catholic scholar must not only
respect these traditions and honestly evaluate the good
contained in them, but, as the Council enjoins, must

'acknowledge, preserve and promote the spiritual and moral goods found among these men as well as the values in their society and culture.'

He set his mind and his heart to this task, and when he made his last and fatal journey to Asia in 1968, he went not only to speak to the East-West Dialogue Conference in Calcutta, but as a 'listening, searching pilgrim.' He anticipated this Asian pilgrimage with much enthusiasm, and said he was going as a man with a 'sense of destiny'. He approached the East with the reverence of a man who felt he had much to learn from its ancient wisdom, and with none of the arrogance sometimes displayed in the Church toward the great religions of the East.

In his prepared remarks for the Calcutta Conference, a few weeks before his death, he wrote:

> I speak as a Western monk who is pre-eminently
> concerned with his own monastic calling and
> dedication. I have left my monastery to come here not
> just as a research scholar or even as an author (which
> I happen to be). I come as a pilgirm who is anxious
> not just to obtain information, not just *facts* about
> other monastic traditions, but to drink from ancient
> sources of monastic vision and experience. I seek not
> only to learn more (quantitatively) about religion and
> about monastic life, but to become a better and more
> enlightened monk (qualitatively) myself. [3]

In statements such as this I find my own arrogance rebuked, my own intransigence softened, and my own intolerance and exclusivism attenuated and converted into something approaching Merton's humility. For it is a humbling experience to find a man whose mind and intuitive abilities are greater than one's own, displaying a humility and openness before the light of Truth wherever it shines.

I was brought up in an evangelical atmosphere which emphasised assurance, proclamation, and personal salvation. That would have been fine if there had been a compensating education in the traditions and insights of other Christian traditions, and an awareness and understanding of other faiths. Merton experienced in his way, and I experienced in mine, the exclusivism, arrogance and 'monopoly of the Gospel' that hardly admitted Christians of other traditions to the kingdom of God, let alone the possibility of salvation for those outside the specifically Christian fold.

In Merton I found a man, a Christian and a monk who not only passed through such stages in his affirmation of true dialogue, but who exemplified in his thought and action the humility of a dedicated scholar and man of God who is also a pilgrim. He continues to minister to me at that level – it is a matter of 'he being dead, yet speaketh', and I continue to find the pilgrimage an exciting, adventuresome and learning experience.

For Merton, Western and Eastern spirituality complemented one another and expressed the universality of the Holy Spirit working throughout mankind. While on the Asian trip referred to above, he met with the Dalai Lama and many Buddhist monks, sharing in their experience of the contemplative dimension which is the inheritance of all men. In such a context he wrote of dialogue-sharing:

> I need not add that I think we have now reached a stage (long overdue) of religious maturity at which it may be possible for someone to remain perfectly faithful to a Christian and Western commitment, and yet to learn in depth from, say, a Buddhist discipline and experience. I believe that some of us need to do this in order to improve the quality of our own monastic life and even to help in the task of monastic renewal which has been undertaken within the Western Church.[4]

Recognition of Ancient Contemplative Heritage

Merton felt that we are in grave danger of losing a spiritual heritage that had been painstakingly accumulated over thousands of years by saints and contemplatives, and that the Western rationalistic approach, together with the emphasis on goods and material 'benefits' in our technological society had much to do with this loss. He felt deeply the disintegration and alienation of our Western society, both in its capitalist and communist forms; and *status quo*, establishment Christianity had no power against such totalitarianism, technological alienation and atheistic materialism. It was the affirmation of profound spiritual values in Zen that particularly attracted him, for he saw in such Asian contemplative traditions an emphasis on the personal which did not pander to individualism, and an awareness of the corporate which did not lead to state-religion or totalitarianism. The emphasis on simplicity of lifestyle, of a pacific attitude to all creatures, the sacredness of all life and the lack of body-mind dualism – all these things attracted him in the Asian Faiths, together with the direct insight and intuitive grasp of experiential awareness rather than the speculative and theoretical knowledge which is emphasised in the West.

He believed that these things are part of the ancient Christian tradition, but are today constantly called in question or denied in the West in the name of progressive and activist Christianity. The Asian contemplative traditions are much misunderstood in the West in Merton's view, and are nearer the mind and heart of Jesus and the gospels than the gospel of social and technological progress which leads to political totalitarianism and social alienation. Speaking of the secular Christianity which is 'activist, antimystical, social and revolutionary', he says, (and remember that he was writing in the midst of America's involvement in the Vietnam War):

> The purpose of the present book is not apologetic; but if it were, I should feel myself obliged to argue in favour of Buddhism against these absurd and unexamined prejudices. I might want to suggest, for instance, that a religion which forbids the taking of *any* life without absolute necessity is hardly 'life-denying', and to add that it is a little odd that this accusation

should be made by people who, some of them invoking the name of Christ, are ravaging a small Asian country with napalm and dynamite, and doing their best to reduce whole areas of the country to a state of lifelessness.[5]

Merton maintains that there is no need for conservative Christians to be suspicious of Asian religious thought because it is 'pantheistic and incompatible with the Christian belief in God as Creator'. He sees the contribution of Asian contemplative thought pointing in the direction of what he calls Christian *panentheism* – that God is intimately present at the heart of creation but that creation does not exhaust His being. This is more biblical to Merton than current *theism*. Also there is no need for progressive Christians to think that all Asian religions are purely and simply world-denying evasions into trance, repudiating matter, the body, the senses and so on, with the eventual result that they are passive, quietistic and stagnant. He maintains that this is part of the Western myth about the mysterious Orient which has no hope of any kind of salvation except from the dynamic, creative, life-affirming, progressive West!

Far from this being the truth, Merton says that the civilisations of India and China – and of other parts of Asia – found it impossible to cope with Western colonialism save by resorting to some of the West's own methods. And he goes on to comment: '. . . the Chinese cultural revolution is itself one of the most radical, most brutal repudiations of the ancient spiritual heritage of Asia.'

Empirical Ego and the True Self

One of the 'universal themes' which Merton takes up time and time again from the Asian Faiths is one which he found many years before in Aldous Huxley[6]. It is that one must distinguish between the carnal 'empirical ego' and the true Self. This was expounded in Huxley as part of the 'Perennial Philosophy' which he saw manifested in all the great world faiths. He stated it:

Man possesses a double nature, a phenomenal ego and an eternal Self, which is the inner man, the spirit, the spark of divinity within the soul. It is possible for a man, if he so desires, to identify himself with the spirit and therefore with the Divine Ground, which is of the same or like nature with the spirit.[7]

Merton understands the empirical ego as an expression of the carnal man, the 'old Adam', fallen and alienated from God, or in the words of the Rhenish Christian mystics, alienated from the Divine Ground of Being. The true Self then is the renewed and enlightened man who manifests the *imago Dei*, the image of God, and is in immediate contact with the Divine Ground in Christ who is the 'new Adam'. He thinks of St Paul's *spirit* or *pneuma* as corresponding to this true Self. If one distinguishes between these two, then there is a deliverance from individualism and egocentricity, and a liberation into true personhood which is also corporate. This is the 'original nature' and 'true face' of Zen which is not restricted to the empirical self, but is in all and above all. And this is not our own egocentric possession of an awareness of self, but 'being's awareness of itself' within us. Neither is this a submission or loss of identity, nor a withdrawal into a spiritual essence with a denial of the created order:

On the contrary it is a recognition that the whole world is aware of itself in me, and that 'I' am no longer limited to my individual and empirical self, still less to a disembodied soul, but that my 'identity' is to be sought not in that *separation* from all that is, but in oneness with all that is. This identity is not the denial of my own personal reality but its highest affirmation.[8]

Merton baptises this ancient part of the universal perennial philosophy into the Christian tradition, and distinguishes between the deep, transcendent self that awakens in the new birth and in contemplation, and the empirical, superficial, external self or ego which we commonly identify with the first person singular.[9] This superficial 'I' is not our real self; it is the worldly, selfish ego which is self-centred in the carnal and worldly sense. The true self is the hidden and mysterious interior person which is 'in Christ' and thus united to God. Thus contemplation is not an exercise of the false ego-consciousness, but is 'a sudden gift of awareness, an awakening to the Real within all that is real. A vivid awareness of infinite Being at the roots of our own limited being.' This means that when the Christian speaks of the new being, of being born again, of transformation by grace and transfiguration, he is speaking a language which is familiar to the other contemplative traditions in the world.

The process of the new birth, in Merton's spirituality, is the gift of grace and not an intellectual exercise or a natural attainment, which is the fruit of our own efforts. The natural has undergone a supernatural birth, has been 'completed, elevated, transformed and fulfilled in Christ by the Holy Spirit.' And taking up the Christ mysticism of St Paul, he says that contemplation is the awareness and realisation, even in some sense *experience*, of what each Christian obscurely believes: 'It is now no longer I, but Christ lives in me'.

One of the reasons Merton takes hold of this theme from the Asian Faiths is that it helps him to repudiate its denial in the Western philosophical tradition which he traces back to Descartes. He sees all such attempts at philosophical abstraction, scholastic reasoning to an objective affirmation of a separate object of deity, as the death of true spirituality, and therefore of the experience of God. The 'God is dead' theologians, for Merton, came to their conclusions because the *experience* of the living God was lost to them. And the reason was that they had objectified God and pursued some objective entity in a philosophical and abstract manner, and this tolls the death-knell of contemplative experience.

Cartesian thought began with an attempt to reach God as object by starting from the thinking self. But when God becomes object, he sooner or later 'dies', because God as object is ultimately unthinkable. God as object is

not only a mere abstract concept, but one which
contains so many internal contradictions that it becomes
entirely non-negotiable except when it is hardened into
an idol that is maintained in existence by a sheer act of
will.[10]

It is this philosophical tradition that Merton blames for a loss
of true religious consciousness in Western Christianity. He sees
Cartesian man 'thinking' with his external, superficial self – the
'I' which is not the true Self of either the perennial philosophy
or the genuine Christian tradition. Therefore, to move in the
philosophical tradition of Descartes is to turn one's back upon
the contemplation that leads to an affirmation of God in the
depths of one's being, where alone he can be found. 'Nothing
could be more alien to contemplation than the *cogito ergo sum*
(*I think, therefore I am*) of Descartes' says Merton:

'I think, therefore I am.' This is the declaration of an
alienated being, in exile from his spiritual depths,
compelled to seek comfort in a *proof for his own existence*
(!) based on the observation that he 'thinks'. If his
thought is necessary as a medium through which he
arrives at the concept of his existence, then he is in fact
only moving further away from his true being. He is
reducing himself to a concept. He is making it
impossible for himself to have any intuition of the divine
reality which is inexpressible. He arrives at his own
being as if it were an objective reality, that is to say he
strives to become aware of himself as he would of some
'thing' alien to himself. And he proves that the 'thing'
exists. He convinces himself: 'I am therefore some *thing*.'
And then he goes on to convince himself that God, the
infinite, the transcendent, is also a 'thing', an 'object'
like other finite and limited objects of our thought![11]

Perhaps Merton lays too much blame at the feet of Descartes,
though he does maintain that this is where that kind of Cartesian
thinking leads. Years earlier, Dan Walsh identified Merton as

an 'Augustinian' rather than a 'Thomist' by nature, and Merton says: 'He meant that my bent was not so much towards the intellectual, dialectical, speculative character of Thomism, as towards the spiritual, mystical, voluntaristic and practical way of St Augustine and his followers.' Merton never appealed to Thomas Aquinas's famous proofs for the existence of God, and in the light of what he says about Descartes, he should repudiate those aspects of Thomism which professes to prove the 'existence of God' by human reason. Perhaps this is an illustration of Merton overstating his case in championing the mystical and intuitive way to God. Merton's understanding of Cartesianism is the very antithesis of true contemplation, for commenting again on Descartes' *Cogito*, he says:

> For the contemplative there is no *cogito* ('I think') and no *ergo* ('therefore') but only *SUM*, I AM. Not in the sense of a futile assertion of our individuality as ultimately real, but in the humble realization of our mysterious being as persons in whom God dwells, with infinite sweetness and inalienable power.

He is really saying that Descartes represents those who have moved away from the existential immediacy of the Bible in which the whole person lives, moves and acts as a unity in intuitive faith. The Western philosophical tradition seems to Merton to have become dry, arid, scholastic and alienated from the sophianic depths of its own wisdom, rooted in the Hebrew and Christian understanding of man's wholeness, so that we are left with a cerebral, thinking machine, which has to think itself back into existence by the Cartesian ploy of *cogito, ergo sum – I think, therefore I am*!

Merton sees the Zen tradition coming to the aid of the West in such a dilemma. He believes that a taste for Zen will enable Western man to come into a new sense of his own unity, ridding himself of the dualism which alienates him from his deepest self. He puts it like this:

The taste for Zen in the West is in part a healthy reaction of people exasperated with the heritage of four centuries of Cartesianism: the reification of concepts, idolization of the reflexive consciousness, flight from being, into verbalism, mathematics, and rationalization. Descartes made a fetish out of the mirror in which the self finds itself. Zen shatters it.[12]

The Wedding of Reason and Intuition

In all this, Merton is not debunking reason in favour of intuition, for if Merton teaches us anything, it is to keep mind and heart together. In considering St Anselm, for instance, and his use of what has been called the 'ontological proof' for the existence of God, he has quite a different attitude to Anselm's philosophising. He sees his eagerness to discover an 'airtight apologetic proof for God's existence' as secondary to the fact that Anselm set out the ontological argument in the context of prayer and intuition. He believes that Anselm could not question the existence of 'Him who is' for his existence required no proof. He sees in Anselm a man who functions at the levels of reason and intuition, so that reason becomes the handmaid of intuition in this respect, though there is an equality in the wholeness of the person.

Contemplative wisdom for Merton is not simply an extrapolation of intellectual or dogmatic principles, but living contact with the loving and infinite source of all being – union with God. And what he believes has come about in the anti-mystical West is that Cartesianism ultimately objectified God, making intellectual atheism possible, and the necessary invention of new 'gods' of science and technology which, though admirable in many respects, can never solve the problems of man's profound being. He sees such men who deify their own scientific wisdom and accomplishments as without wisdom, without the intuition that enables man to return to the root of his being. And he makes this judgement:

. . . the claim of science and technology to expand the capacity of the human person for life and happiness is fraudulent, because the technological society is not the least interested in values, still less in persons; it is concerned purely and simply with the functioning of its own processes. Human beings are used merely as means to this end, and the one significant question it asks in their regard is not *who* they are but *how* they can be most efficiently used.'[13]

Merton realises that it is no use appealing to such men with a reaffirmation of ancient static and classic positions, whether Christian or Asian. As he says: 'Hellenic categories are indeed worn out, and . . . Platonising thought, even revivified with shots in the arm from Yoga and Zen, will not quite serve the modern world.' These words come from his extended essay *The New Consciousness* in which he has sought to integrate a clear Christian Faith together with the profound insights from the Asian Faiths. He is therefore moved to outline the kind of fundamental needs which he feels must be met with a renewed contemplative perspective. These needs are fourfold, and they have to do with man in community, with man's ordinary and everyday living, and with an integration of all man's faculties, body, intellect and spirit. Merton's outline is an agenda for a renewed Christian contemplative life which embraces all that is best in all the great spiritual traditions, earthed quite concretely in our common humanity.

Contemplative Faith – Compassionate Life

Merton has always brought me to this point – I enjoy reading him, I follow him imaginatively, creatively, theologically in the premises and implications of his contemplative teaching. And then comes the crunch! He says: 'So what!' It becomes clear that the practical implications of God loving the world means that God became man. So the practical implications of wide-open ecumenical dialogue and sympathy mean

engaging mind and heart, becoming incarnate in this situation.
Merton's fourfold outline goes like this!

1   Man's need for COMMUNITY: 'a genuine relationship
    of authentic love with his fellow man.' That means
    bringing the mind and heart of contemplation to bear upon
    the critical problems which threaten man's very survival
    as a species: war, racial conflict, hunger, economic and
    political injustice, etc. Neither East nor West have been
    contemplative enough – quietist indifference on the one
    hand, and technological manipulative power tending to
    corruption on the other must give way to Gospel-
    compassion, which expresses *community*.

2   Man's need for an adequate understanding of his
    EVERYDAY SELF in his ordinary life. By this Merton
    means that there must be an end to mere idealistic
    philosophies on the nature of man if they do not make
    his ordinary and concrete existence more bearable, more
    compassionate, more human. All people should come to
    embrace and love their simple humanity and rejoice in
    being simply human. Merton feels this because he denied
    his simple humanity during his first monastic years and
    it was the fault of his religion! It was a happy day for him
    when he could embrace his humanity and realise, in the
    shopping precinct of Louisville, that he was no different
    to other men. He let go his holy illusions with a laugh:
    'Thank God, thank God that I *am* like other men, that
    I am only a man among others. To think that for sixteen
    or seventeen years I have been taking seriously this pure
    illusion that is implicit in so much of our monastic
    thinking.'

This means that contemplative theology must make man's
everyday life more meaningful at every level, beginning here
and now, in affirming the basic goodness of our common
humanity. Men, women and children can then enjoy being
who they are in themselves, and in their relationship to each
other.

3   Man's need for a WHOLE AND INTEGRAL EXPERI-
     ENCE OF HIS OWN SELF. This means his body, his
     imagination, his emotions, his intellect, his spirit. It means
     WHOLENESS. It means sexuality, relationship between
     the sexes, maleness and femaleness. It means enjoying his
     bodily functions in relation to himself, his fellows, the
     earth. It means diet, health, exercise, housing. It means
     intimate physical relationship and chastity. It means
     aesthetic appreciation, emotional acceptance and
     affirmation, study, learning and finding his own level of
     soul-enhancing work. It means the realm of *spirit* – which
     involves all artistic creativity, prayer, meditation, con-
     templative experience and profound awareness of
     God – for everyone. And it means the INTEGRATION
     of ALL these things.
4   Man's need for LIBERATION from his inordinate self-
     consciousness. This means a deliverance from himself –
     that is his obsessive egocentric self which is full of guilt
     or pride or hatred or alienation, or a mixture of all of this.
     Here is indicated the need for salvation in its widest sense,
     to be saved from himself, from his sin – to be cleansed,
     forgiven, renewed, empowered, enlightened and united
     to Love.

This is a world-shaking agenda, and is too big for one
person, for one nation, for one culture. Merton envisages the
evolution of a new consciousness under the Spirit of God – only
then could the task be truly envisioned, let alone attempted.

He does not substitute 'Thy Kingdom come' with 'give us
more time' as an optimistic humanist of the nineteenth century
would do. He realises that on a purely human level sin and
alienation prevent the task which only divine love and grace
can accomplish anyway. And on that level he awaits the
coming of Christ in glory, when the kingdom of this world
shall become the Kingdom of our God and of his Christ. But
that kind of eschatology must not be used to evade these basic
issues, for that is as bad as lapsing into passive, quietism in
a needy world.

The Way Ahead

Merton never spells out specific personal or social action, but rather gives direction. He expects the renewal of the heart and mind, the wedding of intellect and intuition, in co-operation with the divine Spirit of God, to inform, enlighten and accomplish the work.

When I ask, in the light of this chapter, concerning the direction he gives, he turns first of all to the Christians, and then to the Asian traditions. The Christian tradition, as he sees it, must be rooted in the Gospel, and there must be a deliverance from the obsessions of egocentric desire and exploitation. The shorthand words for these counsels are faith and repentance. And that involves the whole revelation of the Christian Gospel from forgiveness of sins, through faith in Christ incarnate, crucified and risen, to new birth, life in God, sanctification and union with the divine Love. And all this must be lived out in the world.

The Asian traditions, for Merton, indicate the 'unworldliness' forgotten in the West. They mean the sacredness of all life, a way of detachment from the evil world system and the profound contemplative dimension of the Asian faiths. And he asks a question here:

> Is the basic teaching of Buddhism – on ignorance, deliverance and enlightenment – really life-denying, or is it rather the same kind of life-affirming liberation that we find in the Good News of Redemption, the Gift of the Spirit, and the New Creation?[14]

He is not asking for doctrinal comparisons and contrasts or for an intellectual synthesis which will only lead to an ideal 'syncretism' which will help neither Christian nor Buddhist. But he is asking for openness, dialogue, trust of other human beings, and the wide and universal perspective of human compassion which is spelled out in love.

The more I have listened to Merton, the more I have taken his direction, the more I have read, studied, meditated about and with those of other faiths, so the more I have understood something of my own humanity, of the integration of intellect and intuition, and something of the profound mystery of the universal Love.

References

1   Merton, *WChTz*, p. 15.
2   Merton, *MZM*, pp. viiif.
3   Patrick Hart, 'Thomas Merton's East West Dialogue', *Monastic Exchange*, Vol. II, No. 4, p. 19.
4   *Loc. cit.*
5   Merton, *ZBA*, pp. 15f.
6   See Merton, *SSM*,
7   Aldous Huxley on 'The Perennial Philosophy'
8   Merton, *ZR*, p. 8.
9   Merton, *SC*, p. 5f.
10 Merton, *ZBA*, p. 23.
11 Merton, *SC*, pp. 6f.
12 Merton, *CGB*, p. 278.
13 Merton, *MZM*, p. 263.
14 Merton, *ZBA*, p. 31

13: *Classic Chinese Thought*

Western Prejudice

Because Merton became a universal Christian he was able to give himself to the religious thought of other cultures and traditions without fear. So instead of suspicious and 'heresy-hunting' attitudes in his investigation into the spirituality of other faiths, he was able with openness and enthusiasm to compare and contrast, to discern and evaluate, to learn and constructively criticise, to the good of the tradition he was investigating and of his own faith and devotion.

The spiritual and philosophical traditions of China lured him with a mysticism and a wisdom that gave rise to exciting contemporary insights in his own pilgrimage. Whenever I found Merton with his head and his heart in the Chinese traditions, whether talking of the early Jesuit missions to China or sharing in the contemplative mysticism of the *Tao*, I was enthused with his enthusiasm, and caught up in the intellectual and devotional excitement of his studies.[1] Always light was shed, either on my own pilgrimage or in ethical and political reflection on the ways of our contemporary world. While Merton was dipping into China third century BC, he was commenting in a parallel manner on present ecumenical, inter-racial, political and intellectual mores.

He reminds us of the imperative need for the West to acquaint itself experientially with the Asian cultural traditions. The West still holds on to its instinctive prejudice that our world and its civilisations are the 'whole world', and that it is our mission to impose our cultural heritage on other continents and peoples. In the 1960s Merton was writing of the emerging strength of the Third World and the future active share of Asia and Africa in directing the course of civilisation and the future of mankind, and although the cities of the West have since experienced a steep rise in their Asian and African populations, attitudes seem rather to have grown worse in many areas.

The first European traders were excluded by the Chinese and Japanese as 'barbarians from the West', and rare were the Europeans who could evaluate and enter into the profound catholicity of Confucian philosophy like the first Jesuits in China. Merton issues a warning mixed with counsel:

> If the West continues to underestimate and to neglect the spiritual heritage of the East, it may hasten the tragedy that threatens man and his civilisations. If the West can recognise that contact with Eastern thought can renew our appreciation for our own cultural heritage, a product of the fusion of the Judeo-Christian religion with Grego-Roman culture, then it will be easier to defend that heritage, not only in Asia, but in the West as well. [2]

One of the first points that Merton makes in relation to China is that there is a Western facile generalisation that there are 'three traditions' corresponding to the 'three religions' of China, viz., Confucianism, Taoism and Buddhism. He makes the point that the oriental religions, while differing in philosophy and belief, have a way of 'interpenetrating quite freely with one another'. It is Merton's aim to get behind the later manifestations of organised, systematised and legalised religion of the Legalists of the third century BC. They were concerned with the unification of China, and by their time the really great period of development for Chinese philosophy had ceased. Therefore, Merton reaches back to the period of the sixth century BC for his sources of classical thought in China, to the persons of Kung Tzu (Mencius), and Lao Tzu (not latinised), the mystic and father of Taoism.

Merton develops the three periods of thought in China, and it is helpful to keep them separate in our own minds, as:

1 *The Taoism of Lao Tzu*. This is the earliest period in which the mystical sense of the *Tao* is found at the heart of the cosmos, and indwelling the man of wisdom and simplicity.

2 *The Ju Confucian School*. This is basically humanist and ethical. It does not deal with the mystery and immediacy of the great *Tao*, but with its 'reflection' in ethical, educational and human relationships.

3 *The Legalism of Hsun Tzu*. If Lao Tzu's Taoism is thought of as 'left', and Confucianism as 'centre', this is certainly extreme 'right'. It is politically totalitarian because it does not affirm the mystical or ethical *Tao*, and therefore becomes a bureaucratic tyranny.

The Taoism of Lao Tzu

Merton sees the classic period of early Chinese thought as contemporaneous with Gautama Buddha in India, Pythagoras in Greece, and in Israel with such prophets of the exile as Jeremiah, Ezekiel and Deutero-Isaiah. This classic period in Chinese thought extended down to the establishment of a unified China in the third century, which was, to a great extent, the work of the Legalists whose form of society brought the most vital and productive age of Chinese thought to a close. Lao Tzu and Confucius manifested great reverence for the past, but Lao Tzu, especially, was suspicious of systematisation or social order as artificial, and was misunderstood therefore as antinomian, which means, in a literal sense, against the rule of law. He saw government, politics, and even ethical systems, however good in themselves, as a perversion of man's natural simplicity and spontaneity. They engendered competitive, self-centred aggression, and led man into delusive ideas about himself, from which came hatreds, schisms, wars and the ultimate destruction of society. As Merton says:

> Lao Tzu's ideal of society was the small primitive community consisting of nothing more than a few villages inhabited by simple, self-forgetful men in complete harmony with the hidden, infallible *Tao*.

It was when the Great Tao declined
That there appeared humanity and righteousness.
It was when knowledge and intelligence arose
That there appeared much hypocrisy.
It was was when the six relations lost their harmony
That there was talk of filial piety and paternal
    affection.
It was when the country fell into chaos and
    confusion
That there was talk of loyalty and trustworthiness.[3]

Lao Tzu is not scorning the values of humanity and righteousness as may seem to be the case, but is affirming that the reality of these virtues are not dependent upon ethical theory, and should exist without self-conscious reflection and self-congratulation. According to Lao Tzu, reflection and self-consciousness are the vitiation of true moral activity, and Merton comments:

As soon as man becomes aware of doing good and avoiding evil, he is no longer perfectly good. Ethical rationalisation makes possible that schizoid division between words and acts, between thoughts and deeds, which (as Hamlet knew well), finally reduces honest activity to complete helplessness, or else lays the way open for political or religious crooks to do all the evil they like in the name of 'righteousness'.[4]

Confucius wanted to set men apart and prepare and school them to be wise men, rulers, 'superior men', but this was the worst way of trying to create a wise and just society in Lao Tzu's view. Merton observes that this kind of thinking is definitely 'left of centre', with a dangerous ring, and is only understood and followed by one who is already on the way to becoming a saint. 'It is a philosophy that would have worked well in the Garden of Eden,' he says, and continues:

and if Adam and Eve had stuck to the *Tao*, there would have been little difficulty for the rest of us in doing so. But from the moment a man is immersed in confusion and carried away by the passions and eccentricities of a bewildered and not always upright society, he has little hope of finding himself merely by shutting his eyes and following the *Tao*. The *Tao* may be within him but he is completely out of touch with his own inmost self. Recovery of the *Tao* is impossible without a complete transformation, a change of heart, which Christianity would call *metanoia*. Zen of course envisaged this problem, and studied how to arrive at *satori*, or the explosive rediscovery of the hidden and lost reality within us.[5]

In another place Merton mentions the fact that Dr John Wu, a Chinese convert to Catholicism confesses that he brought Zen, Taoism and Confucianism with him into Christianity, and in his Chinese translation of the New Testament, he opens the Gospel of St John with the words: 'In the beginning was the Tao.' Merton affirms the idea of the *Tao* in one form or another as central to all Chinese thinking, and makes the differentiation between the 'great *Tao*, which is invisible and incomprehensible, and the lesser reflection of *Tao* as it manifests itself in human life. He draws attention to the fact that Lao Tzu himself distinguished between the Eternal *Tao* 'that which cannot be named' which is the nameless and unknowable source of all being, and the *Tao* 'that can be named' which is the 'Mother of all things'.[6]

There is a certain correspondence with the apophatic theology of the Eastern Fathers here, where a distinction is made between the mysterious and unknowable essence, nature or inner being of God on the one hand, and his energies, operations or acts of power on the other, which can be known and experienced. In that tradition, God's inner essence is forever beyond our comprehension, but his energies, life and power saturate the cosmos and are directly accessible to us. In Lao Tzu's *Tao Te Ching*, he observes that if there is a correct answer to the question: 'What is the *Tao*?' it is: 'I don't know'.

Tao can be talked about but not the Eternal *Tao*,
Names can be named, but not the Eternal Name,
As the origin of heaven and earth it is nameless:
As 'the Mother' of all things it is nameable.[7]

The result of the apparent anarchy which seems to be implicit within such Taoist doctrine referred to above was that it had little to offer to the man who struggled with the problem of society. It offered a certain evasion from society, a kind of escape upward into the transcendent, and Merton speaks of such anarchist tendencies in Taoism playing into the hands of the extreme right wing of Chinese thought – the Legalists, the builders of a totalitarian China, using much the same tactics, in Merton's view, as those used by Mao Tse-tung!

The Ju Confucian School

But in the centre was the school of thought led by Kung Tzu (Confucius). The *Ju* school was very wary of the seemingly antinomian tendencies of the extreme left, represented by the Taoism of Lao Tzu, but instead sought to place supreme value upon the human person and his relations with other persons in society. Merton makes a caustic comment:

This of course sounds quite modern – because one of our illusions about ourselves is that we have finally discovered 'personality' and 'personalism' in the twentieth century. Such are the advantages of not having had a classical education, which would do us the disservice of reminding us that personalism was very much alive in the sixth century BC, and that, in fact, it existed then in a much more authentic form than it does among us with our 'personality tests' and 'personality problems' (the ultimate carving of the Taoist uncarved block!)[8]

The *Ju* or Confucian doctrine, is basically humanist and personalist, and its development was intellectual, ethical and

social. Kung Tzu's disciple Meng Tzu, gave expression to
his basic belief in the fundamental goodness of human nature
in his 'Ox Mountain Parable'.[9] For Meng Tzu this fundamental goodness was destroyed by evil acts and had to be
restored by right education in 'humaneness'. Merton
contrasts Meng Tzu's teachings in this parable with the
coercive teaching of the Legalists:

> The great man, said Meng Tzu, is the man 'who
> has not lost the heart of a child'. This statement was
> not meant to be sentimental. It implied the serious
> duty to preserve the spontaneous and deep natural
> instinct to love, that instinct which is safeguarded by
> the mysterious action of life itself and of providence,
> but which is destroyed by the willingness, the
> passionate arbitrariness of man's greed. In contrast
> to Meng Tzu were Mo Tzu and the Legalist school,
> which wanted men to be forced into the path of an
> abstract universal love by the force of punishment
> (the Legalists). Since, according to them, man was
> basically evil, his evil tendencies had to be harnessed
> and exploited by the power of the ruler.[10]

The Ox Mountain, once thickly wooded, was desecrated
by men with axes. When the trees began to grow again,
they set their flocks to graze upon it, and they ate the green
shoots, so that no-one would believe that the mountain had
once been wooded. So man, who is naturally inclined to
virtue, is overcome by his own actions within a greedy and
grasping society. The consequence is that he is so completely
held by such actions that all evidence of his innate goodness
has been destroyed, and he appears to be naturally evil.

The Confucian ideal was a society governed by a just
and 'human-hearted' prince who could bring out the
concealed goodness in his subjects, and the Confucian system
of rites was meant to give expression to the natural and
human love which is the only guarantee of peace and unity
in society. And this unity is produced not by coercive

imposition from without, but from within men themselves.

Merton is quick to point out that this must not be interpreted as a 'facile utilitarian pragmatism', but as manifesting a sacred sense of the 'will of heaven' inscribed in the very nature of man. And he comments: 'Kung therefore respected the *Tao*, but unlike the Taoists he did not concentrate on the *Tao* alone. He set his gaze clearly on man.' That is why the later Chuang Tzu believed that the *Tao* on which Confucius set his heart was not the 'great *Tao*' that is invisible and incomprehensible. Merton makes the distinction:

> It was a lesser reflection of *Tao* as it manifests itself in human life. It was the traditional wisdom handed down by the ancients, the guide to practical life, the way of virtue . . . Lao Tzu distinguished between the Eternal *Tao* 'that cannot be named', which is the nameless and unknowable source of all being, and the *Tao* 'that can be named', which is the Mother of all things'. Confucius may have had access to the manifest aspects of the *Tao* 'that can be named', but the basis of all Chuang Tzu's critique of Ju philosophy is that it never comes near to the *Tao* 'that cannot be named', and indeed takes no account of it.[11]

When eventually the Confucian thought was deeply influenced by Taoism the various human and ethical aspects of the *Tao* could and did become fingers pointing to the invisible and divine *Tao*, but as Confucianism developed, there was a deterioration which divided and sub-divided the idea of *Tao*, until it became simply a term indicating an abstract universal principle in the realm of ethics. Merton observes:

> All China, at least all the ruling class of China, was supposed in theory to be educated on Confucian lines: but many, and not the least successful of Chinese statesmen, were men who, with an outward facade of *Ju*, were inwardly either pedants or rigid and heartless conformists, or unprincipled crooks.[12]

The Confucian teaching, then, which is in the centre, believes in the inherent goodness of human nature, seeking to educate it by a human and sacred culture which expresses love. This *Ju* school does not seek to interfere with human nature, but to help it.

On the extreme left are the Taoists who are less concerned with men and more with *Tao*. They were suspicious of education and help, and felt that the hidden *Tao* would manifest itself as the hidden and inscrutable presence in man if only man would not interfere. Merton sums up the teaching:

> The mystics then preached a way that is not a way, a 'returning to the root', a deep respect for reality in its primitive and inscrutable state as an 'uncarved block'. Theirs was a way of 'non-action', which is falsely interpreted as pure quietism when in reality it is a policy of non-interference and an abstention from useless and artificial action.[13]

He makes it clear that their non-action is actually a non-activism, and their antinomianism (inherited by Zen) is only apparent and must be carefully and properly understood.

The Legalists: Hsun Tzu

At the opposite extreme are the Legalists who not only interfere with the course of nature, but do so as thoroughly and completely as possible. Organisation and law, objective decrees and sanctions replace subjective spontaneity, with a system of rewards and punishments. Merton shows their complete antipathy to both Lao Tzu and Meng Tzu:

> In general, the Legalists took a pessimistic view of man: his nature could not be left to itself because it was evil, and hence it had to be whipped into good action, against its own spontaneous instincts, by absolute authoritarianism. This ineradicable selfishness of human nature could not be corrected, and to try to

correct it, or bring it back to a supposed primitive order and rightness, as did Meng Tzu, was a delusion. No, the Legalist would simply accept the inevitable and *make use* of man's depravity, his greed, his fears, his lusts, his self-interest in order to bring about certain political ends. These ends can best be summed up in the one word: *power*[14]

Merton traces Chinese Legalism back to the Confucian scholar Hsun Tzu (third century BC) who though outwardly loyal to the *Ju* school, was completely agnostic and sceptical. It is said of him that 'the Chinese people lost their faith in Hsun Tzu's time and have not yet found it.'[15]

The human heartedness of *Ju* is of no use to Legalism, and there is no real concern for moral or supernatural sanctions. Law replaces morality, religion and even conscience, and relies on punishment for its execution. The only standard is the subjective will of the ruler, with no objective standards of right and wrong. Thus a system of espionage emerges, and even language means nothing except what the ruler wants it to mean. The ruler is not responsible to heaven or to *Tao*, and therefore changes his mind when convenient to himself. Merton says of such a regime: 'The goal of Legalism is to make the state so powerful that all its enemies are wiped out. Then there will be peace.' And he adds cryptically: 'Where have we heard that before?' He maintains, therefore, that the Legalist psychology and methods of the third century BC in China are very close to the methods of totalism today, whether Communist or Fascist.[16]

Chinese Wisdom and Biblical Sapientia

As we have seen, the main difference between the *Ju* (Confucian) school and the Taoists was that the latter were concerned with the hidden, eternal, metaphysical *Tao*, and the former with the ethical *Tao*. What we in the West call the 'natural law', referring to the basis of Confucian teaching, is not to be taken to mean a law abstracted or deduced from our nature, but the *Tao* itself. It is the ethical *Tao*, the way

of man, in the Confucian sense, not the metaphysical *Tao* or
the hidden, mysterious God. Merton refers to one of the four
Confucian classics, the *Doctrine of the Mean*, or *Chung Yung*,
a kind of Confucian reply to Taoism, and explains:

> The point of the book is that at the very center of
> man's being is an intimate, dynamic principle of
> reality. It is not merely a static concept or essence, but
> a 'nature' constantly seeking to express its reality in
> right action. In this way, the hidden reality of heaven
> communicates itself to the man who is in harmony
> with it by his actions. *Reality* is the goal, and reality in
> fact is the 'axis' or 'pivot' of man's being. The
> 'superior man' is one who finds this axis in himself
> and lives always centered upon it. Other men do not
> find the center, the axis, and spend their lives
> aimlessly carried this way and that by winds of fortune
> and of passion. Their center is not in themselves but
> somewhere outside them, and their lives are
> consequently a turmoil of frustration, self-seeking and
> confusion.[17]

Merton is not slow to point out that this kind of teaching
has so much in common with the sapiential wisdom of the
Old Testament, as well as with the Zen kind of teaching set
out in the gospels:

> The starting point of Kung's teaching is that there is a
> transcendent and objective reality (the metaphysical
> nature of which is never discussed) called 'heaven'.
> And there are other realities, the changing, contingent
> realities of earth and man, which can be in order or in
> disorder. They are in order when they are in accord or
> in 'harmony' with 'heaven' – with the ultimately real.
> They are in disorder when they are out of harmony
> with the highest principles, with the will of heaven.
> One might compare this to the doctrine of the
> sapiential books of the Bible, as well as with the Gospels.[18]

He makes the point that the teaching of Kung Tzu is more than a philosophy – it is a wisdom – not a doctrine but a way of life impregnated with truth. One only comes to know the doctrine by living the truth, and this truth is such that it contains the whole meaning of existence both for the person and for the society in which he finds a place.

Merton sees the Confucian spirit as something which is present metaphysically, pervading the whole of life, although nothing is said or can be known of the *Tao* in itself. This must be translated into the living experience of man in society by moral conduct, and there must be a celebration of such within the earthly society, with beauty and solemnity. The celebratory rites for Kung Tzu 'were the visible expression of the hidden reality of the universe'. When a man participates in such celebration by the performance of these rites, he is awakened, grows and is transformed, as a person, and as an integral part of his society.

Merton likens such ethical teaching to the unspoken pre-suppositions of St Thomas Aquinas, who, though using the technical language of Greek philosophy, is nevertheless fully concrete in the sapiential sense because he is a Christian contemplative. He is not 'a Platonic contemplative in love with incorporeal essences, but a Christian contemplative, who sees the divine light in every being. For everything exists ''insofar as it is known by God.'' '[19]

Scholastic Deterioration

Theologies and philosophies are subject to scholasticism and therefore to deterioration. Merton underlines the fact that we must remain aware that sacredness is the inner motivation at the heart of Kung Tzu's doctrine. If we miss this, it opens the way to secularisation, and this is what he believes happened in the scholastic revivals of *Ju* philosophy in which technical aspects were emphasised at the expense of living reality.

There is abundant manifestation of the powers of Legalism in the forms of totalitarian Communism and Fascism, and the concept of the Person as developed by classic Confucianism is one which he deems valuable. The Legalist conforms to the ruler's will. He serves a policy of power and self-assertion, involving the development of aggressiveness, astuteness, diplomatic skills and the ability to 'succeed'. Personality, in this sense, is the power to impose oneself and one's wishes upon others. For Kung Tzu this is illusory and unhealthy because it is unreal. Not that it is wrong by some abstract standard, but a man who acts like this is untrue to himself and to 'heaven', whose will is embedded deep in his heart. Such a man does not know himself because he has not reached the very root of his being.

The purpose of Kung Tzu's teaching was to form a 'governing class of humane and enlightened scholars', and Merton quotes Christopher Dawson's positive consideration of the effect of Confucianism on Chinese civilisation:

> The result (of Confucianism) has been that in China alone among the advanced civilizations of the world, the law of nature has not been a philosophical abstraction but a living force which has had a religious appeal to the heart and conscience of the people . . . In this way Chinese civilizations seem to have solved certain fundamental problems of the social and moral order more successfully than any other known culture.[20]

A Future Synthesis

As Merton looks to the future of the *Ju* philosophy in China, he acknowledges that although there have been Chinese thinkers who have led movements of strong reaction against the *Ju* philosophy since the fall of the Manchus and the end of the empire, there are also other currents of opinion. Some have sought to penetrate *Ju* in the form of an official, national religion, which Merton believes to be incongruous and absurd. But even in spite of the rise of Chinese Communism, with its emphatic reaction against the traditional social elements of Confucianism, there are appeals among some Communist

writers to *The Great Learning* and other Confucian classics as
sources for a living Chinese thought. It is certain that the rigid
and inflexible form which Confucianism acquired after
centuries of interpretation is not a living option. It is also true
that Mao Tse-tung was on record as detesting Confucius, but
his days are over, and the future may well have place for an
adapted *Ju* philosophy in modern Chinese thought and life.

But be that as it may, Merton sees the main interest in,
and survival of Confucianism outside of China, in its influence
on the West. He states:

> We hopefully look forward not to an age of eclecticism
> and syncretism, but to an age of understanding and
> adaption that will be able to synthesize and make use
> of all that is good and noble in all the traditions of the
> past. If the world is to survive and if civilization is to
> endure or rather perhaps weather its present crisis and
> recover its dimension of 'wisdom', we must hope for a
> new world culture that takes account of all civilized
> philosophies. [2] [1]

In Taoism and Confucianism, Merton recognises the
reflection of 'the light that lightens every man', affording old
and forgotten insights into the current life and experience of
Christian Faith itself. There is much precedence for this, and
Merton fears that unless the Christian contemplative and
scholar gives himself to the task of understanding, conserving
and communicating these ancient insights, they may be lost
to the specific lands of their origin, and to the whole world.
Speaking again of a man like Dr John Wu, Merton says:

> Dr Wu is able not only to translate Lao Tzu's words
> but also to interpret his life. He is remarkable as a
> Catholic who has brought over into his fervent life of
> Christian faith all the humility, the sense of dependence
> on the unseen, and the sapiential awareness of the
> hidden patterns of life which, in Taoism, foreshadowed
> their fulfilment in the Gospel of Christ. [2] [2]

Dr Wu is engaged in translations of the thought of Lao Tzu, presenting, in Merton's view, a 'Confucian kind of Taoism' and he sees in Dr Wu's work on the *Tao Te Ching* a correspondence between Christian and Taoist teaching:

> One hesitates to use the word supernatural in connection with Chinese thought, yet the fact that the *Tao Te Ching* distinguishes a *Tao* that can be known and spoken of from the *Tao* which is unknown and unable to be named authorizes us to find here something that corresponds with our notion of God above and beyond the cosmos. After all, did not Dr Wu, when he translated the Gospel of John into Chinese thirty years ago, start out with the words: 'In the beginning was *Tao*, and *Tao* was with God, and *Tao* was God.'?[23]

This whole concept has to do with an experiential theology in the 'wisdom' tradition, more amenable to the sapiential writers of the Old Testament than with Plato or Parmenides. Merton illustrates the affective aspects of such an understanding by reference to an ideogram which represents the *TZU* in Lao Tzu (Master Lao). The *TZU* ideogram means both 'master' and 'child', and the same ideogram is combined with another in the word *haiao*, meaning filial love. 'A master is a child, who, like Lao Tzu, knows how to draw secret nourishment in silence from his "mother" the *Tao*.'[24]

Such a master is not one who merely learns and repeats authoritative forms of words from a tradition, but 'one who has been born to his wisdom by the mysterious all-embracing and merciful love which is the mother of all being'. His is not a science of intellectual penetration, wrestling for itself the secrets of heaven, but one who waits in littleness and silence upon the existential mystery of life itself. Merton illustrates the obscure meaning of the *Tao* in Dr John Wu's translation of the *Tao Te Ching*, much of which brings to mind the apophatic theology of the Eastern Church:

We make doors and windows for a room;
But it is these empty spaces that make the room
    liveable . . .

Look at it, but you cannot see it!
It's name is *Formless*.

Listen to it, but you cannot hear it!
It's name is *Soundless*.

Grasp at it, but you cannot get it!
It's name is Incorporeal.[25]

The *Tao* is the formless Form, the imageless Image, the
'fountain spirit' of inexhaustible life, never drawing attention
to itself. It does its work without noise or recognition. It is
utterly elusive and when you think you have caught a glimpse
of it, what you have seen is not the *Tao*. And like the Holy
Spirit in the Christian tradition, it is the source of all, and all
things return to it, 'as their home'. The whole meaning of life
lies in the discovery of this *Tao* which can never be discovered,
and this is no intellectual quest but a transformation of one's
whole being. This transformation is brought about by union
with the *Tao*. One 'reaches' the *Tao* by 'becoming like' the
Tao; 'the *Tao* is at once perfect activity and perfect rest'.[26]
Merton describes the passivity of the 'sage' in which there
is a yielding of worship and recognition of the mysterious *Tao*
in and through which the *Tao* manifests itself in local and
concrete situations:

The sage, then, accomplishes very much indeed because
it is the *Tao* that acts in him and through him. He does
not act of and by himself, still less for himself alone.
His action is not a violent manipulation of exterior
reality, an 'attack' on the outside world, bending it to
his conquering will: on the contrary, he respects
external reality by yielding to it, and his yielding is at
once an act of worship, a recognition of sacredness, and
a perfect accomplishment of what is demanded by the
precise situation.[27]

Merton cannot help drawing parallels with the Christian Faith. The man of *Tao* is like a newborn babe, having nowhere to lay his head, like one born of the Spirit, living in the Spirit and hidden in the love of God. The primitive intuitions of such a tradition are in the form of a dimension of wisdom orientated to contemplation. The religious vacuum in our education in Europe and America stands in need of such perspective and spirituality, Merton observes, and on this even our physical survival may depend.[28]

As he draws together the threads of his reflections on Classic Chinese Thought, Merton points the way forward, not only to a sympathetic understanding on the part of Western Christianity, but to a profound sharing and cross-fertilisation of all the great Faith-traditions of our world:

> The Christian scholar is obligated by his sacred vocation to understand and even preserve the heritage of all the great traditions insofar as they contain truths that cannot be neglected and that offer precious insights into Christianity itself. As the monks of the Middle Ages and the scholastics of the thirteenth century preserved the cultural traditions of Greece and Rome and adapted what they found in Arabic philosophy and science, so we too have a far greater task before us. It is time that we begin to consider something of our responsibility. Jesuit scholars have already pointed the way by contributing to the numerous excellent translations of Oriental texts. Benedictines can hardly find it difficult to understand and to admire the tradition of Kung Tzu, which has in it so many elements in common with the tradition and spirit of St Benedict.[29]

References

1 See 'Classic Chinese Thought', and The Jesuits in China', in *MZM*.
2 Merton, *MZM*, p. 46.

3 *ibid.*, pp. 48f.

4 *ibid.*, p. 49.

5 *ibid.*, p. 50.

6 Merton, *WChTz*, pp. 20ff.

7 Merton, *MZM*, p. 73.

8 *ibid.*, p. 51.

9 *ibid.*, pp. 66ff.

10 *ibid.*, p. 66.

11 Merton, *WChTz*, pp. 20f

12 Merton, *MZM*, p. 53.

13 *ibid.*, p. 54.

14 *ibid.*, pp. 54f.

15 quoted by Merton in *MZM*, p.55.

16 *ibid.*, p. 57.

17 *ibid.*, p. 59.

18 *Loc. cit.* See also *OB*, pp. 16–23 and 50–61.

19 Merton, *MZM*, p. 62.

20 quoted in *MZM*, p. 64.

21 *ibid.*, p. 65.

22 *ibid.*, p. 70.

23 *ibid.*, P. 72.

24 *ibid.*, pp. 73f. This theme of the hiden *Tao* in the cosmos is expounded by Merton in many places. See especially John Howard Griffin and Thomas Merton, *A Hidden Wholeness*, *passim*.

25 Merton, *MZM*, pp. 73f.

26 *ibid.*, p. 74.

27 *ibid.*, p. 76.

28 In spite of Merton's disclaimer that he does not intend 'Christian rabbits to appear by magic out of the Taoist hat', one cannot help being impressed by the analogies of the Christian life of faith which emerge in Merton's treatment of the sage's life in the *Tao*. See *WChTz*, pp. 10, 24f.

29 Merton, *MZM*, p. 76.

14: Taoist and Desert Fathers

Merton loved two particular groups of people – the 'Taoist Fathers' who flourished around the third and fourth centuries before Christ, and the 'Desert Fathers' who flourished around the third and fourth centuries after Christ. The first group are represented in Merton's *The Way of Chuang Tzu*, which he called his favourite book, and the second group by his *The Wisdom of the Desert*.

They are books of personal and communal wisdom, and both represent direct and *immediate* experience. I was going to write *spiritual* experience but hesitated because so many of the stories and parables recorded are of down-to-earth experiences and earthly emotions of simplicity, humility, anger, humour, repentance, sagacity. The whole of human life is earthly and spiritual in these traditions, and the direct experience is both personal and communal. In another context, Merton underlines the importance of direct and personal experience, the kind of immediate insight which anchors the monk within himself and is independent of rules, regulations and legalistic religion, whether of a Buddhist, Taoist or Christian kind! He refers to a kind of anti-monastic statement attributed to the Buddha in one of his last discourses. Knowing that his master's death was imminent, his favourite disciple, Ananda, asked him to leave final instructions probably as a rule or in the form of esoteric teaching or methods, as the founder of an Order might do. This the Buddha refused to do, declining to be thought of as the leader of an Order which would depend upon his instructions, and Merton records part of the answer:

So, Ananda, you must be your own lamps, be your own refuges. Take refuge in nothing outside

yourselves. Hold firm to the truth as a lamp and a
refuge, and do not look for refuge in anything besides
yourselves. A monk becomes his own lamp and refuge
by continually looking on his body, feelings,
perceptions, moods and ideas in such a manner that he
conquers the cravings and depressions of ordinary men
and is always strenuous, self-possessed and collected in
mind. Whoever among my monks does this, either
now or when I am dead, if he is anxious to learn, will
reach the summit. [1]

Of course this is not an argument against grace or
revelation, but an urging to direct insight, personal experience,
rather than a reliance on external means, dogmatic
propositions, ascetic systems or legalistic religious bondage.
This sort of direct experience and insight is what is represented
for Merton in the life and writings of the Taoists and Desert
Fathers.

Universal Monastic Outlook

Merton feels perfectly at ease among the Taoist community
and the Desert Fathers because he enjoys a certain community
of temper with them, reaching back over the centuries and
alive today in all contemplative people who love simplicity
and have achieved or seek a certain authenticity of life. He
put it like this:

I have been a Christian monk for nearly twenty-five
years, and inevitably one comes in time to see life
from a viewpoint that has been common to solitaries
and recluses in all ages and in all cultures. One may
dispute the thesis that all monasticism, Christian or
non-Christian, is essentially one. I believe that
Christian monasticism has obvious characteristics of its
own. Nevertheless, there is a monastic outlook which is
common to all those who have elected to question the
value of a life submitted entirely to arbitrary secular

presuppositions, dictated by social convention, and dedicated to the pursuit of temporal satisfactions which are perhaps only a mirage. Whatever may be the value of 'life in the world' there have been, in all cultures, men who have claimed to find something they vastly prefer in solitude.[2]

Merton finds this outlook or monastic temper quite clearly manifested in Taoist thought with its source in Chuang Tzu and the *Tao Te Ching*, and in the Desert Fathers as reflected in the *Verba Seniorum* which is a collection of the words and parables of the hermits of the desert, and the various *Lives* of the Fathers such as Athanasius's *Life of Antony* and Cassian's *Conferences*.

The joy of Merton's introduction, translations and paraphrases of these two groups is his experiential approach. He appreciates and revels in their playfulness and humour, in their rebelliousness and asceticism, in their opting out of the contemporary corrupt society in order to affirm a new and vital humanity which is not based upon worldliness, possessions and temporal power. Far from apologising for his attitude, especially in enjoying Chuang Tzu's life and teaching, he says:

I simply like Chung Tzu because he is what he is and I feel no need to justify this liking to myself or to anyone else. He is far too great to need any apologies from me. If St Augustine could read Plotinus, if St Thomas could read Aristotle and Averroës (both of them certainly a long way further from Christianity than Chung Tzu ever was!), and if Teilhard de Chardin could make copious use of Marx and Engels in his synthesis, I think I may be pardoned for consorting with a Chinese recluse who shares the climate and peace of my own kind of solitude, and who is my own kind of person.[3]

Discipline and Spontaneity

Merton makes the point that there is a contemporary dissatisfaction with conventional spiritual patterns and with ethical and religious formalism. There is a desperate need, not only in the Church but also in the world, to recover spontaneity and depth in terms of authentic human and spiritual experience. This is open to both opportunity and danger. Merton follows the Taoist and Desert Father emphasis on the importance of the person, but he does not thereby endorse individualism. There is a kind of reading of both these traditions which seeks for spontaneity without discipline, 'high experience' without asceticism, and 'instant' emotional satisfaction without commitment, surrender and compassion. Speaking of the quest, especially among young people for spontaneity and authenticity with Western 'beat Zen', he says:

> Western Zen has become identified with a spirit of improvization and experimentation – with a sort of moral anarchy that forgets how much tough discipline and what severe traditional mores are presupposed by the Zen of China and Japan. So also with Chuang Tzu. He might easily be read today as one preaching a gospel of license and uncontrol. Chuang Tzu himself would be the first to say that you cannot tell people to do whatever they want when they don't even know what they want in the first place.[4]

In any case, Chuang Tzu's philosophy is essentially religious and mystical and belongs to the context of a society in which every aspect of life was seen in relation to the sacred. It is easy to see how Merton could discern 'life in the Spirit' reflected in Chuang Tzu's description of *The Man of Tao*:

The man in whom Tao
Acts without impediment
Harms no other being
By his actions
Yet he does not know himself
To be 'kind', to be 'gentle'.

The man in whom Tao
Acts without impediment
Does not bother with his own interests
And does not despise
Others who do.
He does not struggle to make money
And does not make a virtue of poverty.
He goes his way
Without relying on others
And does not pride himself
On walking alone.
While he does not follow the crowd
He won't complain of those who do.
Rank and reward
Make no appeal to him;
Disgrace and shame
Do not deter him.
He is not always looking
For right and wrong
Always deciding 'Yes' or 'No'.
The ancients said, therefore:

The man of Tao
Remains unknown
Perfect virtue
Produces nothing
'No-Self'
is 'True-Self'.
And the greatest man
Is Nobody. [5]

Spontaneity and discipline run together in such a man as this. He appears to know and live and act according to the charism of the moment, producing joy or wisdom or a work of creativity just as a flautist may produce melody effortlessly. But there is an alternation and pattern of discipline and spontaneity that is both a gift and a work, and superficial men take what they see for the whole.

In one of the Desert stories, a religious layman came across a group of relaxed and happy desert monks, and he disapproved because they were not exercising themselves in 'godly asceticism' of some kind. Merton gives the story:

> Once Abbot Anthony was conversing with some brethren, and a hunter who was after game in the wilderness came upon them. He saw Abbot Anthony and the brothers enjoying themselves, and disapproved. Abbot Anthony said: Put an arrow in your bow and shoot it. This he did. Now shoot another, said the elder. And another, and another. The hunter said: If I bend my bow all the time it will break. Abbot Anthony replied: So it is also in the work of God. If we push ourselves beyond measure, the brethren will soon collapse. It is right, therefore, from time to time, to relax their efforts. [6]

These were not anarchic individualists, though of course there were some rogues in the desert as there are everywhere. But these men who inhabited the deserts of Egypt, Palestine, Arabia and Persia in the fourth century were the first Christian hermits who fled the pagan world and the newly 'established' and decadent Christian religion in the quest for authentic spiritual life. As Merton comments: 'The fact that the Emperor was now Christian and that the 'world' was coming to know the Cross as a sign of temporal power only strengthened them in their resolve.' They didn't believe in the concept of an officially 'Christian state' – politics and religion didn't mix in that sense for them. They knew that the practice of Jesus' teaching would lead to head-on collision

with the power-hungry and idolatrous state. I say they were
not anarchic individualists, but this is what Merton says of
them:

> The flight of these men to the desert was neither
> purely negative nor purely individualistic. They were
> not rebels against society. True, they were in a certain
> sense, 'anarchists', and it will do no harm to think of
> them in that light. They were men who did not believe
> in letting themselves be passively guided and ruled by
> a decadent state, and who believed that there was a
> way of getting along without slavish dependence on
> accepted, conventional values. But they did not intend
> to place themselves above society. They did not reject
> society with proud contempt, as if they were superior
> to other men . . . The Desert Fathers declined to be
> ruled by men, but had no desire to rule over others
> themselves. [7]

They did not believe in the divisions of successful rulers
who imposed their will and those who were subjected to them
being imposed upon. Their society was one of equality under
God, and authority was spiritual, charismatic, manifested in
wisdom, discernment and bearing fruit in experience and love.
It must also be remembered that they did not reject the
authority of their bishops, though it is not clear that they
missed them!

The 'man of Tao' is often more clearly anti-political,
preferring obscurity and solitude. He does not seek political
domination, though he does recognise that the Tao 'which
inwardly forms the sage, outwardly forms the King'. Hui Tzu
was Prime Minister of Liang. He thought Chuang Tzu was
intriguing to supplant him, and when Chuang Tzu visited
Liang, police were sent to apprehend him. Chuang presented
himself before Hui Tzu of his own accord, and in *Owl and
Phoenix* it is clear what he feels about solitude and Liang
politics:

Have you heard about the bird
That lives in the south
The Phoenix that never grows old?

This undying Phoenix
Rises out of the South Sea
And flies to the Sea of the North,
Never alighting
Except on certain sacred trees.
He will touch no food
But the most exquisite
Rare fruit,
Drinks only
From clearest springs.

Once an owl
Chewing a dead rat
Already half-decayed,
Saw the Phoenix fly over,
Looked up,
And screeched with alarm,
Clutching the rat to himself
In fear and dismay.

Why are you so frantic
Clinging to your ministry
And screeching at me
In dismay?[8]

Indwelling Spirit

There was a freedom among the desert dwellers which Merton
appreciated, and at times must have envied. His own yearning
for solitude and a hermitage was only partially granted, and
he knew the strange and mysterious movement of the
indwelling Spirit which called him into the wilderness. Contrasting the cenobites (monastery dwellers) with the eremites
(wilderness dwellers) he says:

The hermits were in every way more free. There was nothing to which they had to 'conform' except the secret, inscrutable will of God which might differ very notably from one cell to another! It is very significant that one of the first of these *Verba* is one in which the authority of St Anthony is adduced for what is the basic principle of desert life: that God is the authority and that apart from His manifest will there are few or no principles: 'Therefore, whatever you see your soul to desire according to God, do that thing, and you shall keep your heart safe.'[9]

Such a dangerous path could be trod by only those who were alert and sensitive to interior guidance in a trackless wilderness. The monk needed faith, detachment and maturity. And his interior visions must be of the Holy Spirit and not of his own inflamed imagination, a symptom of the pseudo-ego. As Merton says:

He has to lose himself in the inner, hidden reality of a self that was transcendent, mysterious, half-known, and lost in Christ. He had to die to the values of transient existence as Christ had died to them on the Cross, and rise from the dead with Him in the light of an entirely new wisdom.[10]

The contrast between formal rule-keeping and pentecostal indwelling is illustrated in the following story:

Abbot Lot came to Abbot Joseph and said: Father, according as I am able, I keep my little rule, and my little fast, my prayer, meditation and contemplative silence; and according as I am able I strive to cleanse my heart of thoughts: now what more should I do? The elder rose up in reply and stretched out his hands to heaven, and his fingers became like ten lamps of fire. He said: Why not be totally changed into fire?[11]

It is the indwelling fire of the Holy Spirit that divinises a man in the eastern Desert Father tradition. The 'law' then becomes interiorised and legalism is swallowed up in a loving interior dynamism.

In the Chuang Tzu tradition, the indwelling Spirit is the *Tao*, and the unnamed and mysterious *Tao* is manifested in the *tao* of relationships, of music, of poetry, or creative work. Merton does not set out to 'christianise' Taoism so that 'Christian rabbits will suddenly appear by magic out of a Taoist hat', but he makes us constantly aware of the basic similarities of experience underlying Desert Father and Taoist spirituality. Like the Christian Orthodox, the Taoists were reluctant to talk about the hidden and mysterious essence of the *Tao*, preferring rather to speak of its manifestations in the ordinary world. In the same series as Merton's book, D. Howard Smith writes of the hidden and mysterious principle of unity:

Taoists believed that the whole cosmos is spirit-fraught, and that there is a spiritual dimension to man himself. Yet few saw reason to believe in a creative, purposive God. The whole universe – gods, spirits, men, living creatures, even the inanimate fields, rocks, hills and streams – were all seen as part of an ever-changing process at the heart of which lay some principle of unity, so hidden and mysterious that its secrets could not be penetrated by human reason or intellect. To seek and find that mysterious principle, to discover it within one's inmost being, to observe its workings in the great universe outside, and to become utterly engulfed in its serenity and quietude came to be the supreme goal of the Taoist mystics. Apprehending it to be ineffable, impalpable and nameless, they nevertheless gave it the name TAO.[12]

'To seek and find that mysterious principle, to discover it within one's inmost being . . .' – that is just what Khing, the woodcarver, exemplifies in one of Merton's Taoist stories:

Khing, the master carver, made a bell stand
Of precious wood. When it was finished,
All who saw it were astounded. They said it must be
The work of spirits.
The Prince of Lu said to the master carver:
'What is your secret?'

Khing replied: 'I am only a workman:
I have no secret. There is only this:
When I began to think about the work you commanded
I guarded my spirit, did not expend it
On trifles, that were not to the point.
I fasted in order to set
My heart at rest.
After three days fasting,
I had forgotten gain and success.
After five days
I had forgotten praise or criticism.
After seven days
I had forgotten my body
With all its limbs.
'By this time all thought of your Highness
And of the court had faded away.
All that might distract me from the work
Had vanished.
I was collected in the single thought
Of the bell stand.

'Then I went to the forest
To see the trees in their own natural state.
When the right tree appeared before my eyes,
The bell stand also appeared in it, clearly, beyond doubt.
All I had to do was to put forth my hand
And begin.

'If I had not met this particular tree
There would have been
No bell stand at all.

'What happened?
My own collected thought
Encountered the hidden potential in the wood;
From this live encounter came the work
Which you ascribe to the spirits.'[13]

This is a clear pattern of Taoist spirituality, and not that of the monk but of an ordinary artisan worker – 'I am only a workman'. And if the workman is able to allow the creative power of the mysterious indwelling *Tao* to manifest itself at the level of ordinary work and relationships in such a way, then the spirituality of third century BC Taoism and that of third century AD Desert Fathers have much in common. Both are the outward manifestations of the mysterious indwelling Spirit.

The Joy of Possessing Nothing

It is not long, in these traditions, before one comes up against the joy of simple poverty. It includes money, attachments, reputation and ambition. There is no desire to possess, to wield power or to climb the social ladders of ambition and reputation. Chuang Tzu has an extended meditation which is full of irony, called *Cracking the Safe*. The part quoted here makes the point:

For security against robbers who snatch purses, rifle luggage, and crack safes,
One must fasten all property with ropes, lock it up with locks, bolt it with bolts.
This (for property owners) is elementary good sense.
But when a strong thief comes along he picks up the whole lot,
Puts it on his back, and goes on his way with only one fear:
That ropes, locks, and bolts may give way.
Thus what the world calls good business is only a way
To gather up the loot, pack it, make it secure
In one convenient load for the more enterprising thieves.
Who is there, among those called smart,

Who does not spend his time amassing loot
For a bigger robber than himself?
The invention
Of weights and measures
Makes robbery easier.
Signing contracts, setting seals
Makes robbery more sure.
Teaching love and duty
Provides a fitting language
With which to prove that robbery
Is really for the general good.
A poor man must swing
For stealing a belt buckle
But if a rich man steals a whole state
He is acclaimed
As statesman of the year.[14]

The 'men of Tao' represented here by Chuang Tzu lived in the time of the 'Warring States' (401–221 BC) – a time of political and social unrest, of intellectual and philosophical ferment. The independent principalities had rulers who sought for a unifying politico-religious philosophy, and advice was sought from the various schools – Confucians, Mohists, Legalists, Sophists, Logicians. For such advice they offered positions of dignity and power, with rank, wealth and reputation to follow. These early Taoists were simply not interested. The ambitious 'schools' were full of ambitious and practical men, and Chuang Tzu affirmed the value of the useless while they waxed eloquent about the useful. Merton quotes John Wu:

To Chuang Tzu the world must have looked like a terrible tragedy written by a great comedian. He saw scheming politicians falling into pits they had dug for others. He saw predatory states swallowing weaker states, only to be swallowed in their turn by stronger ones. Thus the much vaunted utility of the useful talents proved not only useless but self-destructive.[15]

The wisdom of the world must count this as nonsense, but there is a hidden wisdom in the words and acts of the Taoists as of the Desert Fathers. They were simple but not naive, and their poverty enabled them to own the world. Merton loved the following story:

> There were two elders living together in a cell, and they had never had so much as one quarrel with one another. One therefore said to the other: Come on, let us have at least one quarrel, like other men. The other said, I don't know how to start a quarrel. The first said: I will take this brick and place it here between us. Then I will say: It is mine. After that you will say: It is mine. This is what leads to a dispute and a fight. So then they placed the brick between them, and one said: It is mine, and the other replied to the first: I do believe that is mine. The first one said again: It is not yours, it is mine. So the other answered: Well then, if it is yours, take it! Thus they did not manage after all to get into a quarrel.[16]

And this story could have as easily come from the Taoist as from the Desert Father tradition:

> Once some robbers came into the monastery and said to one of the elders: We have come to take away everything that is in your cell. And he said: My sons, take all you want. So they took everything they could find in the cell and started off. But they left behind a little bag that was hidden in the cell. The elder picked it up and followed after them, crying out: My sons, take this, you forgot it in the cell! Amazed at the patience of the elder, they brought back everything into his cell and did penance, saying: This one really is a man of God![17]

These men neither needed the security of possessions, nor lived in fear of losing anything. There is a blessedness in possessing nothing, and a joy in being fearless. As Merton says: 'They neither courted the approval of their contemporaries nor sought to provoke their disapproval, because the opinions of others had ceased, for them, to be matters of importance. They had no set doctrine about freedom, but they had in fact become free by paying the price of freedom.'

A Way of Simplicity

Childlikeness does not mean childishness. Simplicity is a way of integrity and openness. Merton points out that the reason the Taoists were able to live and act simply from the heart was because they had attained a certain maturity and experience, so that following their inward desires was a following of compassion and truth – like Augustine's 'Love and do what you will'. The difference between Chuang Tzu and Confucius was that the latter lived by rules, regulations, rituals and external norms, though he professed to live by the *Tao*. Chuang Tzu believed that the Tao on which Confucius meditated and by which he lived was not the great, mysterious *Tao* that is unnameable, invisible and incomprehensible, but a lesser reflection as it manifests itself in human life – second-hand traditional wisdom, rules of virtue and religious and ritualistic customs. As Merton says:

> Chuang Tzu held that only when one was in contact with the mysterious *Tao* which is beyond all existing things, which cannot be conveyed either by words or by silence, and which is apprehended only in a state which is neither speech nor silence could one really understand how to live. To live merely according to the '*Tao* of man' was to go astray.[18]

This *Tao* of man is not the *Tao* of Heaven. It is an ethical *tao*, and as Confucianism developed, it continued to divide and subdivide until it became merely a term indicating an abstract and universal ethical principle. So there developed the '*tao* of fatherhood', the '*tao* of wifeliness' and in human relationships became akin to the Golden Rule of treating others as you should be treated by them. Yet when Confucian thought became deeply influenced by Taoism, these various human *taos* could become fingers pointing to the divine and mysterious *Tao* itself. The '*tao* of painting' for instance was thought of as expressing the ultimate principle of unity and harmony in the universe.

So while Confucianism and the other 'schools' of the time were becoming complicated in their particularity and sub-divisions, and tied to political and ambitious projects, the Taoism represented by Chuang Tzu kept mind and heart on the centre. In *The Turtle* story, Chuang Tzu not only illustrates the Taoist rejection of political ambition, but points to the better way of simplicity and ordinariness.

Chuang Tzu was fishing in Pu river with his bamboo pole. The Prince of Chu sent two vice-chancellors with a formal document which said: 'We hereby appoint you Prime Minister.' Chuang Tzu held his pole, and gazing upon the river, told them about a sacred tortoise which had been sacrificed three thousand years before, wrapped in silk and laid upon a precious shrine-altar in the temple, venerated by the prince.

'What do you think?' he asked, 'is it better to give up living and exist in a sacred shell to be venerated in a cloud of incense, or to live as a plain turtle, dragging its tail in the mud?' Merton records the rest of the story:

> 'For the turtle,' said the Vice-Chancellor,
> 'Better to live
> And drag its tail in the mud!'
> Go home!' said Chuang Tzu.
> 'Leave me here
> To drag my tail in the mud.'[19]

This does not indicate political naivety, but rather a certain sagacity and humour in dealing with human relation-ships on a personal and a corporate level. Chuang Tzu believed that all life is sacred, recognising the spiritual dimension, and he sought to probe into the being of things in affirmation of that unifying centre to all existence – the *Tao*. His poking fun at the Confucians and Mohists of the day and his constant debate with the logicians stimulated political thought. He would have said that 'small is beautiful' and this would have been reflected in small self-governing groups of inter-dependent villages, living close to the earth and manifesting the compassion and rhythm of the mysterious *Tao*. As D. Howard Smith says:

> Disillusioned by the scheming, intrigues and sycophancy of the feudal courts, and highly critical of the social conventions, elaborate ceremonial, moral precepts, and detailed rules of behaviour which formed a veneer to cover hypocrisy and self-seeking, the early Taoists contrasted the artificialities of man-made institutions with the ordered sequences of natural processes. They were horrified by the enslavement of the peasantry, the wasteful and destructive wars, the endless jockeying for position and power. They believed that man, like all other creatures, must learn to conform to the spontaneous and natural processes of birth, decay and death, and become attuned to a cosmic rhythm. Freedom, peace and happiness for all men could only be attained by conformity to natural and not man-made laws . . . man's most prized possession is life itself. Their aim was to be left alone to enjoy life in freedom, preserving their own inner integrity.[20]

So when Merton presents Chuang Tzu as saying: 'Leave me here to drag my tail in the mud', he was not stating the case of a recluse (for Chuang Tzu was in constant debate), but of a people who did not want bureaucratic interference with the natural rhythms of a 'simple' and primitive existence.

Constantly, Merton gives us a window into the kind of 'leaving things alone' mentality that governed the best of the Desert Fathers, but he also shows the beginnings of a more legalistic attitude to obedience and corporate control that is opposed by the true contemplative:

> A brother in Scete happened to commit a fault, and the elders assembled, and sent for Abbot Moses to join them. He, however, did not want to come. The priest sent him a message, saying: Come, the community of the brethren is waiting for you. So he arose and started off. And taking with him a very old basket full of holes, he filled it with sand, and carried it behind him. The elders came out to meet him, and said: What is this, Father? The elder replied: My sins are running behind me, and I do not see them, and today I come to judge the sins of another! They, hearing this, said nothing to the brother but pardoned him.[21]

Humour and Sagacity

There was, about Merton, a great sense of humour, wit and mischief. This did not endear him to many of his early camp-followers who expected a pious asceticism in keeping with monastic solitude. Poker-faced and pious hermits eventually go mad or immoral! But within and through Merton's humour was a profound wisdom – it was not just laughing at the devil or gently poking fun at the serious enemy, but endeavouring to see that he needed the opposition to clarify his own thought and help him to see the other side, by what Merton calls 'the principle of complementarity'. Perhaps that's what St Paul meant when he maintained that good could come out of opposition and heresies.

Merton relates this humorous little story from the Chuang Tzu tradition, called *Three in the Morning*:

> When we wear out our minds, stubbornly clinging to one partial view of things, refusing to see a deeper agreement between this and its complementary opposite, we have what is called 'three in the morning'. What is this 'three in the morning?'

A monkey trainer went to his monkeys and told them: 'As regards your chestnuts: you are going to have three measures in the morning and four in the afternoon.'

At this they became angry. So he said: 'All right, in that case I will give you four in the morning and three in the afternoon.' This time they were satisfied.

The two arrangements were the same in that the number of chestnuts did not change. But in one case the animals were displeased, and in the other they were satisfied. The keeper had been willing to change his personal arrangement in order to meet objective conditions. He lost nothing by it!

The truly wise man, considering both sides of the question without partiality, sees them both in the light of *Tao*. This is called following two courses at once.[22]

The Desert Father tradition also manifested a dry sense of humour, like the story of the two monks who tried to quarrel and didn't succeed, or like the two who met a nun at a stream, and without a word, one of them put her on his back, waded across, set her down, and they went on, in different directions. After half an hour the second monk said to the first: I don't think you should have carried that nun on your back across the stream.' The second came back with: 'Oh, I put her down half an hour ago – you've been carrying her ever since,.'

Merton reflects here the humour of God, and certainly as I read these stories I feel within myself not only the stimulation of a genuine humour which is shot through with profound wisdom, but I also feel the way in which the Lord plays his game with me – with the same mixture of humour and wisdom that causes me to laugh at myself first, and then at our stupid and lovable humanity. Here are glimpses of the Incarnation – when God became man it was utterly serious – an act that made archangels tremble – but it was also an act of divine humour. That divine humour was part of Merton's pilgrimage and saved him from sliding from discouragement into despair. He recognised it not only in creation, but in the saving Gospel, and in the Taoist, Zen, Buddhist, Hindu, Jewish and Desert Father traditions. The eremitic (desert) hermit tradition has special humorous stories of its own against the cenobitic (monastery) tradition. Merton especially appreciates the story of one canny hermit who was visited by some cenobitic monks who ate everything he had in his hut. During the night he heard them planning to go on to another hermit to do the same, so the next morning he gave them this message to give to his brother hermit: 'Be careful not to water the vegetables'.

They delivered the message and the second hermit understood! He got them to weave baskets right up until the evening time, and then he added some extra psalms to the usual number, saying that they did not eat every day in the desert, but for a change they would have supper that day. He gave them some dry bread and salt with a 'special treat' of a mixture of a little vinegar, salt and oil. After supper they started with psalms again, right through almost until dawn, when he said: 'Well, we can't finish all our usual prayers, for you are tired . . . you had better take a little rest.' When the first hour of the day came they wanted to leave the hermit, but he resisted and said: 'Stay with me, I cannot let you go too soon, charity demands that I keep you for two or three days.' Merton concludes the story: 'But they, hearing this, waited until dark and then, under cover of night they made off.'[23]

With Thomas Merton as guide, it is clear that this spirituality and simplicity is a universal way and perspective. It is simply the good soil and the ideal context in which the Gospel can be understood. It is part of the world as natural and good and holy, and not part of that world which is sinful, alienated and system-dominated. As Merton says:

> The whole teaching, the 'way' found in these
> anecdotes, poems and meditations, is characteristic of a
> certain mentality found everywhere in the world, a
> certain taste for simplicity for humility, self-effacement,
> silence, and in general a refusal to take seriously the
> aggressivity, the ambition, the push, and the self-
> importance which one must display in order to get

along in society. This other is a 'way' that prefers not
to get anywhere in the world, or even in the field of
some supposedly spiritual attainment. The book of the
bible which most obviously resembles the Taoist classics
is Ecclesiastes. But at the same time there is much in
the teaching of the Gospels on simplicity, childlikeness,
and humility, which responds to the deepest aspirations
of the Chuang Tzu book and the Tao Te Ching.[23]

Freedom and Joy

It is difficult to know what *most* attracted Merton in these two
groups of 'way out' characters, the Taoists of third/fourth
centuries BC, and the Desert Fathers of the third/fourth
centuries AD. But the word that springs most readily to mind
is *immediacy*. There was a directness and immediacy of spiritual
experience – indeed of all experience which was the basic
material of their spirituality and way of living. Theirs was not
a religion of authority, book-study, legalism or inherited
tradition. They did not despise these, though sometimes poked
fun at obsession with any of them – but they needed first-hand
experience. It was the living God or no god at all!

Thomas Merton's life was like this. One cannot appeal to
his love of immediacy and use it to back up or justify a
clamouring for 'instant' spirituality (which is one of the heresies
of today). I have learned from Merton not to try to write 'a
book on prayer for busy people'. There *must* be a demand for
direct, immediate and valid experience, but it is always within
the context of discipline, asceticism, and a total surrender to
the grace of God, because there is a gift-like quality in the
spirituality of the two groups illustrated in this chapter.

Merton enjoyed reading about them, for it reflected his own
attitudes and lifestyle. He enjoyed translating, paraphrasing,
expounding the heart of their spirituality and lifestyle, and he
enjoyed communicating and commending such writings. His
enjoyment was at the heart of his communication but at the
same time, it became an exercise in wide ecumenical sympathy,
and promoted human understanding in such a way that

unsuspecting 'pious' readers were drawn into a like sympathy, so that the rubble of prejudice was cleared away, and the springs of human feelings began to flow freely.

This freedom from bigotry and religious exclusivism begets a true humility which is universal, and once one has reached such a place, then freedom and joy are natural, and spontaneous sharing is the outcome. Merton mingles the traditions in his estimation of this humility:

> One may call this humility 'cosmic', not only because it is rooted in the true nature of things, but also because it is full of life and awareness, responding with boundless vitality and joy to all living beings. It manifests itself everywhere by a Franciscan simplicity and connaturality with all living creatures. Half the 'characters' who are brought before us to speak the mind of Chuang Tzu are animals – birds, fishes, frogs, and so on. Chung Tzu's Taoism is nostalgic for the primordial climate of paradise in which there was no differentiation, in which man was utterly simple, unaware of himself, living at peace with himself, with *Tao*, and with all other creatures.[24]

Thomas Merton's explorations into the climate of ancient Taoism and Desert Father spirituality lured me into an appreciation and sympathy that enhanced my own Christian spirituality and made me even more aware of the universal temper of my perspective. It continues to do this, so that the direct and immediate nature of my own spirituality is something which I now value at a profound level, and this, in turn, enables me to commend and stimulate it in others.

References

1 Merton, *MZM*, p. 218.
2 Merton, *WChTz*, p. 10.
3 *ibid.*, pp. 10f.

4 *ibid.*, p. 16.

5 *ibid.*, p. 91.

6 Merton, *WD*, p. 63.

7 *ibid.*, pp. 4f.

8 Merton, *WChTz*, p. 95.

9 Merton, *WD*, p. 6f.

10 *ibid.*, p. 7.

11 *ibid.*, p. 50.

12 D. Howard Smith, *The Wisdom of the Taoist Mystics*, pp. 5f.

13 Merton, *WChTz*, pp. 110f.

14 *ibid.*, pp. 67f.

15 *ibid.*, p. 25.

16 Merton, *WD*, p. 67.

17 *ibid.*, p. 59.

18 Merton, *WChTz*, p. 21.

19 *ibid.*, pp. 93f.

20 Smith, *op. cit.*, pp. 4f.

21 Merton, *WD*, p. 40.

22 *ibid.*, p. 44.

23 Merton, *WChTz*, p. 11.

24 *ibid.*, p. 27.

Part V: Personal Evaluation

15: Merton as Guide and Friend

Simply Being Human

I believe I speak for many thousands of people when I say
that Merton acted for me as a catalyst in setting me free
from the modes and limitations of thought that had been
laid down by my own tradition. Because he was a pilgrim-
adventurer, moving from his early circumscribed ways of
monastic thinking in the pre-Vatican II Roman Church into
areas of broad humanitarian and ecumenical appreciation,
he gave hope to many others who were locked in party
prejudices or traditional fundamentalism.

Therefore, he represented to me a kind of liberator, but
one who could be trusted to pursue new paths of thought,
with reverence and understanding for the old. He affirmed
both tradition and revolution, but filled these words with
new meaning. By 'tradition' he did not mean ecclesiastical
customs that were outworn, tending towards stagnation and
decay, and which had no relevance or meaning for the
contemporary Christian. He thought of it, rather, as the
handing-down or passing-on of the life-giving breath of God
in the Church. 'The living tradition of Catholicism is like
the breath of a physical body,' he says. 'It renews life by
repelling stagnation. It is a constant, quiet, peaceful revolution
against death.' 'Revolution' is the turning upside down of
worldly, materialistic values which have invaded the Church,
and returning to the basic principles of a gospel-life. Merton
applies this principle to theological understanding as well
as to Christian lifestyle. It is *orthodoxy* as well as *orthopraxis*,
and both are revolutionised by the life-giving power of the
Holy Spirit – and this is a return to the true tradition of

the Church. He spells it out in his essay 'Tradition and Revolution':

> The life of the Church is the Truth of God Himself, breathed out into the Church by His Spirit, and there cannot be any other truth to supersede and replace it. The only thing that can replace such intense life is a lesser life, a kind of death. The constant human tendency away from God and away from this living tradition can only be counteracted by a return to tradition, a renewal and a deepening of the one unchanging life that was infused into the Church at the beginning.
>
> And yet this tradition must always be a revolution because by its very nature it denies the values and standards to which human passion is so powerfully attached. To those who love money and pleasure and reputation and power this tradition says: 'Be poor, go down into the far end of society, take the last place among men, live with those who are despised, love other men and serve them instead of making them serve you. Do not fight them when they push you around, but pray for those that hurt you. Do not look for pleasure, but turn away from things that satisfy your senses and your mind and look for God in hunger and thirst and darkness, through deserts of the spirit in which it seems to be madness to travel. Take upon yourself the burden of Christ's Cross, that is, Christ's humility and poverty and obedience and renunciation, and you will find peace for your souls.'
>
> This is the most complete revolution that has ever been preached; in fact it is the only true revolution, because all the others demand the extermination of somebody else, but this one means the death of the man who, for all practical purposes, you have come to think of as your own self.[1]

This understanding of tradition and revolution is post-Vatican II thinking, and it was revolutionary for Merton because he had been caught up in the kind of ecclesiastical conservatism that formed around this kind of monastic life as barnacles gather on the hull of a ship. He had experienced a devaluation of his simple and ordinary humanity as he became imprisoned in a monastic outlook that lacked the integration of the sacred and the secular, in a platonic separation of the world of spirit from the world of matter. After more than sixteen years in monastic life, Merton makes an unusual domestic trip into Louisville which leads to an immense theological discovery:

> In Louisville, at the corner of Fourth and Walnut, in the center of the shopping district, I was suddenly overwhelmed with the realization that I loved all those people, that they were mine and I theirs, and we could not be alien to one another even though we were total strangers. It was like waking from a dream of separatedness, of spurious self-isolation in a special world, the world of renunciation and supposed holiness. The whole illusion of a separate holy existence is a dream. Not that I question the reality of my vocation, or of my monastic life: but the conception of 'separation from the world' that we have in the monastery too easily presents itself as a complete illusion: the illusion that by making vows we become a different species of being, pseudoangels, 'spiritual men', men of interior life, what have you . . .
>
> To think that for sixteen or seventeen years I have been taking seriously this pure illusion that is implicit in so much of our monastic thinking.[2]

What Merton is bewailing, of course, is the sliding away from the primitive monastic vision – the monks he writes about in both the Taoist and Desert Father traditions, both BC and AD were eminently social and human in the most profound sense. They enabled the ungodly and materialistic world to understand what it is to be truly human. And rejoicing in the simple humanity Jesus manifested is a deliverance from religious fundamentalisms and philosophical separatedness. When Jesus shared at an intimate level with the 'immoral woman' in John's gospel, he offended both the social and religious sensitiveness of the disciples, but he displayed an exhilarating freedom in simple human relationship. 'A false and divisive sacredness or super-naturalism can only cripple man,' says Merton. I recognised the truth in this kind of writing, and like Merton, I found I needed to 'unlearn' much of what had been imposed upon me in the religious realm.

The simplicity and wonder of simply being ordinary and human is a great gift, and Merton has helped me to unlearn, to return to my beginnings, and to live in the simple spontaneity of relating to others on the basic level of humanity, not on the grounds of a shared theology or philosophy which, by its nature, excludes others. This is of doctrinal and practical importance at the two extreme poles of the catholic and the evangelical in the Church today, especially as the multi-racial society is part of our situation, calling upon us to relate in basic humanity and compassion with those who are of different ethnic and religious traditions to our own.

Let me give two illustrations of how this perspective of Merton's works out in different contexts. Belonging to an Amnesty International Group in Glasgow some years ago, I attended the annual meeting where were gathered people from many groups of different religious and humanitarian backgrounds. I got into conversation with a small group of people who told me they were atheists because of the kind of God represented to them by the teaching and lifestyle of the Christian Church. I listened to them, increasingly aware of the sincerity of their stance, and the tremendous human compassion that they revealed in their support of Amnesty and other healing and reconciling agencies. As we shared and discussed, I was constrained to say: 'Look, I don't believe in the kind of God you don't believe in – for the same reasons!' And we found so much common ground, so much joy in sharing, so joyful an appreciation of one another's humanity that it was clear that we were participating in what I could only call the fellowship of the Holy Spirit.

Then hitching along the A303 in Somerset some while back, a lorry driver, whose curiosity had been aroused by my brown Franciscan habit, asked: 'Could you say in one sentence what your attitude is in the world today?' I said that it would be impossible for me to do this without clear reference to the centrality of Christ, but that I would try. 'In one sentence,' I said, 'I would say that I seek to be open and compassionate to all people on the basis of our shared humanity.' 'But that's amazing,' he cried, 'I've never heard anyone say anything like that before.' I hastened to confess that I did not manage actually to live that out, but that it is my desire and intention to do so. And then began an animated, joyful and productive conversation. And I must admit that I frequently get more joy, more sense, more down-to-earth reality in such conversations than I find in religious talk-shops that I sometimes have to attend. Pseudo-religion and mere religiosity masks simple humanity, and encourages the projection of pious or intellectual images – which the Bible calls hypocrisy.

Merton was not, of course, expounding anything new, but simply returning to the simple humanity of Jesus in the gospels. But to find a man who was experiencing increasing freedom from both secular and religious trappings, and addressing one's common humanity was refreshing and liberating. Jesus did it in the context of the Judaism of his day, Merton did it in the early repressive monasticism of his day, and we are called upon to do it in the context of our own exclusivisms or fundamentalisms of whatever kind they are. Do not let your theology or your philosophy cut you off from friendship and sharing with other human beings – whether you agree in opinion or not! We are not saved by our opinions but by the grace and love of God.

The tendency in parts of the Christian Church is still to sustain a certain exclusivism of the elect, and be open to others inasmuch as they are potential converts. There is even a cult of cultivating friends to influence them into your brand of the Faith. This is spiritual blackmail – have nothing to do with it! At best, of course, it is not like that. In many ways the Christian Church ecumenically seeks to reach out a compassionate and social hand to all people on the basis of their humanity, of whatever creed, colour or culture. Certainly Thomas Merton enabled me to see more clearly that the basis of openness of heart and mind must not be religion or ideology, but a simple acceptance of the humanity of one's fellow. And that, for me, was a return to my early and childhood intuitive understanding.

True Catholicity

Merton's understanding of catholicity also underwent a sea-change as his pilgrimage unfolded. The *aggiornamento* renewal of Vatican II stimulated such thinking, enabling him to relate at a profound level, not only with other Christians, but with people of other Faiths. There were universal implications in the great world Faiths for Merton, and James Baker points this out:

> Merton was himself a true Catholic, but he admitted that it was only in the last few years of his life that he became one. In the early days of his profession of faith, the days so well described in *The Seven Storey Mountain*, he felt that the Church possessed ultimate and sacred truth, that it held in trust the final revelation of God in Christ, and that it must call the world to itself for salvation. In those days he rejected the world outside the Church and had no apparent interest in establishing dialogue with it. But upon his emergence from the enforced silence of the 1940s he began to listen as well as speak to the world and to make friends with many of the world's citizens, and much later he would say that it was only then that he became a true Catholic. [3]

Merton found that as he was able to say 'yes' to everything that is good and true and beautiful in the world, so he was affirming the basic unity and integration in himself, resolving tensions and being delivered from a proud individualism. This is the language of his heart: 'I will be a better Catholic, not if I can *refute* every shade of Protestantism, but if I can affirm the truth in it and still go further.' In going further he embraced Hindus, Muslims, Buddhists – indeed the whole religious and contemplative traditions which followed the love of God. And in taking such a stance he was not affirming a vague friendliness, careless of truth, compromising orthodox theology and leading to a vapid syncretism. He was rather sensing and following the Holy Spirit in all that was true and good and loving, and therefore manifesting God's grace in the world.

Lest it be thought that in such openness no one can be taken seriously or in depth, let's look at Merton's attitude in action towards classic Protestantism. He reveals his deep appreciation of salvation *fides sola*, *by faith alone*, while at the same time being aware of the danger of faith cut off from good works:

> The religious genius of the Protestant Reformation, as I see it, lies in its struggle with the problem of justification in all its depth. The great Christian question is the conversion of man and his restoration to the grace of God in Christ. And this question in its simplest form is that of the conversion of the wicked and the sinful to Christ. But Protestantism raised this same question in its *most radical form* – how about the much more difficult and problematic conversion, that of the pious and the good? It is relatively easy to convert the sinner, but the good are often completely unconvertible simply because they do not see any need for conversion.[4]

Merton quite clearly sees the need, not simply to attain good habits, become outwardly pious, or adopt the language (or opinions) of the 'saved'. All these can be subtle evasions of conversion – what is needed, as Merton says, is a *new creature*, 'becoming a totally new man in Christ and in the Spirit.' He does a simple but succinct exposition of the Protestant and Catholic positions on the necessity for true faith followed by the works of grace, pointing out the dangers of both positions in neglect of the other. Then he goes on:

> Those who are faithful to the original grace of Protestantism are precisely those who, in all depth, see as Luther saw that the 'goodness' of the good may in fact be the greatest religious disaster for a society, and that the crucial problem is the *conversion of the good to Christ*. Kierkegaard sees it, so does Barth, so does Bonhoeffer, so do the Protestant existentialists.
>
> As a Catholic, I firmly hold of course to what the Church teaches on justification and grace. One cannot be justified by a faith that does not do the works of love, for love is the witness and evidence of 'new being' in Christ. But precisely this love is primarily the work of Christ in me, not simply something that originates in my own will and is then approved and rewarded by God. It is faith that opens my heart to Christ and His Spirit, that He may work in me. No work of mine can be called 'love' in the Christian sense, unless it comes from Christ. But 'the good' are solely tempted to believe in their own goodness and their own capacity to love, while one who realizes his own poverty and nothingness is much more ready to surrender himself entirely to the gift of love *he knows* cannot come from anything in himself.[5]

What causes me to respond with joy when Merton listens and responds to the reformation tradition is that he not only understands the truth (and error) of Protestant witness, but he relates it to the Catholic tradition in such a way as to correct the 'Roman blind spots' of Catholic theologians who had not really listened to their opponents. Merton's method was one of listening for truth and love, for they cannot be divorced, and then responding within the same context.

There was a twofold attitude behind this universal perspective. The first was a total lack of fear in openness to truth wherever it was to be found; and the second was a profound desire to share the truth as he understood and experienced it in his emerging pilgrimage. Fear lies behind most of our distrust of others who do not hold the same opinions as we do, and Merton's example is one of a man at unity in himself, with his roots into the love of God, and therefore unafraid of total openness in charity.

This universal perspective was both attractive and infectious as far as I was concerned. There is a certain understandable exclusivism built into a robust catholic or evangelical faith, which affirms quite basically the uniqueness of Christ and the revelatory nature of God's disclosure in him. But in tracing one's theological attitude to the historical Jesus himself, it is clear that Merton's twofold perspective is more akin to Jesus than to the Church's increasing exclusivism. Jesus had nothing to fear, and he was totally open to all, desiring to radiate the love and compassion of God. He was conditioned by his own Jewish roots and perspective, but his vision and attitude was universal.

The present situation is dramatically different, with the major Faiths living together 'cheek by jowl' in our contemporary world. As I endeavour to live out the Gospel in such a world I realise that the image of Jesus has been parochialised and emasculated by the Western Church. But I also am increasingly aware of the 'Merton perspective' which frees us to see the glory of the eternal Christ reflected in all the positive insights of the great Faiths. As Merton said of the missionary enterprise of the Church – it is not only that we carry the Gospel-news of the crucified and risen Jesus of the Christian tradition to those who have never heard, but that we are also prepared to discover and treasure the hidden Christ within the sophianic traditions of other cultures and Faiths.

Christianity can only profit by such insights, and the cross-fertilisation which is then possible can only enrich catholic and ecumenical understanding in their widest sense. This is, for Merton, synthesis, not syncretism – an appreciation of ancient and proved insights that serve to deepen the understanding of one's own faith, not a confused mish-mash of divergent and contradictory doctrines. But even the doctrinal differences reflecting the particular philosophical ethos in which they have been formulated do not stop Merton from entering into a contemplative understanding an experiential level. James Baker spells this out:

> While the obstacles to dialogue on the doctrinal level might be insurmountable, it would be possible to discuss openly and frankly the disciplines and rewards of the contemplative life, which is basically the same in all religions, and from that to move to even more important subjects. Zen Buddhist monks and Christian Cistercians he explained, because they are so similar in their simplicity, austerity, uncompromising poverty, manual labour, and common life, would be able to understand each other more easily than Buddhist and Christian theologians. And so Merton began, through his personal activities and writings, to establish dialogue with Eastern thinkers, especially monks. He hoped that by his example he might lead other Catholics to confront the Orient, learn to appreciate its rich heritage, and begin to think beyond their religion to the larger religious family of man. He wrote in his Asian Journal that he hoped to find on his trip 'the great solution' which probably meant the true religious synthesis that he always believed both possible and desirable.[6]

Cross-Fertilisation

This is the process by which Thomas Merton gained insights from open dialogue and sharing with representatives of cultures and traditions not his own, and by which they learned at the same level, the lifestyle and theology of a Christian contemplative monk. The dialogue is based on friendship, and the friendship on an acceptance of common shared humanity. This is the lesson which I have endeavoured to imbibe from Merton, and which has stimulated thought and opened up experience in the widening of my own horizons.

For instance, last Sunday at our 'open tea' at Glasshampton monastery, we had invited a group consisting of a Church of the Nazarene pastor and his family. Then, uninvited, but very welcome, there appeared a group of a dozen or so men and women Sikhs from the Birmingham Gadwara (temple), complete with turbans, saris and specially cooked Sikh food for distribution. Also accompanying them was their 'sant' or holy man, and as the Rule of St Benedict encourages, we received the guests as the Christ. After sharing together our food (avoiding certain proscribed items), I was asked by the Sikhs to talk about Christian meditation. The Christian guests asked if they could 'sit in' too, so we all went into the Chapel, most of us sitting on the floor before the altar.

So I talked to the group (some of the Sikhs needed their interpreter) about relaxation posture, breathing, heartbeat – about the Holy Spirit as the breath of God, the importance of the dying and rising Jesus in our spiritual experience of new birth, and about the Jesus Prayer. Then the Sikhs put doctrinal and practical questions to me, and I to them. It was a happy experience of sharing, openness, cross-fertilisation and seed ideas, resulting in a new awareness and of joy and prayer together. Their 'sant' and I embraced with mutual blessings at the conclusion of our Chapel session, and with an exchanging of gifts and greetings, the Sikhs went on their way – after we had received and extended invitations to join together again soon.

Thomas Merton had prepared me for such unexpected blessings as these, because of the experimentation in his lifestyle, and the content of his writings about World Faiths. He was the kind of ecumenical pioneer that I could trust as a guide and friend in this area, and his optimism concerning the outcome of such fruitful dialogue was once again demonstrated, both on a theological and practical level.

The Christian pastor and his wife stayed longer than the Sikhs, and wanted to talk about the experience, which was entirely new to them. They had come from the evangelical, even fundamentalist, section of the Christian Church. The first observation of the pastor was to the effect that these Sikhs seemed to be seekers of God in a more sincere and earnest manner than many nominal Christians. And the discerning comment of his wife was that she had closely observed the 'sant' guru man and had felt the warmth and wisdom of the Holy Spirit within him, as far as she could judge. 'But,' she asked, 'how can I square that with the words of Jesus: "No man comes to the Father but by me"?'

Here was a paradoxical situation of confessing the reality of spiritual life in this holy man who was not specifically confessing the historical Jesus as the source of that life, though of course the Sikhs would hold Jesus to be a prophet of God. It was the kind of problem that the Christian Church has not yet sorted out, and which hinders any real acknowledgement of genuine experience of God in the spiritual life of worthy adherents of other Faiths.

My suggested explanation to her was one that I had learned from my own experience, guided by the Merton perspective referred to above. It went like this:

You remember that Jesus' words are found in the *Gospel of St John*. In that same gospel, Jesus says: 'Before Abraham was, I am'. He was not there speaking simply of the historical Jesus who began to be at Bethlehem, but of the eternal Christ or Logos of the Prologue of that gospel. So may not Jesus have been speaking of the eternal Christ or Logos in relation to those who come to the Father? For certainly Abraham, Isaac, Jacob, Moses – all the Old Testament saints came to the Father through the eternal Word or Logos – for he was the agent of creation, and he is the true Light that enlightens everyone who comes into the world. They did not come through the historical Jesus, for Bethlehem was far into the future. And certainly Sikhs acknowledge Jesus as a holy prophet of God and do not simply reject him. So all those who approach the Father in sincerity and truth are drawn by the Holy Spirit and come through the eternal Word, for there is no other way to approach the Father. And not only so, but when the eternal Word became incarnate in the historical Jesus, then what he accomplished for our redemption not only covered all the Old Testament patriarchs and saints, but covers all those who will at last be saved.

As I shared this suggested explanation of the paradox, her face lit up. The fact was that she *wanted* to affirm doctrinally what she had felt intuitively. She wanted the universality of God's love to embrace the Sikh men and women with whom she had talked for the first time in her life, and she and her husband left the monastery with a whole new dimension of theological thought and experience which would have to be worked out in mind and heart, and in compatibility with the Gospel of our Lord Jesus Christ, understood now at a new and profound level.

This is the kind of catalyst that Thomas Merton is. This is why, in claiming him as guide and friend, I gladly acknowledge the integration of his life and words as a factor of influence and example of my own. When Merton entered into a life-giving dialogue with Daisetz Suzuki, the Buddhist, on Christianity and the Zen tradition, he spoke of a sense of the breakdown of duality and a renewed sense of the unity of all things. The following words of Merton need to be seen in the whole context of their dialogue to be fully understood, but the second paragraph conveys a wonderful sense of the ordinariness of our humanity with which we began this chapter:

Zen implies a breakthrough, an explosive liberation from one-dimensional conformism, a recovery of unity

which is not the suppression of opposites but a
simplicity beyond opposites. To exist and function in
the world of opposites while experiencing that world
in terms of primal simplicity does imply if not a
formal metaphysic, at least a ground of metaphysical
intuition. This means a totally different perspective
than that which dominates our society – and enables
it to dominate us.

Hence the saying: before I grasped Zen, the
mountains were nothing but mountains and the rivers
nothing but rivers. When I got into Zen, the
mountains were no longer mountains and the rivers
no longer rivers. But when I understood Zen, the
mountains were only mountains and the rivers only
rivers.[7]

References

1 Merton, *SC*, p. 112.
2 Merton, *CGB*, pp. 153f.
3 James Baker, *Thomas Merton Social Critic*, pp. 128f.
4 Merton, *CGB*, p. 165.
5 *ibid.*, pp. 165f.
6 Baker, *op. cit.*, pp. 137f.
7 Merton, *ZBA*, p. 140.

16: The Meaning of Merton's Death

The Circumstances

Thomas Merton died suddenly on 10th December, 1968, during a Monastic Conference in Bangkok. John Moffitt edited the published proceedings of the Conference. He writes:

> Two days after Thomas Merton's death, four not very large crocodile-like creatures living in the lake came out onto the grass. There, in sight of several of the monks, including Dom Rembert, one of them seized and consumed a dog. It seemed strange to me, in retrospect, to recall that in an Indian parable about the inevitability of death, the form taken by the god of death to complete his mission was that of a crocodile. [1]

Just two hours before his death, Merton gave a lecture to the assembled conference before two television teams, entitled 'Marxism and Monastic Perspectives'. In his concluding remarks he said: 'I believe the plan is to have all the questions for this morning's lectures this evening at the panel. So I will disappear.' And that is just what he did!

At about 1.40 p.m. he took the ten-minute walk over to the cottage where he was staying with three other delegates. Shortly afterwards Dom Celestine Say OSB, the Benedictine prior from the Philippines entered the cottage and went into the bathroom. A few minutes later the French monk, Dom Francois de Grunne OSB, knocked on the bathroom door and asked Dom Celestine if he had heard something like a cry and the fall of a heavy object. On receiving a negative reply he returned upstairs.

At about 3.50 p.m. he wanted the cottage key, so he went to Merton's room, knocked on the door, and receiving no reply he peered in. Merton was lying on his back in the far left corner, wearing only a pair of shorts; and on top of him lay one of the tall standing fans. There was a smell of burning, and sparks were shooting from the switch box. The alarm was raised and Dom Odo Haas OSB, from South Korea, burst in and tried to lift the fan from Merton's body. He received a strong electric shock and his hands became paralysed and stuck to the stem of the fan until it was unplugged. He was saved from death because of his insulating footwear.

There was a large and deep burn extending on Merton's right side, from the top of his shorts to his armpit – and he was dead. The two abbots gave Merton general absolution. Within minutes a nun-doctor came and verified the death as caused by electrocution or heart failure, and the Abbot Primate administered extreme unction at 4.10 p.m. Sister Pia Valdri, secretary of the International Benedictine Organisation AIM (Aide à l'Implantation Monastique), wrote to John Moffitt:

I believe that no one can say with certainty what caused Father Merton's death . . . One cannot say his death was caused by electrocution, as many newspapers have said, and one cannot say, either, that it was the result of a heart attack. Probably – but only probably – a heart attack began it and electrocution completed it. In fainting, the father may have dragged with him the large fan, which in falling was damaged and caused a short circuit. That is as far as we can go with our deductions. That would explain why Father Merton's hands were not burned and not glued to the fan . . . I believe that no one can say more about this mysterious death, by which God wished to mark one of his elect. 'This is my servant in whom I am well pleased.'[2]

The Meaning of Merton's Death

This experience of sudden death – being plunged into bereavement, and especially the cutting off of a great man's life at the peak of his achievements and energies, is a strange and shocking thing. How can we make sense out of the execution of a man like Dietrich Bonhoeffer, the assassination of men like the Mahatma Gandhi or Martin Luther King? And what are we to say about the seemingly totally fortuitous electrocution of Thomas Merton?

It was just before 1.00 p.m. that Abbot James Fox saw the monastery jeep pull up at his hermitage on 10th December, which was his birthday. He had resigned as Abbot of Gethsemani in January and was now living as a hermit a few miles south of the Abbey. He was surprised to see emerging Brother Patrick, Merton's secretary, and Brother Lawrence, secretary to the new Abbot Flavian Burns. He could only think they were come to greet him on his birthday, and it was with shocked amazement that he received the news: 'I looked at both Br Patrick and Br Lawrence in utter bewilderment. I saw only too clearly that indeed they were not joking. They were in deep sorrowful sincerity. Then I sat down repeating over and over: 'What a loss – what a loss.'

The manner of Merton's death was in my mind when, planning my postgraduate theological writing on Merton in 1970, I made the journey to the Cistercian Abbey at Nunraw in Scotland. Being welcomed by the old Abbot, he said, in the course of conversation, that Merton's death was within the will of God. 'The Lord took him', were his words, and this just confirmed what was written on Merton's ordination card in 1949, from Genesis 5:24: 'He walked with God, and was seen no more, because God took him.'

This was not a fortuitous or accidental death – it contained, for me, a deep and hidden meaning. It was not a tragedy but a triumph. Someone called it a Zen-like death that Merton would have appreciated. Certainly there were ironies about it, as one of the Gethsemani monks pointed out.

Merton used to inveigh against monster machines, yet it
was a big electric fan that really caused his death; Merton
was always writing against military complex, yet it was the
U.S. Army officials who took charge of his body in Bangkok,
provided the embalming and coffin, and then flew his body
home in a U.S. Air Force plane!

This makes a seeming nonsense of all that Merton longed
for. When I recall the immediate impact I felt on reading
his *Contemplative Prayer*, which was among the last things he
wrote, and the seminal essay, 'The Cell', and 'Philosophy
of Solitude',[3] I cannot believe that such experiential
discernment about the hermit life and solitude in God is
unfulfilled. And of course it is not unfulfilled – for Merton's
death was his entrance into the eternal solitude which is
participation in the fulness of the divine life of the Holy
Trinity. But my expectation was that Merton could have
overcome his compulsive writing, and the kind of gregari-
ousness that hindered his hermit vocation, and entered into
the kind of solitude that he longed for in the depths of his
being.

What I am seeing now, in the light of his death, is that
he blazed the trail for others. He was among the first pioneers
of a revival of the hermit life in the bosom of the Western
Church, and because of his influence, teachings and writings,
Abbot James Fox (retired 1968), and Abbot Flavian Burns
(retired 1973), both Abbots of Gethsemani, did what he
profoundly desired for himself – became hermits, without the
compulsive obstacles that Merton found to be part of his
temperament.

I am now convinced, in retrospect, that there is meaning
and providential pattern in Merton's death, and I am enabled
to see much more clearly, not only because of his positive
discernment and communicative teaching on solitude (though
that is the primary thing), but also because of his own inability
to actually live out the lonely austerities of the hermit life.

Positively, Merton's discernment, research, writings and
experience have shaken me to my foundations. I am drawn
inexorably to the hermit tradition for myself. Merton, under

God, has stirred up the fires of solitude within my own being. When I read the writings mentioned above, and Merton's section 'The Case for Eremitism' (wilderness/solitude), in *Contemplation in a World of Action*, I am powerfully stimulated at three levels of my being – *intellectually* by reason of the painstaking research, *emotionally* by the fire in Merton's belly, and *spiritually* by the clear light of the Holy Spirit, evidencing the *vocation* expressed within those studies.

But negatively I find myself becoming aware of Merton's inability to actually get down to it when the crunch came. And this points up similar obstacles in myself, and the awareness of apprehension, fear and vulnerability when faced with the loneliness, austerities, psychological and spiritual conflict and darkness which is part of this way.

For instance, in 1955, when Merton heard that the State Forestry Department of Kentucky was to erect a very tall Fire Tower on one of Gethsemani's highest knobs, he got typically enthusiastic about it being an ideal hermitage. The tower was made of steel with a large glassed cabin on the top. Inside was a telephone and a short wave radio, and the warden's only job would be to watch and communicate any forest fire so that it could be pin-pointed exactly and dealt with. Merton climbed to the top when it was under construction, was hypnotised by the 360 degree view of the surrounding woodlands, and the next day went to see Abbot James Fox.

'Reverend Father,' he said, 'the Forestry Department of Kentucky will need a Fire Warden. That tower, with its trap door at the top, will be absolutely ideal for a hermitage. I could lock myself in without any fear of intrusion. What do you say – let me give it a try.'

Abbot Fox reminded Merton that he had no authority to grant this, that Merton could not absent himself permanently from the Divine Office in choir, and that he had encountered difficulties about monks breaking enclosure to wander in the woods, let alone living permanently in the tower like a Simon Stylites.

Merton would not accept a refusal, and persuaded Abbot

Fox to put his case to the General Chapter of the Cistercian
Order meeting in France just after this conversation.

Abbot Fox listened and was persuaded, and amazingly
he got full permission from the Abbot General of the
Order – but the outcome showed what canny discernment
was revealed in such permission. He said to Abbot Fox,
'OK, but with this condition, that Fr Louis be 100 per cent
hermit – that is, not be a cenobite (monastery brother) in
the morning and a hermit only in the afternoon.' 'Merci
beaucoup, Mon Reverendissime Pere,' replied Abbot Fox,
I'll tell Father Louis what you said.'[4]

When Abbot Fox arrived back in Gethsemani, Merton
went to see him, and he spelled out the permission and the
condition. At first Merton was radiant. 'Terrific – terrific,'
he said, 'I never expected it.' And Abbot Fox says:

'Although his expressions of gratitude and delight were
quite prolific, I seemed to sense that, now he was actually
confronted with the reality of living alone in the tower, he
was a little hesitant.'

Three days later, Merton came again to see Abbot Fox.
'Reverend Father,' he said, 'you have need of a new Father
Master of Novices. I've been giving it deep and prayerful
thought. If you so judge, I'll be willing to take the job,
and thus help you out.' Abbot Fox was immensely relieved
because he had great misgivings about Merton's solitude
in the tower, though he had given Merton complete freedom
to choose it. But now he saw how things were, and accepted
Merton's offer, saying that there were two conditions – one,
that he would keep the job for three years, and two, that
he would give no conferences on becoming hermits to the
novices. Fox comments: 'At this he laughed and laughed.
I laughed also. He knew what I meant . . . This appointment
seemed to lift a tremendous load off his heart.'

Merton kept this job for ten years, and it was not until
1965 that he began to spend long periods in the cinderblock
cabin on a wooded hill not far from the Abbey which became
his hermitage, though never in complete seclusion.

Merton's Pattern for My Life

The above episode reveals three areas of my own life which have to be examined, and they are parallel to Merton's own experience. They are:

1 The gregarious nature of Merton's lifestyle;
2 The delight and ability he had in communication, teaching, preaching and group work;
3 The compulsive nature of his writing.

These three areas have to be examined in the light of the challenge and call to the hermit life. The attitude of the monk or religious will indicate *a*) whether a hermit vocation in complete solitude is indicated (and this will be rare) or *b*) whether there is a vocation to periods of withdrawal and solitude which do not necessitate complete enclosure and is open to forms of communication.

There was tension in Merton's mind about this as indicated by the above incident, and it was thought by his superiors and fellow-monks that complete enclosure would not have been possible for a man of Merton's temperament anyway.

I am aware that most readers of this book will not feel a vocation to the hermit life, or even to long periods of wilderness solitude. Nevertheless, my own reflections on Merton's pattern for my life cannot but serve as an analogy for the solitude we all need. The monk and hermit live in microcosm the life of every man. So let me take the above pattern step by step.

First of all, the matter of Merton's gregarious lifestyle. John Eudes Bamberger, one of his fellow-monks, has written much of Merton's sheer enjoyment of company, intellectual stimulation and social intercourse that was life-blood to him. He comments that in spite of Merton's unvarying and intense attraction to solitude, he was one of the most sociable of men, who had an absolute need for human society. When he was most himself, and in order to be most himself, he would require, with considerable regularity, to meet with people with whom he could converse on subjects of the most diversified kind. Bamberger says: 'As intense as his longing for solitude and silence was – and this too was a very real, urgent necessity for him – it had always struck me that in an out-and-out battle, if it ever came to that, his social instinct would easily win the day.' And yet life without solitude for Merton would have been unendurable. As Bamberger adds: 'The entrenched, semi-conscious conflict between these two needs remained, active and intense, till the end.'[5]

I see a similar pattern, though on a lesser scale, in my own vocation, which has carried me from lay-preaching and group leadership at sixteen years of age, into busy hospital work, university, the Christian ministry in Wales, Scotland and England, and into university Chaplaincy work until I came to the Anglican Society of St Francis in 1975. After some hesitancy between postulancy and noviciate, I have lived in four of the Society's friaries, and between 1982 and 1984 was allowed to experiment with two separate periods of six months' hermit life in Dorset and North Wales. Thus, there have been times of intense communication in evangelism, retreats, conferences, preaching and teaching, and at the time of writing I find myself Guardian of the Society's contemplative house of prayer in Worcestershire.

Like Merton, I appear to be pre-eminently gregarious – but know also the loneliness that is first of all part of the human condition, but which also indicates the absolute necessity of solitude and a contemplative orientation. It was this dimension which carried me as an observer to the Hermit Symposium held at St David's, Wales, in 1975, and over the last decade this orientation to the solitary life has caused me to suspect a vocation in that direction.

The gregarious nature of my lifestyle is neither the basic or most important part of my life – it derives from my interior solitude which is basic and primary. Yet I appreciate the dialectic involved in these words of Merton's concerning the scholastics under his care:

The best of them, and the ones to whom I feel closest, are also the most solitary . . . All this experience replaces my theories of solitude. I do not

need a hermitage, because I have found one where I
least expected it. It was when I knew my brothers
less well that my thoughts were more involved in
them. Now that I know them better I can see
something of the depths of solitude which are in
every human person, but which most men do not
know how to lay open either to themselves or to
others or to God.[6]

Secondly, like Merton, I take great delight in communication. To communicate experience and truth enthusiastically,
especially that which has been life-giving for me, is one of
the great joys of life. And this joy continues in preaching,
teaching and novice-training. I do not doubt my ability in
these areas, and though I have drastically and necessarily
reduced the workload in public ministry, the joy remains.
Merton's abilities and experiences were wider than mine
and his horizons were larger, but our joy in communication
is comparable.

In 1975 I was faced with a possible post as lecturer in
Christian doctrine at the University of Glasgow, but I
withdrew my application after a time of prayer (and some
straight talking about vocation from the principal of the
Edinburgh Episcopal College!). This withdrawal was in
favour of the religious life and the dimension of prayer. That
choice determines my present situation at an even deeper
level today.

Thirdly, the matter of writing. Merton was amazed when
The Seven Storey Mountain became a best-seller, and that fact
firmly established him as one of the most prominent spiritual
writers of the second half of this century. My own writing
is much more modest, but from 1985 I have written four
sizeable books and four small books in a series on spirituality,
and they have filled a real ecumenical need and been well
received. When I speak of the negative elements in Merton's
influence on my life, I recall his words to Abbot Fox: 'I
am most grateful that you put no obstacles to my writing.
If ever I were forbidden to write, I would soon land in a

mental hospital.'[7] It was as compulsive as that!

At present, I do not see my writing as a serious obstacle to the solitary vocation which opens up before me. But the vocation is the one thing necessary, and if writing (and by that I mean publishing) were to interfere with, or negate, it, I would stop writing, though I would expect guidance in this from my spiritual directors.

Like Merton, I enjoy writing – both for myself and for communication and sharing of the knowledge and experience of God (theology and spirituality). I do see that there may well be the demand for complete anonymity and hiddenness in the hermit life. If this becomes clear as part of my own path, then it would demand silence in every respect. As Merton pointed out, the ways of the hermit tradition are various, and the pattern of the hermit's vocation may be what is called *idiorhythmic*, which may be translated as a private or personal rhythm of life, or may be freely paraphrased as 'doing your own thing'. But this is not licence, for 'your own thing' must be God's thing! When St Augustine said 'Love and do what you will', then Pelagius, the moralist, was outraged because he did not have the theological understanding to perceive that, by 'love', Augustine meant total dedication to the will of God in the power of the Holy Spirit. And this conditioned the will of the lover!

Merton himself did not (and perhaps could not) take the path of complete seclusion, and his solitude was never total. Even when he was granted use of the hermitage in the Abbey grounds from 1965 it was used first as a place of dialogue and shared prayer and later, when he spent longer periods of prayer there, he went to the Abbey for a main meal and to collect mail. Merton researched, planned and wrote much on the contemplative and hermit life, but much of it he did not actually pursue for himself, though I believe he yearned to do so. I wonder about the development of his vocation if he had returned from Asia. I cannot help believing that he would have sought permission to live in complete seclusion at least for an extended period.

I have no way of *knowing* which way my own vocation

will take me, but there is certainly a 'next stage' which will possibly mean a whole year of complete seclusion, out of which will arise the awareness of yet another stage on the contemplative path.

This whole discussion arises for me out of Merton's sudden death, for he had reached the age which I am now approaching. He was traversing, pioneering, the contemplative ground shared among the world's great contemplative Faiths. He was suddenly taken – and I say to myself – I am suddenly left! Of course, I merely stand in Merton's shadow, and though I have still some illusions about my own 'spiritual path', I also know I am an ordinary man, and a sinner! Nevertheless, I feel myself to be validly upon the same path that Merton trod, and part of the meaning of his death for me is that I feel myself called to take up the torch that he was compelled to lay down – at least for *this* life. He felt himself to be on the very edge of a great breakthrough, a new discovery and synthesis of the contemplative traditions. His breakthrough and discovery came in the form of death, and he was suddenly catapulted into the dimension of eternity. As far as I can judge, my path is to continue that way 'in my body' and I find a particular relevance in the fellowship, writings and discernment of this man, with almost the feeling of being called to carry on where he left off.

The Loneliness of Merton's Death

Part of the sadness of the manner of Merton's death was its very solitude. He was not only part of the Asian Monastic Conference, but its main speaker on 10th December, 1968, and within an hour of the end of his important lecture he was lying dead and alone. His death was in solitude.

This fact is one which for me is salutary. This is the way I think he would have wanted it. I am also aware that if the path of the solitary is the one which I travel, and if what seems to be a growing vocation within my own soul is objectively genuine, then the possibility is that I shall die alone. It is as salutary a thought as the reminder of the words spoken on Ash Wednesday, when the priest dips his finger in ash, making the sign of the cross on the penitent's forehead, with the words:

> *Memento, homo, quia pulvis es,*
> *et in pulverum reverteris.*

> Remember, man, that you are dust,
> and unto dust you will return.

Merton was well aware of his own mortality, and his theology of nature allowed him to think of death as the natural boundary of our mortal life. But if the body returns to the dust, the spirit returns to God who gave it. This was the great adventure which called out to him from the depths of solitude. He knew the validity and reality of the way; he had even mapped out parts of it for others to travel; he was on the way himself, and at the time of his visit to Asia he looked for this powerful breakthrough and synthesis of East and West on the level of contemplative and religious experience. The rending of the veil of his body was the rending of the veil of eternity, and he began the great adventure into the nearer presence of God and ultimate cosmic glory. The tensions and conflicts of life in the body had come to an end, and there was no more talking or writing to be done. Instead there was the wordless and silent entry into the ineffable presence of God – and that defies description.

A lonely death in a foreign land was fitting for one who sought for so long the solitude which he had only just begun to embrace before that sudden death. I remind myself that the primary thing for Merton was that solitude already exists within the man of prayer, and that geographical solitude is worse than useless unless interior solitude is a present experience. And communication regarding solitude is a nonsense unless one presumes that it is part of every human life and quest, for 'why write about solitude in the first place' he asks. And then answers: 'Certainly not in order to preach it, to exhort people to become solitary. What could be more absurd? Those who are to become solitary are, as a rule, solitary already . . . all men are solitary. Only most of them are so averse to being alone, or to feeling alone, that they do everything they can to forget their solitude.'[8]

'The possibility of his death was not absent from his mind,' said Abbot Flavian Burns in the homily after Merton's death. 'We spoke of this before he set out – first jokingly, then seriously. He was ready for it. He even saw a certain fittingness in dying over there amidst those Asian monks, who symbolised for him man's ancient and perennial desire for the deep things of God.[9] And recalling Merton's own words, Abbot James Fox thinks of Merton's death as prophetic, solitary and poor:

> Everything that touches you shall burn you.
> Do not ask when it will be,
>   or where it will be
>   or how it will be.
> On a mountain or in a prison
> or in a desert or in a concentration camp
> or in a hospital or at Gethsemani.
> It does not matter.
> So do not ask me, because I am not going to tell you.
> You will not know, until you are in it.
> But you shall taste the true solitude of My anguish
>   and of My poverty.
> I shall lead you into the high places of My joy and you
>   shall die in Me.
> And find all things in My Mercy, which has created
>   you for this end . . .
> that you may become the brother of God.
> and learn to know the Christ of the burnt men.[10]

References

1 John Moffitt (ed), *A New Charter for Monasticism*, (1970), pp. 9f.

2 *ibid.* p. 84.
3 These two essays are found in *CWA*, pp. 252 – 259, and *PML*, pp. 43 – 73.
4 Patrick Hart, *Thomas Merton, Monk*, p. 150.
5 *ibid.*, p. 40.
6 *SJ*, p. 328.
7 Hart, *op. cit.*, p. 155.
8 Merton, *PML*, p. 44.
9 Hart, *op. cit.*, p. 220.
10 *ibid.*, p. 158.

17: The Pilgrimage Continues

On the Borderland

Merton's experience of solitude from 1965 to his death in 1968 served to increase his sense of solidarity with all that is human. He learned a little more compassion and humility for himself, and entered more deeply into the pain and suffering of the world. His writings about this are not ivory tower pieces of prose, but are based on his experience of hermitage solitude. While desiring deeper solitude in God, his concern for the pain of the world and responsibility within his own nation was clear. In June, 1965, he stayed overnight in hospital in Lexington, and his reaction to the current newspapers and *Life* magazine was one

> . . . full of helicopters in Vietnam, white mercenaries in the Congo, marines in San Domingo. The whole picture is one of an enormously equipped and self-complacent white civilization in combat with a huge, sprawling colored and mestizo world (a majority) armed with anything they can lay their hands on. And the implicit assumption behind it all, as far as *Life* and apparently everyone else is concerned, is that 'we' are the injured ones, we are trying to keep peace and order, and 'they' (abetted by communist demons) are simply causing confusion and chaos, with no reasonable motives whatever. Hence, 'we', being attacked (God and justice are also attacked in us) have to defend ourselves, God, justice, etc. Dealing with these 'inferior' people becomes a technical problem something like pest extermination.

In a word, the psychology of the Alabama police
becomes in fact the psychology of America as a
world policeman.[1]

Merton did not think of himself as a total pacifist, but
increasingly felt that Christians must practise non-violence,
and that some should bind themselves to follow the way
of peace exclusively, as an example to others. 'I myself as
a monk do not believe it would be licit for me ever to kill
another human being even in self-defence,' he said, 'and
I would certainly never attempt to do so.' He had not had
the opportunity to think the matter through thoroughly,
though he was clear in his own mind about the use of nuclear
weapons. In his cyclostyled 'Cold War Letters', he wrote:
'I think that nuclear war is out of the question. It is beyond
all doubt murder and sin, and it must be banned forever.'
He found consistency difficult in this area, but certainly as
a man of the Gospel he was adamant in his criticism of
all political power based on wealth and violence. Speaking
of the readiness of the United States and the Soviet bloc
to contemplate the use of nuclear weapons not only in defence,
but increasingly as a possible pre-emptive first-strike, he
maintained that this was a commitment to a policy of
genocide:

There are activities which, in view of their possible
consequences, are so dangerous and absurd as to be
morally intolerable. If we co-operate in these
activities we share in the guilt they incur before
God. It is no longer reasonable or right to leave
decisions to a largely anonymous power elite that is
driving us all, in our passivity, towards ruin. We
have to make ourselves heard. Christians have a
grave responsibility to protest clearly and forcibly
against trends that lead inevitably to crimes which
the Church deplores and condemns. Ambiguity,
hesitation and compromise are no longer permissible.
War must be abolished.[2]

These are dangerous words as far as the 'state' is concerned, when that state in its political realities is based upon territory, power, money, ambition and therefore violence. This is not the kind of writing and protest that the establishment expects from a contemplative, and Merton was told by his superiors to keep quiet. But the theological quest for Merton is synonymous with the truly human quest. Merton sought an awareness of the divine presence renewing and transfiguring the natural order and human experience. The consequences of this were participation in social and political criticism, the pursuit of justice and truth in every dimension of human life, and the dedication of all his powers in the service of love, manifested in compassion. I appreciate Merton's humour immensely, but I don't always think he communicates well when he becomes ironic, though you can see what he means:

> I am told by a higher superior: 'It is not your place to write about nuclear war: that is for the bishops.'
> I am told by a moral theologian: 'How can you expect the bishops to commit themselves on the question of peace and war, unless they are advised by theologians?'
> Meanwhile the theologians sit around and preserve their reputations. Pretty soon they will no longer have any reputations to preserve. [3]

From his schooldays, Merton was attracted by the character and teaching of Gandhi, and became a vociferous opponent of the Vietnam war. Such books as *Faith and Violence*, while maintaining this stance on war and peace, with a whole dimension on social criticism and the profound sensitivity of being a believer in a godless world and godless Church, also bore witness to an even more powerful vocation to contemplative prayer. Within that book he reveals his awareness of the personal and corporate hypocrisy of the Church in relation to the issues of war, race, violence and belief. He writes warmly to a Buddhist monk who suffered in

Vietnam, and pens an open letter of apology to an unbeliever, with the compassion of conflict and love born of common and mutual honesty.

All this, together with his literary/poetic awareness, mutual international exchanges, and his experience of the contemplative traditions of the great world Faiths, deepened his hunger for God in prayer and solitude. This is not seen in a negative withdrawal from the world, but rather in a positive engagement with men of philosophy and sanity in all the great intellectual disciplines of the world. He immersed himself in the existentialist novelists and writers, and shared with those who were able to diagnose the chaotic dilemma of a violent and sick world, affirming a real place for the man of prayer in the midst of the chaos:

> This is an age which by its very nature as a time of crisis, of revolution, of struggle, calls for the special searching and questioning which are the work of the monk in his own heart: he plunges deep into the heart of that world of which he remains a part, although he seems to have 'left' it. In reality the monk abandons the world only in order to listen more intently to the deepest and most neglected voices that proceed from its inner depth.[4]

Using the language of the secular philosopher Heidegger and the theologian Paul Tillich, he believed that the monk shares with the secular existentialist the feeling of *angst*, dread, which bears the nature of ontological anxiety, an expression of the human condition in its alienation from true Being in God. He uses ordinary, common language, philosophical language, theological language, at different times and in different ways, to speak of man's lostness, loneliness, suffering and pain. He seeks, as a man of love and prayer, to enter deeply into such lostness with the suffering and crucified Christ, and to carry the hope of the risen Saviour into the darkest situation.

The facing of such existentialist dread as is man's

contemporary dilemma is evaded in our contemporary Western society, and the monk's special vocation, says Merton, is to descend into such depths for himself and on behalf of society, as a sign and witness to the ultimate meaning of human life. 'This is precisely the monk's chief service to the world,' he writes, 'this silence, this listening, this questioning, this humble and courageous exposure to what the world ignores about itself – both good and evil.'

> The monk who is truly a man of prayer and who seriously faces the challenge of his vocation in all its depth is by that very fact exposed to existential dread. He experiences in himself the emptiness, the lack of authenticity, the quest for fidelity, the lostness of modern man, but he experiences all this in an altogether different and deeper way than does man in the modern world, to whom this disconcerting awareness of himself and of his world comes rather as an experience of boredom and spiritual disorientation. The monk confronts his own humanity and that of his world at the deepest and most central point where the void seems to open out into black despair.[5]

But unlike unregenerate, secular man, the monk need not despair, but is able to transform the black abyss into a place of hope by prayer and love. He faces the worst and discovers in it the hope of the best. From the darkness comes light. From death, life. 'From the abyss there comes unaccountably, the mysterious gift of the Spirit sent by God to make all things new, to transform the created and redeemed world, and to re-establish all things in Christ.'

In August, 1967, Pope Paul VI requested from Merton a 'message of contemplation to the world', thereby affirming that Merton was one of the few men who, in Pope Paul's view, lived on this borderland between the life of prayer and the needy world. Merton composed his statement, with a personal letter to Dom Francois Decroix, the intermediary.[6] This covering letter is very revealing as Merton says that he can only respond rapidly and spontaneously, and that there are no experts in the field of prayer, but only sinners writing to sinners. We do not leave the world by our contemplative life, Merton maintains, but simply live hopefully at a deeper depth for our brothers and sisters in the world.

He says that he was more sure of 'answers' when he was a young, raw monk, without any mature experience of our sad but wonderful world. 'As I grow old in the monastic life and advance further into solitude,' he says, 'I become aware that I have only begun to seek the questions.' But then Merton, in the simplicity of his response, makes it clear that he understands the questions at depth, and they are universal and urgent questions of existence, of life and death:

> My brother, perhaps in my solitude I have become as it were an explorer for you, a searcher in realms which you are not able to visit – except perhaps in the company of your psychiatrist. I have been summoned to explore a desert area of man's heart in which explanations no longer suffice, and in which one learns that only experience counts. An arid, rocky, dark land of the soul, sometimes illuminated by strange fires which men fear and peopled by specters which men studiously avoid except in their nightmares. And in this area I have learned that one cannot truly know hope unless he has found out how like despair hope is.

Merton then goes on to apologise that the Church has often misrepresented the love of God, and affirms that the suffering and compassionate Jesus is present in all men, women and children. Hope must be based not on our goodness but on God's love, irrespective of our merits. 'No one on earth has reason to despair of Jesus, because Jesus loves man, loves him in his sin, and we too must love man in his sin.'

As the letter continues, it reveals the human dimensions of Merton's mature thought, the gentle yet unsentimental compassion that flows out of the depths of his being, and shows that the man of solitude and prayer is one who bears the pain of the world as Jesus did, and channels the love, light and glory of God back into the world, as Jesus did.

A Truly Human Pattern

This letter goes on to become a pattern not only for the man or woman who feels a powerful vocation to the life of solitary prayer (and such people are rare), but for anyone who seeks to deepen his humanity. It is quite clear that for Merton the key and centre of it all is the divine Love, and that compassion comes streaming forth, pouring itself out within the hearts of ordinary people. So it is as we relate in the mutuality of love in all its forms that our humanity reaches its own fulfilment and reflects the divine. 'It is the love of my lover, my brothers or my child that sees God in me, makes God credible to myself in me. And it is my love for my lover, my child, my brother that enables me to show God to him or her in himself or herself.' So the contemplative life is the true life of our humanity. It means that we are made for love, and even our sin and despair cannot ultimately contradict it.

The sign and pattern of all this is God becoming man and dying for love, drawing us to himself in his own anguish and taking upon himself all our sin and pain. But that is not the end. It includes the raising up into glory of all those who will look to him in hope and love. Merton closes the letter now addressed to 'brother in the world':

The message of hope the contemplative offers you, then, brother, is not that you need to find your way through the jungle of language and problems that today surround God: but that whether you understand or not, God loves you, is present in you, lives in you, dwells in you, calls you, saves you, and offers you an understanding and light which are like nothing you ever found in books or heard in sermons.

This is Merton at his best. He is profoundly contemplative,
an heir of the monastic contemplative tradition which searches
the depths of our precious humanity, and the depths of the
mystery of God. And all this is to do with the dimension
of experience, not of scholastic speculation. At the same time
Merton is a man of the world, sharing the world's anguish
and pain, the world's aspirations and yearnings as it looks
at and listens to the establishment image and speculative
verbosity of the Church. He longs to initiate the 'brother
in the world' into the dimension of God-experience, and
with powerful words of encouragement, enthusiasm and
enlightenment he finishes the letter:

> The contemplative has nothing to tell you except to
> reassure you and say that if you dare to penetrate
> your own silence and risk the sharing of that solitude
> with the lonely other who seeks God through you,
> then you will truly recover the light and the capacity
> to understand what is beyond words and beyond
> explanations because it is too close to be explained:
> it is the intimate union in the depths of your own
> heart, of God's spirit and your own secret inmost
> self, so that you and He are in all truth One Spirit.
> I love you, in Christ.

Here is the contemplative who was asked from the pinnacle
of his contemplation, to speak to a needy world. And what
he does is to say that he is simply an ordinary man, and
in any case, a sinner. But the word he has to speak is one
of loving encouragement – that if we are one in the fallenness
of our humanity, we are also one in the glory of our universal
call to love. All men can experience the intimate union in
the depths, the secret of the inmost self where God's Holy
Spirit dwells.

I am greatly encouraged as I experience my own vulnerability, conflicts and tensions as I am drawn deeper into
contemplative prayer, for they are reflected in Merton's own
experiences. He refuses to serve as an enlightened guru to

the contemplative or the eremitic life. He says that the only way to love is to love, and the only way to pray is to pray. The only way I shall learn the ecstasy and awesomeness of solitude is to live it out. There are, of course, warnings about the common pitfalls in the Church's monastic tradition, and there are guidelines set down by the Desert Fathers, and in Merton's record of his own pilgrimage. But the way cannot be learned from books alone, but must be lived out in loneliness and pain, in glory and in wonder. Writing to one woman who looked to him for some guidance in this way, Merton said:

> I am not going to try and be guru to you about solitary life. I understand your yearning for it, obviously. With a great deal of prayer, humility, willingness to be changed and transformed interiorly, to be quieted down, etc., and to do all the rest that God asks of you as time goes on, you will doubtless prepare to meet His grace. What are you looking for me to do? Tell you you are not an eccentric? If you need someone to tell you that, you are not by any means ready for solitude. But if you get up in the air about my saying so, it will confirm my saying it. In other words, take it easy. Take what God gives and trust Him. He will do the rest.[7]

The way is by trial and error. There are few valid road maps because each vocation is different, and each one has in himself his own devils to fight with. But each one too has the true spiritual guru who is the Holy Spirit indwelling the heart. If this is not the basis of Christian experience, then prayer in solitude can become a ghastly experience of isolation and madness.

Then in Merton there is the delightful dash of humour which is true sanity. 'No hermit is ordinary,' he says, 'we are all cracked in slightly different ways, that's all. The first thing is to accept ourselves as we are and God's grace as it is given.' Of course, this matter of interior knowledge, the assurance of your vocation, standing on your own feet, not looking to others for continual affirmation – all this together with your own awareness of interior spiritual experience of God, is but one side of the coin. We do need help from the great tradition, from those who have travelled the way before us, and from spiritual direction within the discipline of the Church. Otherwise, we become spiritual vagrants or eccentrics imprisoned in our own narcissistic image – leading ultimately to madness. But the balance will right itself as long as there is the awareness of the two poles of personal experience and spiritual direction.

Sharing the Journey

Merton knew from the beginning that if he shared his own story, it would shed light on the spiritual journey of other pilgrims. This has been my experience too. The more I have shared with novices, brothers and sisters in community, other Christians and especially with non-Christians in the world, the more I have experienced feed-back. Nearly all such feed-back has been positive, and even disagreements have been enthusiastic. There is a way of disagreeing which is stimulating and positive, promoting deeper respect on both sides.

I hitched a lift on the M4 motorway from Bristol to London, and was picked up by the Marxist group of Bristol University, travelling by minibus to a Marxist rally. I accused them, with a huge grin on my face, of pinching and twisting a basic Christian principle laid down in Acts 4:32: 'From each according to his ability, to each according to his need.' We did battle together, argued, and enjoyed it. A friar in a brown habit was an unusual sight on the M4 in their experience, but then a minibus full of budding Marxists was a new experience for me. The enjoyment and duelling was mutual, and we learned from one another. I mean, I acknowledged the hypocrisy and double-dealing of the Church – but here was a case of the pot calling the kettle black! I had to be willing to expose myself, to be vulnerable, to take them seriously, to attack and defend in charity, and to LISTEN . . .

Merton is like that when he tells his story, and especially when he is dealing with the tensions and conflicts that surrounded his 'deeper into solitude' longing. He never really achieved it, and whether he would have done so in this life is another matter of speculation, for not only did so many people and commitments hold him back from solitude's depths in the last three years, but he fell in love with 'S', his hospital nurse. The whole story of that beautiful and sad struggle only endears him to me more closely, in understanding his loveable, common and vulnerable humanity. [8]

Because he had tensions, conflicts and a powerful and gregarious love of people, it makes me follow him all the more sympathetically, reading between the lines of his writings and actions, laughing and weeping with him. If it were not for the fact of his vocation he would have fallen into despondency and quit. But because he was who he was, displaying such honesty and integrity, it encourages me 'who also am a sinner' to respond to that deepest inward call to solitude, which will carry me I know not where.

My own journey is, at the same time, infinitely easy, overflowing with joy, wonder and gratitude, and infinitely difficult – heavy with loneliness, struggle and confrontation with powers of darkness. Merton's own warnings tell me that I do not ultimately need him, for with an assurance of God as Father, Christ as Saviour, the indwelling Spirit as counsellor, and with scripture and solitude I shall find the way. I have no doubt of this, and realise that these are the great ultimates for me – summed up in the words 'God alone'. But it is a great gift for me to realise that I am part of the wholeness of the universal human search; part of the contemplative tradition in the Church; part of my own Franciscan community. Also, I am immensely grateful to God not only for the ancient monastic tradition, but especially for the witness of the Desert Fathers and the Celtic monks, and more particularly for the story of Thomas Merton. He was aware of these truths too, for he says that the monastic hermit has, as his first duty, to live happily and without affectation in his solitude. He owes this not only to himself but to his monastic community which has afforded him the opportunity to try it out:

> The monastic hermit realizes that he owes his solitude to his community and owes it in more ways than one. First of all the community has bestowed it upon him, in an act of love and trust. Second, the community helps him to stay there and make a go of it, by prayers and by material aid. Finally the hermit 'owes his solitude' to the community in the sense that his solitary life with its depth of prayer and awareness is his contribution to the community, something that he gives back to his 'monastic Church' in return for what has been given him.[9]

If the hermit can live in tranquillity without affectation, Merton sees this as a great gift to the world. He sees modern Western man being exploited by an unhealthy social system which exacerbates man's fear of boredom and exploits it. He runs from one unsatisfying product to another, afraid of the terror of what may be revealed in silence and solitude, for 'the terror will rise up again and he will have to buy something else, or turn another switch, or open another bottle, or swallow another pill, or stick himself with a needle in order to keep from collapsing.'

The hermit lives in simplicity, without a 'happiness machine' to solve his problems. Rather he faces his boredom and his fears with no other resources than those he has within himself. This is the simplicity of maturity, which participates in a basic simple life, giving the body to manual work, the mind to meditation and the spirit to contemplation, in a simple co-mingling which manifests a basic unity.

The hermit lives the pattern of Christ's life in prayer and silence, in the temptation in the desert and adoration on the mountain. He learns Christ's agony in Gethsemane, his glory on Mount Tabor and his dying on Calvary. I recall, as I write, the midnight mass of Easter during my six months of solitude on Anelog at the tip of the Lleyn Peninsula. I emerged from my stone cottage a few minutes before midnight on Holy Saturday, 1984. I stood quietly in the night stillness before the unlit pile which was to be my Easter bonfire, and began the mass of the Resurrection, crying out the words into the wind and darkness of the mountain: 'CHRIST IS RISEN! HE IS RISEN INDEED!' And the new light was struck, the fire was lit, and began to blaze, and I sang aloud with great joy:

> Up from the grave He arose
> With a mighty triumph o'er His foes;
> He arose a victor from the dark domain,
> And He lives forever with His saints to reign.
> He arose! He arose!
> Alleluia! Christ arose!

I found myself entering into the reality of the Gospel experience of Jesus in ways I had only *imagined* previously. I have told elsewhere of the harrowing experience of treading the 'Stations of the Cross' upon the top of the bare mountain, and the glory and wonder of days, weeks and months of meditative experience along the mountain paths high over the Irish Sea and the splendour and heaviness (how often the mood changed) of Bardsey Island rising up from the sea. My experience and style are quite different from Thomas Merton's, but both our books, *The Sign of Jonas*, and *A Hidden Fire* bear witness to a deepening of experience and a heightening of sensitivities to the grace and mercy of God calling us into contemplative prayer.

I am not too heavenly-minded to be of any earthly use, but I certainly find that Merton constantly calls me back to the affirmation of simple and ordinary tasks, and to the stripping away of false spiritual illusions. I have learned, with him, to cope with my eccentricities with humour, and to avoid madness. These are eminently sane words:

> Solitude is not a satisfactory setting for concerted,
> thoroughgoing madness. To be really mad, you need

other people. When you are by yourself you soon get tired of your craziness. It is too exhausting. It does not fit in with the eminent sanity of trees, birds, water, sky. The silence of the woods forces you to make a decision which the tensions and artificialities of society may help you to evade forever.[10]

One of the rewarding things I find now that I am 'back in circulation' for a while is that 'ordinary secular sinners' get very excited about solitude, and prove themselves to be often more discerning than 'believers'! They want to know about my motivation, about deprivation, expectation – about material and economic things like diet, keeping clean, keeping fit, keeping sane, and about the spiritual dimension – about the mystery of God, joy, hope, fulfilment in a dark world like this. All this is exciting for me to communicate, because I can *feel* the hunger and thirst in them. I sympathise with their longings, and weep and laugh with them in their hopes and fears. I also find that many of them have strong (and responsible) objections to the Church as an institution and organisation, and they are actually full of glee when I talk about the reality of God's presence in solitude. Thomas Merton talks about the exaggerated legalism and institution-alism of the Roman Catholic Church today in the attempt to dominate Christians by fear – and though he overstates his case, and similar things may be said about the Anglican and other churches of Christendom, he is right in saying that good and honest people are driven away from the visible Church because they cannot, in conscience, meet demands stupidly forced on them by incompetent officials. He sees a similar thing happening in the social and political areas where society has a way of enlarging demands to the point where it arrogates to itself complete power over everyone and everything. In such contexts as these, he sees the wholesome witness of the hermit having something powerful to say:

The man who can live happily without snuggling up at every moment to some person, institution, or vice is there as a promise of freedom for the rest of men. And that perhaps is one of the only reasons why the solitary can be so bitterly resented, especially by a certain type of Christian for whom the Church is mere institution and womb.[11]

He understands the hermit life as a response to the love and mercy of God, and envisages the hermit saying: 'I have known and experienced the goodness of God to me in Christ in such a way that I have no alternative but this total response, this gift of myself to a life alone with God in the forest.' And this actually becomes a proclamation of the Gospel non-verbally as he goes on to say: 'And this witness is at the same time the purest act of love for other men, my gift to them, my contribution to their joy in the good news of Jesus Christ, and to their awareness that the Kingdom of Christ is in the midst of us.'

So for me, my human journey has been a spiritual pilgrimage, and the horizon lengthens to a Western sunset that beckons me on to a further sunrise in eternity. I have understood in my heart the mystery and the love of God since a small child wandering on the Welsh coast. At twelve years of age I had a simple but lasting experience of Christ as personal Saviour and Lord. At sixteen I entered into a dimension of the Holy Spirit that has kept me on the way through joy and sorrow. Over the last decade, from within the religious life, I have continued a life of witness, preaching and instruction, but have been drawn more and more into a deeper life of prayer. In 1982, and then in 1983/4 I spent two periods of six months' solitude. Now, since 1984, I have been Guardian of the Franciscan House of Prayer at Glasshampton, Worcestershire, being too busy, but with great joy. Now I feel myself just on the edge of a new discovery of prayer in the dimension of solitude.

The formal request has yet to be made, the conditions and context has to be worked out, the place and time is not yet clear, but the fact of such solitude is deep within me – and demands a concrete and committed response. I find it terrifying and exciting, and expect the reader to share some of my feelings in all this.

Thomas Merton shared his pilgrimage with me, and continues to minister to me in his writings and from the communion of saints. And I share my story with you, believing that the overlapping of our experiences will only serve to deepen, sharpen and intensify the longing for God in prayer and love.

References

1 Michael Mott, *The Seven Mountains of Thomas Merton*, p. 415.

2 Quoted in *Continuum*, p. 266. The correspondence between Merton and James Forest during the last seven years of Merton's life indicates Merton's increasing opposition to nuclear arms and the advocacy of non-violence. See William H. Shannon, (ed), *The Hidden Ground of Love*, pp. 254–308.

3 Merton, *CGB*, pp. 289f.

4 Merton, *CP*, pp. 24f.

5 *ibid.*, pp. 27f.

6 See Shannon, *op. cit.*, pp. 154–159.

7 *ibid.*, pp. 529f.

8 The story is clearly and sympathetically told in Mott, *op. cit.*, pp. 435–454.

9 Merton, *CWA*, p. 242.

10 *ibid.*, p. 245.

11 *ibid.*, p. 246.

Epilogue: This Is It[1]

The book is finished, and I am filled with that kind of feeling I have known before – that of wondering if I could *ever* communicate that which is in the depths of my being. And there is something particularly mysterious and painful in writing of my life in the shadow of Merton's and of the solitude that plagued and enamoured him.

I write these words in my usual writing place in Glasshampton monastery which looks out to the Spanish Chestnut tree I referred to in *Fulness of Joy* in December, last year. It was stark and bare under a winter sky. I talked about it again in April of this year when I wrote the chapter 'Contemplation and the Cosmos' in this present book. It was then budding in the springtime of hope. And now it is September, and the prophesied fruitfulness has come. It is so covered with foliage and spiky chestnuts in their thousands that the immense trunk cannot be seen. 'A tree gives glory to God by being a tree,' says Merton, and this is why I am drawn to it on this beautiful and melancholy autumn day.

This tree is the context of my reflection today as I look back over this book, over Merton's life and death, and into my own heart. I have once again read Merton's powerful essay 'The Cell', and together with his 'Philosophy of Solitude' it has confirmed in me that which I have always known – that like the Chestnut tree, I will be drawn dynamically and inexorably deeper into the interior solitude which leads to the ultimate fruitfulness of union with God in love.

Merton's meditation on the tree also speaks to me of the *kairos*, the opportune moment, which for the tree is every moment – this is it – according to the season, but which bears a cyclic relationship to fruitfulness in the dying of the year.

All this is confirmed in 'The Cell', for whereas Merton is
writing of the solitary sitting in his cell and learning the
painful and necessary lessons of solitude, I am reminded
that St Francis, in my own tradition, said that the body
is the cell and the soul is the hermit who dwells therein.
This means for me that I am always in my cell, but not
always inwardly aware of it. It also confirms Merton's words
in the essay:

> Patiently putting up with the incomprehensible
> unfulfilment of the lonely, confined, silent, obscure
> life of the cell, we gradually find our place, the spot
> where we belong as monks: that is of course
> solitude, the cell itself. This implies a kind of
> mysterious awakening to the fact *that where we actually
> are is where we belong*, namely in solitude, in the cell.
> Suddenly we see 'this is it'.

This is it! If you have travelled the pages of this book
with me, you will have discovered a little of the greatness
and vulnerability of the man who for me has been a special
kind of guide and soul friend. He suffered much at the hands
of the world, in terms of loneliness, unfulfilled yearnings,
misunderstanding and a certain isolation. He suffered too
because of his interior vocation which was only partially
fulfilled, and I empathise with him at this level because I
feel much the same at this point.

And yet this is it! These words affirm for me the positive
value of Merton's life in all its vicissitudes, and they confirm
in me the fact that I have needed to live out all the experiences
of my own life, and have been able, more than most, to
share the human and divine riches which are part of me.
And by that very fact I have been left dumb in certain
respects, meaning that I cannot share that which is deepest,
most true and most filled with the yearning for love.

Merton said that man is made in such a way that he
cannot live happily without love, and went on to warn that
a man who chooses religious solitude from any other motive

is in danger of becoming obsessed by the inner frenzies of self-hatred, and will project a loveless life of unhappy frustration and destructiveness. Merton's understanding of solitude was a life of love, and a life of special love, for it is centred upon God, and overflows directly from the source – God's love for humankind in Christ.

From my two prolonged periods of solitude, I feel that I simply responded to an overwhelming call which erupted from within – summed up in the word *vocation*. So my understanding of solitude, like Merton's, is not a life dedicated to asceticism, philosophical reflection or abstract contemplation, nor merely to study, work, writing or prayer. It is simply a response to love which looks for no rational justification within the Church or the world. It is a response and a surrender to love – being able to do no other.

From where I am today, within the world, the Church, and as a member of a Franciscan Order, I see this response as a further manifestation of the dynamic process which has moved and guided me from childhood. I have no guarantee that if I seek permission to test a vocation to the *eremitical* (solitary) life, it will be granted. But that does not cause me any anxiety, for if what I feel and know within my own heart is interpreted truly, then it will happen, for it must. The grace which has called me, keeps me.

And that grace will draw me on, ever deeper into the divine Love. I am under no illusion concerning the loneliness, darkness and conflict that lies on the path ahead. If that were not the way, it would be a false way, but as 'this is it' has been the pattern of my pilgrimage up to the present, so it will continue to be.

I have used the word *dynamic*, but I do not consider the vocation of a hermit to be a kind of spiritual *dynamo* to produce prayers of the quantity and quality that justifies his existence or contribution to the Church's apostolic mission. Neither did Merton. The vocation is simply to love, in God. With all the inevitabilities of conflict, illusion, sinful evasion and confrontation with dark powers, the work of sanctification will continue until the divine Love becomes the ground and source of the hermit's life, and he loves God in all things, and all things in God. This is the classic 'mystical way' of purgation and illumination, leading to union. In such a process he will taste of the cosmic union which is the ultimate vocation of all humanity – the goal of all creation in Christ. Theologically, St Irenaeus, following St Paul, enunciated it most clearly, and Merton among contemporary men of prayer, sought to embrace it most closely in the vocation to solitude. He once spoke of it as the experience of 'the unspeakable beating of a Heart with the heart of one's own life,' using the analogy of a living organism to communicate the vitality, spontaneity and interior reality of his own experience.

None of this is individualistic, though it is intensely and intimately personal. Merton castigates the world-denying isolationist, locked into the narcissism or self-hatred of his own stubborn will. He understands solitude, in the true hermit, as an experience that is shared by everyone, though most people evade it in this life. The solitary lives for himself and for the world, and all the self-denials and asceticism which may be involved are simply obstacles upon the way which are encountered and overcome for the sake of Love. He knows his own potential for evil and alienation, and has entered into a saving experience of forgiveness and new birth in Christ by the power of the Holy Spirit. But that is just the beginning – for then, out of compassion for the universe and for love of humankind, he responds to the call to solitude, into the healing silence of the wilderness (not without its travail and conflict) for the healing of the wounds of the entire world, beginning with himself.

The world is full of words, and this book adds to the volume of them – but it also bears witness to the wordless dimension of contemplation for all the people of God. Many people in the world, and too many in the Church, will think of the hermit as a failure, outside the activist plans and projects of busy people, with no power status or political influence. Merton even says that some who consider themselves contemplative often cherish a secret contempt for the solitary, for he lacks 'that noble security, that intelligent depth, that artistic finesse' which the academic contemplative seeks in his sedate respectability!

And that brings us to the failure of the Cross. It is there, at Calvary where the sinner finds forgiveness, and there that the fulness of God's love is revealed. The dying and rising of Jesus is the pattern, not only for the solitary, marking the whole of his life, but for every Christian. The light and shadow of the Cross is over all our lives, and the failure which is manifested there, together with the resurrection light within the darkness, is the faith by which we all must live.

We all experience the present darkness of our world, but the vision which I have endeavoured to share in this book is one which has no easy and facile answers, but which affirms a living faith from within the perplexity of our poor world, anchored within the love of God. Words of Merton's which express his faith and my meaning come, appropriately, from his *Thoughts in Solitude*:

> My Lord God, I have no idea where I am going. I do not see the road ahead of me. I cannot know for certain where it will end. Nor do I really know myself, and the fact that I think I am following your will does not mean that I am actually doing so. But I believe that the desire to please you, does, in fact, please you, and I hope I have that desire in all that I am doing. I hope that I will never do anything apart from that desire. And I know that if I do this, you will lead me by the right road, though I may know nothing about it. Therefore, I will trust you always though I may seem lost and in the shadow of death. I will not fear, for you are ever with me, and you will never leave me to face my perils alone.

References

1 Merton, *CWA*, p. 254.
2 Merton, *TS*, p. 70.

Other Marshall Pickering paperbacks

THE SACRED DIARY OF ADRIAN PLASS AGED 37¾
Illustrated by Dan Donovan

Adrian Plass

A full-length, slide-splitting paperback based on the hilarious diary entries in Christian Family magazine of Adrian Plass, 'an amiable but somewhat inept Christian'. By his own confession, Adrian 'makes many mistakes and is easily confused', but a reasssuring sense of belonging to the family of God is the solid, underlying theme.

THE HORIZONTAL EPISTLES OF ANDROMEDA VEAL
Illustrated by Dan Donovan

Adrian Plass

Adrian Plass, diary-writer *sans pareil* returns! This time he finds much to amuse him in the letters of Andromeda Veal, precocious eleven year old daughter of a Greenham woman, and shrewd commentator on her local church and the wider world.

Andromeda is in hospital with an undisclosed complaint. She seizes her chance to write all those letters that had to wait before – to, 'Gorgeous Chops', 'Ray Gun', 'Rabbit' Runcie, the Pope, and even Cliff Richard.

At the same time her friends of Sacred Diary fame write to her: Gerald with his mysterious 'persunnul problem', Mrs. Flushpool, Leonard Thin, and also the local MP who vows that she 'can be sick in our hands'! She is also the lucky recipient of letters from conscientious Bible student Charles Cooke who finds 15 texts for every word of 'I hope you get better soon', and a large Christian organization whose aims appear to change from letter to letter. Of course Andromeda's illness gives her a chance to think more seriously about God too, even to the extent of writing him a letter.

All of this is interspersed with new diary entries from Adrian Plass' inimitable diary writer and Dan Donovan's hilarious illustrations.

OFF THE CHURCH WALL

Rob Portlock

A hilarious collection of cartoons by Rob Portlock, depicting the unusual ways in which people choose to behave in church!

ASSEMBLED IN BRITAIN

Stewart Henderson

Assembled in Britain strengthens Stewart Henderson's reputation as one of Britain's leading Christian poets. His sharp, earthy style communicates Christian truth effectively and arrestingly.